D1271213

# The Politics of Inclusion and Empowerment

*Also by Birte Siim*

CONTESTED CONCEPTS IN GENDER AND SOCIAL POLITICS (*ed. with Barbara Hobson and Jane Lewis*)

GENDER AND CITIZENSHIP: POLITICS AND AGENCY IN FRANCE, BRITAIN AND DENMARK

*Also by John Andersen*

Social and System Integration and the Underclass. In I. Gough and G. Olfsson (eds.), CAPITALISM AND SOCIAL COHESION

Postindustrial Meritocracy or Solidarity. In *Acta Sociologica* No. 4. 1999

Gambling Politics or Successful Entrepreneurialism? – The Orestad in Copenhagen. In F. Moulart, E. Swyngedouw and A. Rodriquez (eds.) THE GLOBALISED CITY

# The Politics of Inclusion and Empowerment

## Gender, Class and Citizenship

*Edited by*

John Andersen
*Department of Social Sciences,*
*Roskilde University, Denmark*

and

Birte Siim
*Institute of History, International and Social Studies,*
*Aalborg University, Denmark*

First published 2004 by
PALGRAVE MACMILLAN
Houndmills, Basingstoke, Hampshire RG21 6XS and 175 Fifth Avenue, New York, N.Y. 10010
Companies and representatives throughout the world

PALGRAVE MACMILLAN is the global academic imprint of the Palgrave Macmillan division of St. Martin's Press, LLC and of Palgrave Macmillan Ltd. Macmillan® is a registered trademark in the United States, United Kingdom and other countries. Palgrave is a registered trademark in the European Union and other countries.

ISBN 1–4039–3238–7

This book is printed on paper suitable for recycling and made from fully managed and sustained forest sources.

A catalogue record for this book is available from the British Library.

Library of Congress Cataloging-in-Publication Data
The politics of inclusion and empowerment : gender, class, and citizenship / edited by John Andersen and Birte Siim.
  p.   cm.
Includes bibliographical references and index.
ISBN 1–4039–3238–7
1. Democracy.   2. Citizenship.   3. Civil society.   4. Globalization.
5. Women in politics.   I. Andersen, John, 1954–   II. Siim, Birte.

JC423.P5662   2004
321.8–dc22

                                                                    2003067263

10   9   8   7   6   5   4   3   2   1
13   12   11   10   09   08   07   06   05   04

Printed and bound in Great Britain by
Antony Rowe Ltd, Chippenham and Eastbourne

# Contents

# List of Contributors

**John Andersen** is Professor of Social Science, in the Department of Social Sciences, Roskilde University Centre, Denmark and worked as an expert for the European Commission from 1991 to 1994 in the third European Anti-Poverty Programme (Poverty 3). His current fields of research are the empowerment of underprivileged groups, urban policy and the inclusive labour market.

**Ann-Dorte Christensen** is Associate Professor of Political Sociology at FREIA Feminist Research Centre, Aalborg University. She has written books and articles on gender, democracy and politics. She participated in the Gender-Empowerment-Politics (GEP) programme, in 1996–2002. She is co-author of *Equal Democracies: Gender and Politics in the Nordic Countries*. She is currently working on the issues of the political identities of young women.

**Ute Gerhard** is Professor of Sociology and Director of the Cornelia Goethe Centre for Women's and Gender Studies at the University of Frankfurt/Main. She is the co-ordinator of the TSER Network, 'Working Mothering: Social Practices and Social Politics'. She has published on women's rights, social policy, the history of women, the women's movement and feminist theory. Her publications include *Atempause. Feminismus als demokratisches Projek* (1999).

**Jørgen Elm Larsen** is Associate Professor of Sociology in the Department of Sociology, University of Copenhagen. He is currently co-ordinator of the Graduate School of Integration, Production and Welfare. He participated in the Gender-Empowerment-Politics (GEP) programme in 1996–2002. His current fields of research are social inclusion and exclusion, activation policy and social work with marginal people.

**Ruth Lister** is Professor of Social Policy at Loughborough University. She is a former director of the Child Poverty Action Group and a member of the Commission on Poverty, Participation and Power. She is author of *Citizenship: Feminist Perspectives* (2nd edn 2003) and *Poverty* (2004).

**Marjorie Mayo** is Professor at PACE, Goldsmith College, University of London. She is co-author (with C. Craig) of *Community Empowerment* (1995). Her recent publications include (with J. Anastacio) 'Welfare Models and Approaches to Empowerment', *Policy Studies* 1, 1999.

**Pauline McClenaghan** was Professor at the School of Social and Community Sciences, University of Ulster, Magee College, Northern Ireland. She has written numerous articles on community development. Her publications include (with T. Robson) *Training for Community Development: The North West Initiative. Achievements and Prospects* (1996).

**Anne Phillips** is Professor of Gender Theory and Director of the Gender Institute at the London School of Economics and Political Science. Her publications include *Engendering Democracy* (1991); *Democracy and Difference* (1993); *The Politics of Presence: The Political Representation of Gender, Ethnicity and Race* (1995); and *Which Equalities Matter?* (1999). She is currently working on issues of gender and multiculturalism.

**Birte Siim** is Associate Professor of Social Science in the Institute of History, International and Social Studies, Aalborg University. She coordinated the national research programme Gender-Empowerment-Politics (GEP), in 1996–2002. She is author of *Gender and Citizenship: Politics and Agency in France, Britain and Denmark* (2000) and has co-edited *Contested Concepts. Gender and Social Politics* (2002). She is currently working on issues of gender, citizenship and multiculturalism.

**Jens Ulrich**, is an Assistant Professor in Democratic Theory in the Department of Economics, Politics and Public Administration, Aalborg University. He has written articles on the theory of democracy, political identity, gender education and modernisation. He is currently working on issues on the research programme Digital Local Democracy.

**Iris Marion Young** is Professor of Political Philosophy, Chicago University. She is the author of many influential books on democracy. Her publications include *Justice and the Politics of Difference* (1990) and *Inclusion and Democracy* (2000).

# 1
# Introduction: The Politics of Inclusion and Empowerment – Gender, Class and Citizenship[1]

*John Andersen and Birte Siim*

## Introduction

Globalisation poses challenges for political and social theory as well as problems for the modern welfare state and democracy in that it demands the development of a new politics of redistribution and recognition. During the 1980s and 1990s a political battle was waged over the restructuring of the welfare state and democracy, followed by an academic debate about the meaning of certain key concepts, including equality, diversity and difference. One controversial issue is how to link the class struggle for greater economic equality with struggles for recognition of difference along gender, ethnicity and sexuality lines. The essays in this volume illuminate the political struggles and academic debates about the inclusion/exclusion of women and marginalised social groups from different policy contexts. The focus is on the different class and gender regimes influencing the interplay of citizenship in different policy context and on different levels of politics.

This contributors discuss the politics of inclusion and empowerment and the paradigms of inclusion/exclusion. One of the objectives is to underline the close link between issues surrounding economic inequality and the recognition of cultural difference. The politics of inclusion – as we understand it – is the productive/innovative linkage of the politics of redistribution and the politics of recognition, which over a longer time span creates sustainable paths to democratic and social development increasing the capacity to handle conflicts arising from economic resources and life chances as well as conflicts about identities. The politics of empowerment concerns the agency and mobilisation dimensions of social and political change. The title of this book, *The Politics of Inclusion and Empowerment*, addresses our leitmotif: discussing the possible plus-sum game between the two.

We define empowerment as the process of awareness and capacity-building, which increases the participation and decision-making power of citizens and may potentially lead to transformative action which will change opportunity structures in an inclusive and equalising direction.

One objective of this volume is to illustrate the new types of social conflict, coalition and transformative action associated with gender relations and other kinds of discrimination according to class, ethnicity and race in the era of globalisation. Another objective is to analyse the capacity of individual citizens and social groups to organise collective action from below, for example at the community level, as well as the scope of NGO activism to influence international decisions and global governance at the national and international levels.

The contributors concentrate on two sets of issues. One set focuses on the transformation of democracy and raises issues about the interplay between political institutions and the participation and formation of the political identities of women and marginalised social groups. The other set of questions focuses on the restructuring of the welfare state and social rights, and raises issues about new forms of exclusion/inclusion and the empowerment/disempowerment of the working class and other social groups. Key concepts linking the two sets of issues are the *recognition, redistribution* and *equal participation* of women and marginalised social groups in deliberations concerning the common good. One of the objectives is to establish a dialogue between research reflecting on specific empowerment traditions and contexts, and meta-theoretical reflections on changes in the 'meta-discourses' of citizenship, inclusion and diversity.

Taking the more diverse and complicated socio-economic and political-cultural picture of late modernity into account, we argue that the politics of inclusion and empowerment must increasingly: (1) be able to address the old issues of social inequality; (2) be able to take new 'particularities' into account; and (3) stimulate the interplay between institutions and the political participation of citizens at different policy levels.

From the social citizenship and exclusion/inclusion viewpoint, the implications of the trend away from national government and towards multi-level governance (Swyngedouw et al., 2003) suggest that the creation and mobilisation of multiple-actor networks is a key issue when it comes to changing the power matrix and strengthening the pressure for a new 'social contract' which includes the socio-economic interests and political participation of excluded groups.

This raises questions about the creation of new types of democratic and inclusive government and governance, which can both integrate actors representing interest at the bottom of the social ladder, and enable the actors to operate across different spatial levels – local, regional, national and global. The latter task is necessary because the forces of exclusion in the era of globalisation operate in complex ways and on many levels. Therefore the 'inclusive forces' committed to democratic and social values cannot operate exclusively at the local, regional or national level (Andersen, 1999).

In the following section we look first at the concepts of inclusion and empowerment in the approach to democratic citizenship. Then we explore the social exclusion and underclass approaches, which are interpreted as two antagonistic scientific and political solutions to welfare politics. Finally, we give a brief résumé of the various chapters which illustrates the different approaches and provides examples of proposals to develop a politics of inclusion and empowerment from different policy contexts.

## Globalisation, democratic citizenship and empowerment

Globalisation undermines democracy and promotes anti-democratic tendencies, and at the same time offers opportunities for public discourse and new forms of democratic participation, which can link local, regional, national and global issues and popular influence. The paradigms of cosmopolitan democracy and feminist universalism have emphasised the need to expand democracy beyond the nation state and to develop universal values of solidarity (Giddens, 1994: 252–3) and global responsibility (Dean, 1996). From this perspective one major challenge today is to foster responsible citizens who are able to transcend existing group identities and strengthen the bonds of solidarity with outsiders through 'reflective solidarity'.

According to Iris Marion Young we need to go beyond deliberative democracy and develop a vision of local and cultural autonomy in the context of global regulatory regimes (Young, 2000: 236). Young argues that a commitment to justice begins with local and particularistic relationships, but in so far as a sense of solidarity is not timeless and natural but constructed, transnational sentiments of solidarity ought to be constructed to correspond to transnational obligations (Young, 2000: 242–3). Young identifies seven regulatory regimes: 1) peace and security; 2) environment; 3) trade and finance; 4) direct investment and capital utilisation; 5) communication and transportation; 6) human rights, including labour standards and welfare rights; and 7) citizenship and migration. One important challenge, which 'glocal' movements like ATTAC and the Social Forums have responded to, is to develop policies across the (sectoral) boundaries between these different regulatory regimes, for example by linking the political regulation of trade and finance with welfare rights. One example is the struggle of poor countries over access to cheap medicine versus the property rights of multinational companies.

In this volume the focus is on the interaction of welfare rights and the equal participation of citizens in local, national and global politics. A key question is how to link the construction of new forms of global governance 'from above' with the formation of political identities of citizens rooted in everyday life problems 'from below'. From a citizenship perspective the challenge is to link the formation of citizens' political identities at the local and global levels with the activism of political agents in local and global civil organisations. The democratic and solidarity challenge of *linking* the local and the global can (preliminary) be conceptualised as the *politics of glocalisation. Tentatively, the politics of glocalisation can be defined as politics based on universal values of solidarity that transcend the nation state and link the local, regional, national and global levels in a supportive way, as well as a vision of social and democratic sustainable development.*

Globalisation presents new challenges to democracy to include diversity and difference through the politics of inclusion and empowerment. The empowerment approach is interdisciplinary and is inspired by Third World action research, community studies (see Marjory Mayo, this volume, chapter 9) as well as by feminist research (Marques-Pereira and Siim, 2002).

Arguably, the 'empowerment' and 'equal participation' of citizens 'from below' approach needs to be reformulated in the current global context. Empowerment has been criticised because of the dangers of voluntarism: a matter of political will detached from social and economic conditions (see Anne Phillips, this volume, chapter 3). It also underestimates the important role of political institutions as 'opportunity structures' facilitating social change (Marques-Pereira and Siim, 2002).

Iris Marion Young's book *Justice and the Politics of Difference* defines empowerment as 'the participation of an agent in decision making through an effective voice and vote' (Young, 1990: 251). The 'politics of difference' links the inclusion of women and marginalised social groups in democracy 'from below'. Empowerment is thus linked to local autonomy and is a means by which to include the participation of oppressed social groups in decision-making at all levels of society. Her vision of democracy rests on social differentiation without exclusion – 'a politics of difference' built on mutual recognition and acceptance of difference, which links the particular with the universal. Young's contribution is useful, because it emphasises social inequalities and the need to include different social perspectives in politics. It is based on a dual need to accept difference and create mutual recognition and a respect that transcends difference – that is, to reinforce as well as to transform existing group identities.

Nancy Fraser (1997) has argued forcefully that justice today requires redistribution *and* recognition. She has proposed a 'perspectival dualist' analysis with two irreducible dimensions of justice. Fraser's critical theory of recognition treats recognition as a question of equal social status: 'What requires recognition is not group-specific identity but the status of the group as full partners in social interaction' (Fraser, 1997). The point is that there is a real dilemma between an ideal about social equality based on socio-economic redistribution and an ideal of equity based on cultural recognition. Both conditions must be satisfied if participatory parity is to be achieved. According to the general principle of participatory parity, democratic justice requires social arrangements that permit all (adult) members of society to interact with one another as peers (Fraser, 2003: 4). We use Fraser's model and the three key concepts of redistribution, recognition and participation as a starting point, taking into account the different developments in Europe and the United States (see Anne Phillips, this volume, chapter 3), as well as the different logics of gender and welfare in Europe (Siim, 2000).

Globalisation has stimulated a debate about cosmopolitan democracy among liberal democrats that gives priority to the reform of global institutions 'from above' (Held and McGrew, 2002) and among radical democrats that emphasizes the need to change the dominant discourses about global issues 'from below' (Dryzek, 2000). One key question is the extent to which NGOs in the international civil society movement have the power to influence global governance. The growing activism of grassroots and international NGOs in the human rights movement has employed globalisation to promote international and collective inquiry and scrutiny of human rights policies and practices. Ackerly and Okin (1999) note that women's rights as human rights activism is a social critique which at the same time acts as an agent of social change. They suggest that the movement is an illustration of international civil society in the form of a network of local, national and international NGOs sharing a common guiding criterion (Ackerly and Okin, 1999:

157–8). From this perspective the women's rights as a human rights movement can be interpreted as an example of the politics of glocalisation, since it has clearly moved beyond the division between national and international NGOs and demonstrated that their combined activism can be effective at the international level.

In the next section we suggest that democracy needs to be strengthened by pluralising the modes and sites of representation and by improving the connection between representation and the participation of citizens in the public spheres (Young, 2000: 132–3). We agree with Fraser that there is indeed a need for a theory and vision of solidarity based on social equality which can overcome the distribution/recognition dilemma with participation at the centre. This can take the form of contextual 'non-reformist reforms' in the sphere of redistribution or recognition (Fraser, 2003: 15).

## The battles over social citizenship – from social class to social exclusion and underclass

The two antagonistic poles in the international political and scientific discourse on new patterns of social inequality and social disorder and strategies to handle the new social divisions are the social exclusion versus the underclass paradigm (see Table 1.1 below).

The term 'social exclusion' is primarily used in European discourse while the concept of an 'underclass' is more often used in the Anglo-Saxon discourse (Andersen and Larsen, 1995). The different meanings of the term 'new poverty' thus offer a window into these political cultures more generally (Silver, 1996: 108).

Within the rhetoric of the EU institutions – closely linked to the promotion of the 'social dimension' when Jacques Delors was president of the EU Commission from the mid-1980s to mid-1990s – the concept of social exclusion became a key concept in the struggles over the direction of EU policy. In EU policy documents social exclusion was defined as 'processes and consequent situations'. More clearly than the concept of poverty, often understood as referring exclusively to income, it states the multidimensional nature of the mechanisms whereby individuals and groups are excluded from taking part in social exchanges, and from the component practices and rights of social integration and of identity (Commission of the European Community, 1993).

In the New Right's 'Moral Underclass Discourse' (MUD) the *underclass* is defined as those who 'are poor from their own choice, influenced by corrupting role models, and by welfare provision that saps personal discipline' (Westergaard, 1992: 576). The social exclusion paradigm addresses the 'exclusionary society' (Lister, 1990) as the problem. Social exclusion is the result of socio-economic restructuring and regression in welfare policy. The new social division is not a product of cultural changes at the bottom, but a product of economic and political changes at the top.

With the exception of Britain, the term underclass has not played a dominant role in European discourse on socio-economic restructuring (Dahrendorf, 1988: 152). In the French debate on 'l'exclus', the term was used as a metaphor for postmodern society's polyphony in which a weakening of common values and the social fabric is emerging (Silver, 1994).

Theoretically, the notion of social exclusion points to a shift in the conceptualisation of poverty from (extreme) class inequality and lack of resources to a broader insider/outsider problematic – that is, a change of focus in the poverty and inequality discourse from a vertical to a horizontal perspective. Some scholars have described it as a shift from a Marxist and Weberian tradition of class (and status) analysis to a Durkheimian 'anomie/integration' discourse (Andersen, 1999). As Levitas (1996) notes, the danger of the inclusion/exclusion discourse comes when it is narrowed to labour market participation and may thus obscure the fact that the positions in which people are 'integrated' through paid work can be extremely unequal.

We argue that the social exclusion approach is fruitful as a relational and differentiated discourse, because it includes *both* horizontal relations of dominance and inequality *and* vertical/hierarchical (class) relations of dominance. As May Daly and Chiara Saraceno argue, the double emphasis on vertical and horizontal relations makes it possible to understand how power not only is a matter of degree, but is also located in a structure of relationships and how differences – in behaviour, personal attributes, lifestyles, and so forth – can be turned into inequalities (Daly and Saraceno, 2002: 96–7). A gender perspective may potentially enrich the social exclusion approach by referring to specific, gender-based risks and vulnerabilities, but the social exclusion approach does not translate easily into a discourse on women (Daly and Saraceno, 2002: 101). Feminist theory and comparative research often prefer the citizenship framework, which emphasises the double inclusion/exclusion of women in the labour market and in politics in order to explain the specific position of women and gender inequality within and across societies (Hobson, Lewis and Siim, 2002).

Compared to the prototype of industrial class society and the golden age of the postwar welfare society, socio-cultural and socio-economic conditions in late modernity for *The Politics of Inclusion and Empowerment* have changed in a number of ways. As discussed above, the role of the nation state as the locus of the political and the pattern of action arising from distinct social formations have to some extent changed. What complicates the picture is that since the 1970s this process has taken place at the same time that the neoliberal rhetoric of 'voting with one's feet' and the neo-conservative rhetoric of 'obligations of citizenship' were emerging.

Within postwar mainstream sociology (for example, the Parsonian tradition) the concept of social integration invites the researcher to view conflicts between collective actors as something to be avoided. In short, the social exclusion/inclusion approach suggests that in an age of flexible capitalism the absence of collective action from the bottom is a problem.

Generally speaking, it can be argued that the ability to organise collective action from the bottom, and therefore to some extent the presence of organised conflictual relationship between the affluent and the less affluent in the struggle over access and control over valued goods in society, is a precondition for arriving at a sustainable, negotiated social contract in society. Informed by classic conflict sociology (Coser, 1956), we suggest a notion of social inclusion and social conflict, which includes the distinction between the exclusionary 'socially unproductive' and the inclusive 'socially productive' types of conflict.

The aim is to stress the positive and innovative functions of social conflict. One way of approaching the problem and challenge of handling the need for recognition of identity differences and particularities (the politics of difference) on the one hand, and recognizing the need for a set of universalistic values and orientations within which differences can be thought and handled on the other, is to speak about *socially productive conflicts*. This way of thinking has similarities with the notion of radical democracy (Mouffe, 1993). The overall aim of this book is to stimulate social and political theory in the above direction.

Below is a brief overview of the various approaches, discourses and policy orientations analysed in the essays that follow. The focus is on establishing a link between the social exclusion (Ruth Lister, Marjorie Mayo, Pauline McClenaghan, David Etherington, John Andersen and

Jørgen Elm Larsen) and democratic citizenship (Iris Young, Anne Phillips, Jens Ulrich, Ute Gerhard, Birte Siim and Ann-Dorte Christensen) approaches. In Table 1.1 the two approaches are contrasted with the competing underclass approach.

## Outline of the book

In 'Situated Knowledge and Democratic Discussions' Iris Marion Young explores the concept of inclusive democracy and the reasons for claiming that social groups and positions should be included in political discussions, especially since some people voice reservations that this 'politics of presence', to use Anne Phillips' phrase, fosters divisiveness and diverts citizens' attention from a common good. The most frequently stated reasons for trying to make sure that all social segments and perspectives attain a real voice in public discussions and decisions have to do with recognition and defence of socio-economic interests. On the one hand, a polity that tries to include all groups, segments and perspectives in their specificity in the processes of political decision-making thereby gives specific recognition to those groups. This is especially important where the polity has a history of marginalising or ignoring certain groups, or of attempting to assimilate them into a single, dominant culture.

Young suggests that a second and more general reason for promoting the inclusion of social segments and perspectives concerns the democratic value of interest promotion. The democratic ideal of political equality asserts that every citizen is the best, if not the only, judge of what is in his or her interest, and that every citizen should have the right and effective opportunity to pursue his or her legitimate interests through the political process. According to Young, social and economic inequalities tend to give significant advantages to some over others in the pursuit of their interests; therefore democratic equity requires compensating for this unfairness so that each citizen has a real opportunity to pursue his or her legitimate interests in the democratic process.

In 'Identity Politics' Anne Phillips traces the debate about group identity. She notes that the key innovation in recent debates on citizenship is the recognition of the exclusionary power of discourses of universality or assimilation that fail to register group difference. This innovation stems largely from what we call 'identity politics', but while identity politics is in one sense inescapable, it is also widely criticised. The most common objection is that it gets the groupings wrong: that it boxes people into inappropriate identities, freezes identities that are hybrid

*Table 1.1*  Comparison of dimensions of democratic citizenship, social citizenship and the underclass

| | Democratic Citizenship | Social Citizenship | Underclass |
|---|---|---|---|
| **Political orientation** | Feminist, communitarianist and multiculturalist | Feminist social democratic/socialist | Neo-liberal and conservative |
| **Theoretical foundation/Inspiration** | Feminist theory, deliberative democracy, theories about multiculturalism, radical democracy | Feminist theory, regulation theory, critical political economy, critical social theory | Neoclassical economics, public choice theory versions of functionalist sociology |
| **Diagnosis and discourse at the macro level** | Multi-level governance, lack of democratic legitimisation and accountability at the transnational level | Post-Fordist economy, welfare state retrenchment, lack of regulation of global market forces | Over-generous welfare state that 'crowds out' market dynamics |
| **Policy orientation** | Democratic inclusion and recognition of difference and diversity through multiculturalist strategies based on equal participation – improving political, cultural and civil rights. Cosmopolitan democracy | Redistribution and inclusion. New opportunity structures: the redistributive 'capability state'. New *social contract*, taking the social costs of post-industrial transformation into account | Politics of deregulation and residualisation of the welfare state. New authoritarianism: strong moral leadership on work ethics and family values |
| **Diagnosis and discourse at the meso level** | Individualisation and democratic fragmentation. An increase in identity politics. Emergence of everyday life politics that focuses on politics from a particular perspective | Social polarisation in the urban space. Erosion of working-class culture and the emergence of the populist New Right. Ethnic and gender-based discrimination in the labour market | Urban underclass due to 'dependency culture', erosion of meritocratic values. Lack of positive role models at the bottom |
| **Policy orientation** | Empowerment/political mobilisation based on new forms of political identities and solidarity. Linking particularism and universalism, gender, ethnicity and class | Empowerment and social capital-building: Linkage of social and economic objectives for policy. Coping with care and work – for example, life and time politics. Adult learning | Extended inequality in order to restore reward structures and incentives Enterprise zones Workfare programmes |

and shifting, and somehow addresses people by the 'wrong' name. The further worry, which Phillips addresses, is that identity politics may be getting the problems wrong, that it may be misplacing the resentments, displacing the inequalities, and thereby encouraging us to sever political from economic power. She argues that despite the relevant critique of assimilationism, the problem is due to the missing linkage between an understanding of misrecognition and socio-economic inequality. The 'identity camp' has lost its transformative potential and has come to function as part of a 'renaturalisation' of capitalism which forecloses more ambitious claims about social justice.

Phillips argues that the massive problem in contemporary mainstream discourse is the absence of a link between redistribution and recognition issues. The paradox is that in the period – at least in most Anglo-Saxon countries – when the gap between the 'haves' and the 'have-nots' is growing, socio-economic equalisation has 'come to be a less compelling objective – in part because it is associated with 'sameness' – and this move has been supported by identity politics who in their criticism of 'false universalisms', missed their initial interest in radical changes of opportunity structures. Phillips argues that a crucial part of the project of political equality is narrowing the income gap between rich and poor, combined with a greater convergence in life-chances. Like Marshall, and his legacy of social citizenship, she argues that democracy 'in its deeper sense' recognises the tension between the universalism of political equality and the persistence of economic and status inequality. From this perspective, democracy is not just a 'mechanism for generating governments', but a deeper claim about status and socio-economic equality of citizens. Phillips discusses empowerment in this framework and warns that we should be careful not to reduce the language of empowerment to voluntarism: a matter of political will completely detached from social and economic condition.

Jens Ulrich argues in 'Deliberative Democracy and Civil Society' that it would be constructive to extend the often narrow definition of civil society found in deliberative theories. He notes that democratic dialogue is highly valued in contemporary debates among critical social scientists and that civil society is seen as a guarantor for a constructive and critical public sphere from where such a dialogue can spring. The question is, however, whether the emergence of late modern society sets new frameworks and conditions for how civil society ought to be defined and localised. The point is that the localising of civil society ought to take, as its departure, a point of reference in the rationality of the dialogue as opposed to the institutionalised roots of the dialogue.

With a feminist Habermasian reading as its starting point, the chapter works towards an understanding of civil society, which both agrees with and repudiates elements of the feminist critique. He argues that Jodi Deans' concept of the hypothetical third is central to an approach that makes it possible to extend the understanding of civil society, while at the same time defending the universalistic element.

In 'Globalisation, Democracy and Participation – The Dilemmas of the Danish Citizenship Model', Birte Siim discusses the challenges to modern democracy presented by globalisation and immigration. She suggests that the Danish gender model can illustrate the dilemma for the participatory model of citizenship between equality and diversity in the era of globalisation. In the first section of her chapter, she looks at the paradox of globalisation on the basis of sociological theories of modernisation. The gendered problem of combining the local, national and global levels of politics is explored on the basis of a recent study of citizenship in Denmark. The study illustrates the dilemma of the participatory model of democracy: citizens feel a relatively high degree of empowerment in relation to local democracy but a sense of competence decreases if we move from the local to the national level, and decreases even more at the European level. This dilemma is gendered, because women tend to be more interested in and feel more empowered by local democracy, while men are more interested in national politics and tend to identify with broader political issues. In the second section Siim discusses the implications of immigration by focusing on the tension between the inclusion of women and ethnic minority groups. It is argued that feminist approaches to the equality/diversity dilemma need to be contextualised and that the Danish case challenges the belief in an automatic link between inclusion based on gender, diversity and difference. Siim argues that there is a need for a feminist universalism based on new forms of solidarity and global responsibilities that link the mobilisation of women citizens around everyday life politics with the development of global solidarities and responsibilities.

In 'The Danish Gender Model: Between Movement Politics and Representative Politics' Ann-Dorte Christensen explores the development of the Danish gender model. She emphasises that the model is closely related to the intersection between movement politics and representative politics. Focusing on these two channels Christensen discusses the differences in women's political identities and strategies. The 'movement channel' is analysed through women's involvement in the peace movement in the 1980s, while the 'institution channel' is examined through the debate about gender quotas in the Socialist People's Party in the 1970s and the 1980s. In the last section of her chapter

Christensen discusses the current changes and challenges to the Danish gender model arising from the construction of new political identities among young women.

In 'Gendered Citizenship: A Model for European Citizenship?' Ute Gerhard argues that the varied vocabulary used to describe the concept of citizenship shows that it is necessary to reconsider the distinctive historical background and legal traditions and to reconstruct citizenship by contextualising its meaning. The chapter elaborates on the German legal theoretical and political differentiation between bourgeois and citizen, between citizenship as legal status and as membership, and discusses the specific meaning of basic rights codified in the German constitution since 1949. The history of women's delayed citizenship, and their struggle for political participation, is analysed with reference to the feminist debate on 'differentiated citizenship' as a multiple or post-national concept substituting for the exclusiveness of a nation state. Against this background Gerhard discusses whether the European Union, with its promise 'to contribute step by step to a construction of an area of freedom, safety and law', might serve as a political opportunity structure for women's participation and full citizenship.

In 'A Politics of Recognition and Respect' Ruth Lister argues that the politics of poverty can increasingly be characterised as a 'politics of recognition and respect' as well as of redistribution. A pivotal demand is for a voice and for participation in political debate and policy development. The first section of the chapter makes a normative theoretical case for this demand, using the concepts of social exclusion, citizenship, democracy, recognition and power and empowerment. The second section describes a number of British initiatives, including the Commission on Poverty, Participation and Power, which both acts as a prefigurative model of what is possible and promotes the case for the participation of people in poverty in decision-making that affects their lives.

Marjorie Mayo in 'Exclusion, Inclusion and Empowerment' addresses the contested concept of empowerment in the current policy context. In the first section of the chapter the concept of empowerment itself is unpacked by looking at the various definitions and how these, in turn, relate to competing perspectives on power in society. Mayo argues that 'community empowerment', 'community participation' and 'empowerment' have become more vital and yet more overtly problematic than ever in the current global context. She traces the connections between neoliberal economic agendas and their consequences on the one hand, and agendas for community participation and empowerment – framed in terms of increasing communities' capacities for self-organisation and self-help, in the face of increasing social needs but decreasing public welfare provision – on the other. While recognising the significance of neoliberal agendas, globally, Mayo emphasises the potential for more radical, transformatory approaches. Faced with pressures for increasing social polarisation (both locally and globally) relatively powerless individuals, groups and communities were nevertheless managing to do more than simply learn how to respond to official programmes – they were learning the rules of the regeneration/development game. There were also examples of their developing strategies to empower themselves, to form their own agendas for development and regeneration in the countries of both the North and the South. Mayo illustrates the potential for women (and men) to develop their own agendas, empowering themselves in ways that would be consistent with feminist approaches to citizenship as processes of active involvement. Mayo also argues that far from representing an alternative to the state on the one hand, and the market on the other, as some protagonists of 'communitarian' approaches have suggested, civil society has been deeply affected by these restructuring processes – with emerging evidence of processes of restructuring and polarisation in the voluntary and community sectors themselves. This raises key questions about who might be being empowered and included and who might be becoming even more marginalised and excluded, and how these processes might relate to social divisions in terms of gender, ethnicity, age, disability and social class.

Pauline McClenaghan's chapter 'Redefining Citizenship: Community, Civil Society and Adult Education' follows the same line of argument. The increasingly important role of community and voluntary participation, as an expression of active citizenship, reflects processes of economic and social transformation associated with globalisation and the socio-cultural imperatives governing state efforts to maintain integration and cohesion in a rapidly changing and competitive environment. The re-emergence of 'community' as a unit concept in social theory and the process of community sector integration into state socio-economic strategies in social and health care and in local economic regeneration, mark the ascendance of a cultural project aimed at creating a social environment in which active citizens take responsibility for themselves and their communities. 'Community participation' and 'empowerment' are increasingly expressed as the twin pillars of social policy interventions aimed at social inclusion and based on synergetic partnerships between community groups, governmental bodies, statutory authorities and other organisational agents. If this cultural project is to mean more than the implementation of lower-cost forms of social problem management, community stakeholders, as well as their professional and private sector counterparts, must see the expression of citizenship in synergy relations with the state as meaningful, worthwhile and legitimate. The analysis draws on research data derived from experience in the field of adult education in the community development at the University of Ulster. The role of community development education in forming a 'habitus' for this expanding social field is critically examined and its potential contribution to increased democratic participation and empowerment accessed.

In 'Welfare, Gender and Political Agency: Comparing Strategies in the UK and Denmark' David Etherington explores women's agency and the strategies deployed by women and social/labour movements in the pursuit of gender equality comparing welfare and workfare/activation in the UK and Denmark. A key argument is that both place and space are important elements in exclusion and mobilisation and this is explored by a focus on gender and workfare in the urban context. Compared with Denmark, there is a *relatively* more developed politics of equality in UK, which can be explained by the legacies of municipal socialism, but also by the national struggles over institutionalised racism. The role of the trade union movement in both countries is crucial, but the relatively advanced developments of women's self-organisation (or the integration of diversity) within the larger British unions are crucial in shaping equality agendas. This tradition has not been embedded in the Danish union movement to the same degree. However, in Denmark the unions engagement with the labour market institutions and corporatist networks does have benefits for women's mobilisation. Therefore, whilst the liberal welfare model in the UK reinforces gender exclusion compared with the more redistributive and equality-based Danish welfare system, there are traditions and innovations around the politics of equality in the UK, which can offer lessons for Denmark.

In 'The Politics of Marginal Space' J.E. Larsen presents a case study of community centres for mentally ill people, drug addicts, alcoholics and lonely people in Kongens Enghave in Copenhagen. The case study illustrates how drop-in centres have contributed to facilitating the creation of socially constructed communities for marginal people which may well be a last resort for making sense of the world and for socialising with others. Rather paradoxically this spatialisation of social policy, or the politics of marginal space, may facilitate rather than counteract 'marginal cultures' and 'risk communities'. Social 'integration' into marginal communities may lead to disintegration in relation to 'mainstream cultures'. On the one hand, overall governmental policy is aiming at the reintegration of marginal people into the labour market and other normalising social institutions. On the other hand, there is a growing awareness among social policy actors and agencies of the impossibility of normalising the social integration of 'outsiders'. A critical perception of the politics of marginal space argues that it represents a new confinement of marginal and deviant people. It is not a physical but a symbolically violent confinement as marginal spaces may produce a common-sense perception about the limitations one is subordinated to in social and physical space. Poor communities with poor people are self-evidently experienced as being condemned to poor services. Although the case study is local in scope, the empirical study illuminates a partly overlooked issue in relation to debates on recognition and redistribution: that certain types of redistribution policies involving recognition of 'marginality' risk reproducing 'cultures of inequality'. Recognition of marginality with limited redistribution can in fact be a way of displacing what is 'different' to marginal spaces within the community. The politics of marginal space may therefore turn out to be a problematic 'discount' version of both recognition and redistribution instead of empowering marginal people and facilitate their inclusion in the community.

John Andersen and J.E. Larsen in 'Social Polarisation and Urban Governance' focus on the often overlooked meso level of politics: local government and urban policy. The case study looks at the struggles over urban government and governance in Copenhagen with reference to the intensive American and European discourse on the new 'urban underclass'.

Urban policy changes are interpreted in an historical context with an emphasis on how the transition to a new post-industrial economy and urban form was mediated via struggles over the form and content of urban planning. The postwar 'golden age' of the 'welfare city' rested on a strong town hall administration and powerful social democratic leadership. During the 1970s the efficiency and legitimacy of this urban regime were challenged by a weakened urban economy and powerful leftist forces and mobilisation from new urban movements. At the beginning of the 1980s political and institutional dislocation fused with a growing financial crisis. This in turn increased the conflicts over additional grants with the state level. From the late 1980s the 'entrepreneurial city' strategy became the new orientation of urban policy, but at the same time, new bottom-up community welfare development programmes came into operation.

They argue that the present urban democracy is a battlefield characterised by a widening gap between:

1. Participatory empowering welfare-oriented community strategies, which target deprived districts, which are based on notions of the *inclusive city*. This trend is founded on a rhetoric with elements of deliberative democracy, social inclusion and citizens' empowerment.
2. Neo-elitist/corporative market-driven growth strategies, which are based on notions of the *entrepreneurial globalised city*, where urban policy becomes a question of facilitation of the 'growth machine'. This trend echoes what Harvey (2000) has termed neoliberalised urban authoritarianism.

The question raised, which goes beyond the urban policy field, is how the logic of social inclusion and democratic citizenship can coexist with the logics of elitist growth machines.

## Note

1. This book is one of the results of the national Danish research project GEP: Gender, Empowerment and Politics, which involved researchers from four Danish universities. GEP was a five-year research programme funded by the Danish National Research Council for the Social Sciences. The book is based on original research and includes three keynote papers as well as selected papers from international experts at the GEP International conference 'New Challenges to Gender, Democracy, Welfare States – The Politics of Empowerment and Inclusion', Vilvorde Kursuscenter, 18–20 August, 2000. We would like to thank the Danish National Research Council for the Social Sciences for its generous support of the project.

## References

Ackerly, B.A. and S.M. Okin (1999). 'Feminist Social Criticism and the International Movement for Women's Rights as Human Rights', in J. Shapiro and C. Hacker-Cordóned (eds.), *Democracy's Edges*. Cambridge: Cambridge University Press.

Andersen, J. (1999). 'Post-industrial Solidarity or Meritocracy?' *Acta Sociologica* 1999: 4.

Andersen, J. and J.E. Larsen (1995). 'The Underclass Debate – A Spreading Disease?', in N. Mortensen (ed.), *Social Integration and Marginalisation*. Copenhagen: Samfundslitteratur.

Commission of the European Community (1993). *European Social Policy. Options for the Union*. Luxembourg: Commission of the European Community.

Coser, L. (1956). *The Function of Social Conflict*. New York: The Free Press.

Craig, G. and M. Mayo (eds.) (1995). *Community Empowerment*. London: Zed Books.

Dahrendorf, R. (1988). *The Modern Social Conflict. An Essay on the Politics of Liberty*. London: Weidenfeld and Nicolson.

Daly, M. and C. Saraceno (2002). 'Social Exclusion and Gender Relations', in B. Hobson, J. Lewis and B. Siim (eds.), *Contested Concepts in Gender and Social Politics*. Cheltenham: Edward Elgar.

Dean, J. (1996). *Solidarity of Strangers. Feminism after Identity Politics*. Berkeley: California University Press.

Dryzek, J. (2000). *Deliberative Democracy and Beyond. Liberals, Critics, Contestations*. Oxford: Oxford University Press.

Fraser, N. (1997). *Justice Interruptus. Critical Reflections on the Post-Socialist Condition*. London: Polity Press.

Fraser, N. (2003). 'Institutionalizing Democratic Justice: Redistribution, Recognition and Participation'. Paper presented at Roskilde University Centre, 30 April.

Friedmann, J. (1995). *Empowerment. The Politics of Alternative Development*. Oxford: Blackwell.

Giddens, A. (1994). *Beyond Left and Right, The Future of Radical Politics*. London: Polity Press.

Harvey, D. (2000). *Spaces of Hope*. Edinburgh: Edinburgh University Press.

Held, D. and A. McGrew (2002). *The Globalisation/Anti-Globalisation Movement*. London: Polity Press.

Hobson, B., J. Lewis and B. Siim (2002). *Contested Concepts in Gender and Social Politics*. Cheltenham: Edward Elgar.

Jessop, B. (1994). 'The Transition to Post-Fordism and the Schumpetarian Workfare State', in R. Burrows and B. Lauder (eds.), *Towards a Post-Fordist Welfare State*. London: Routledge.

Levitas, R. (1996). 'The Concept of Social Exclusion and the New Durkheimian Hegemony'. *Critical Social Policy*, 16, 46.

Lister, R. (1990). *The Exclusive Society. Citizenship and the Poor*. London: Child Poverty Action Group.

Marques-Pereira, B. and B. Siim (2002). 'Representation, Agency and Empowerment', in B. Hobson, J. Lewis and B. Siim (eds.), *Contested Concepts in Gender and Social Politics*. Cheltenham: Edward Elgar.

Mouffe, C. (ed.) (1993). *Dimensions of Radical Democracy: Pluralism, Citizenship, Community*. London: Verso.

Siim, B. (2000). *Gender and Citizenship: Politics and Agency in France, Britain and Denmark*. Cambridge: Cambridge University Press.

Silver, H. (1996). 'Culture, Politics and National Discourses of the New Urban Poverty', in E. Mingione (ed.), *Urban Poverty and the Underclass*. Oxford: Blackwell.

Swyngedouw, E., F. Moulaert and A. Rodríguez (eds.) (2003). *The Globalized City*. Oxford: Oxford University Press.

Westergaard, J. (1992). 'About and beyond the Underclass: Some Notes on Influences of Social Climate on British Sociology Today'. BSA Presidential Address, 1992. *Sociology*, 26, 4.

Young, I.M. (1990). *Justice and the Politics of Difference*. Princeton: Princeton University Press.

Young, I.M. (2000). *Inclusive Democracy*. Oxford: Oxford University Press.

# 2
# Situated Knowledge and Democratic Discussions

*Iris Marion Young*

Recent political theory has focused more attention than before on the importance of taking special measures to assure that socially or economically disadvantaged groups or social segments are included in processes of political discussion and policy formation in ways that make their voices audible as an expression of the specificity of their situation. This reflects recent practice in a number of political movements that acknowledge that fairness is as important in processes as it is to outcomes. While most political processes still need significant improvement to approximate this ideal, the issue has been seriously raised in the last few decades, and substantive reforms have taken place in some democracies in an attempt to address problems of *de facto* exclusion.

Those interested in deep and inclusive democracy need to be clear on the reasons for claiming that social groups and positions should be included in their specificity in political discussions, especially since some people voice reservations that this 'politics of presence', to use Anne Phillips' (1995) phrase, fosters divisiveness and diverts citizens' attention from a common good. The most frequently stated reasons for trying to make sure that all social segments and perspectives attain a real voice in public discussions and decisions have to do with recognition and the defence of interest. On the one hand, a polity that tries to include all groups, segments and perspectives in their specificity in processes of political decision-making thereby gives specific recognition to those groups. This is especially important where the polity has a history of marginalising or ignoring some groups, or of attempts to assimilate them to a single dominant culture.[1]

A second and more general reason for promoting the inclusion of social segments and perspectives concerns the democratic value of interest promotion. The democratic ideal of political equality states that every citizen is the best, if not the only, judge of what is in his or her interest, and that every citizen should have the right and effective opportunity to pursue his or her legitimate interests through the political process. While differentiating legitimate from illegitimate interests is a difficult business, which I do not wish to explore in this chapter, let us say for now that a legitimate interest is any expressed interest, the satisfaction of which will not violate the basic rights of others. Because social and economic inequalities tend to give significant advantages to some over others in the pursuit of their interests, democratic fairness requires compensating for this unfairness so that each citizen has the effective opportunity to pursue his or her legitimate interests in the democratic process.

The goals of recognising all members of the polity in their specificity and affording them all opportunities to pursue their legitimate interests are good reasons for advocating special attention to the inclusion of otherwise disadvantaged or marginalised social segments. Both these reasons, however, can nurture the fears of divisiveness and diversion from a commitment to a general good that critics of so-called 'identity politics' invoke. In this chapter I wish to explore a less often cited but, I think, equally important reason why democratic discussions and decision-making processes ought to take special measures to assure that the voices and perspectives of all social segments can have an effective voice in which they express their opinions and judgements from the specificity of their position and experience. Such inclusion, I will suggest, enables wiser and more just decisions, because it increases the knowledge available in the decision process and helps promote a shift in the perspective of everyone from self-regard to a more objective view, which takes into account the legitimate interests of everyone. This third reason, that is, can help allay fears that a politics of presence turns us away from public commitment towards divisive interest group competition.

To explicate how an interest in political inclusion promotes wise and just judgement I rely on ideas derived from feminist epistemology. Writers such as Donna Haraway, Lorraine Code, Sandra Harding and Ismay Barwell have criticised what Haraway calls a 'god's eye' conception of the process of attaining reliable knowledge, which assumes that there is a standpoint transcending the particularities of history and social position from which the truth can be ascertained. They theorise instead what Haraway calls 'situated knowledges', which I interpret as a conception of objectivity as constructed from the partial and situated perspectives of differently positioned social actors. My argument applies this feminist epistemology to the knowledge and judgement that ideally ought to result from inclusive democratic processes. I will conclude with a brief discussion of how this interpretation of inclusive discussion might be applied to debates about human rights.

## The subject of political decision: judgement

In what follows I assume the general model of democratic process that has come to be called deliberative democracy. In the larger project to which this essay is related, I argue that some statements of the ideal of deliberative democracy privilege argumentative forms of communication too much, and tend to assume norms of order, dispassionateness and consensus (see Young, 2000: chapters 1 and 2). Nevertheless, I agree with proponents of a deliberative model of democracy that making room for inclusive discussion of issues and opinions is better for democratic outcomes, partly because democratic agenda-setting and policy formation should not be considered merely as the aggregation of preference, but as the search for the best answers to collective problems. Participants in democratic decision-making ought not to think of themselves simply as registering a subjective preference or opinion, but as together looking for informed and well-considered answers to questions. Along the lines of a Deweyian understanding of democracy, the democratic process ideally should be a form of inquiry and the results a kind of knowledge (see Dewey, 1927; Honneth, 1998: 87–95). Since my project here is to apply some ideas of feminist epistemology to arguments for the inclusion of socially differentiated voices and perspectives in democratic discussions, it is useful to ask just what sort of inquiry democratic discussion is.

Political philosophers often write as though the solution that participants in democracy seek to political problems is a principle or set of principles. John Rawls' formulations of the task of deliberative democracy as that of seeking an 'overlapping consensus' among diverse groups with differing moral and metaphysical commitments is the most famous of these accounts. On a Rawlsian view, the fundamental problem of politics is determining the principles of justice that diverse society members can agree on to guide the design of their political institutions. While Rawls denies that these principles should come into play to adjudicate every possible issue of justice within institutions, his model of democratic process nevertheless gives us the picture of a well-ordered democratic polity as one in which discussion seeks either to ascertain the correct principles for guiding institutions and evaluating policies or seeks to apply these principles to particular issues and situations. Many others who think and write about the democratic process implicitly assume that the knowledge democratic inquiry seeks is knowledge of general principles and their application. Call this the legal model of democratic knowledge.

Other theorists and public officials appear to assume that if democracy is at least partly a process of inquiry to try to solve collective problems, then its knowledge is technical. Suppose the problems are poverty or industry emitting too many pollutants into the air. The task of the policy sciences is to develop a sanction and incentive structure that will motivate various segments of the society to behave in ways that lead to the result of raising the incomes of the lowest or reducing pollution. Political leaders, then, must have knowledge of economics, chemistry and meteorology, as well as sophisticated behavioural science. If good policy is the product primarily of technical knowledge in this sense, however, the inclusion of all citizens in democratic discussion on an equal basis would seem to be an impediment rather than an aid to inquiry.

While the technical model of democratic knowledge once held considerable influence, it has lost credence in recent years, partly because experts have lost confidence that they can in fact solve many of mass society's problems, and partly because citizens' movements have sometimes shown that technical knowledge is at best only a part of what is needed for wise and fair policy-making. Environmentally motivated movements, such as the ones against nuclear power and around the siting of hazardous facilities, have been particularly successful in establishing that the point of view of technical expertise is rarely neutral from a social point of view, and that ordinary citizens can face the problems of what to do about energy needs or hazardous waste if given the chance.

The model of democratic knowledge as solving problems technically precludes understanding the process of discussion as having a normative aspect. The legal model does indeed understand the subject of democratic discussion as normative. By focusing on processes of discovering and applying principles, however, this model invites us to imagine a more abstract and comprehensive decision situation than politics usually exhibits. It is rare that participants in actual political conflict are struggling over basic principles of justice. They are more often worried about what actions to take to address immediate or long-term problems. Considering political debate and its resolution as aiming at agreement on a set of principles that can then be applied to solve problems, moreover, gives too general an understanding of the subject of political discussion. A social problem or conflict has more particularity than such a model can allow, deriving from a particular historical trajectory and the particular social actors and their relationships.

I wish to follow political theorists such as Jennifer Nedelsky in suggesting that the goal of democratic political discussion should be understood as that of arriving at *judgements* rather than principles or technical solutions. Democratic inquiry consists in members of a polity together considering their situation, ascertaining the place and interests of the different people in it, and trying to make a judgement about what course of action would be best for addressing these particular problems with these particular actors in these particular relationships. Like the formulation of preferences, and unlike principles, judgements remain related to the particularity of participants and their situation. Unlike the formulation of preferences, however, and more like principles, judgements are a form of *objective* discourse in the sense that they are claims made to a public for which an audience expects reasons that can be examined and criticised, and about which people can be persuaded to change their minds.

If we consider the main object of democratic inquiry to be political judgements, then, we retain the particularity of situated action in politics, but we can also say that the process is aiming at a kind of knowledge or wisdom. Considering the desired outcome of democratic discussion as good judgement, moreover, retains a place for both principles and technical know-how in the process of policy-making. To the extent that people require justification from one another for their claims and proposals, they must often appeal to principles and values of justice. Appeals to principles of justice have a more pragmatic function in political interaction than many theories of justice attribute to them. Where practical judgements are the result at which discussants aim, appeals to principles of justice are steps in arguments about what should be done. Similarly, technical knowledge may often be useful in choosing among alternative courses of action, but the technical conclusions are properly only steps towards judgements that also include concerns about fairness and appropriateness.

Nedelsky recommends adopting Hannah Arendt's ideas about the character and importance of judgement. Arendt takes from Immanuel Kant the idea that judgement is a kind of thought that is neither general nor singular, neither deductively certain nor merely subjective, but is a form of discourse that claims general acceptance about situated affairs. Judgement derives its claim to generality and objectivity not from bringing particulars under a universal, according to Arendt, again taking her cue from Kant, but rather from an enlargement of thought that comes from considering the perspectives of many differently situated people. In the argument that follows I rely on such a notion of enlarged thought.[2]

## Difference, knowledge and objectivity

A key feature of the normative ideal of deliberative democracy is that deliberation facilitates the transformation of the desires and opinions of citizens from an initial partial, narrow or self-regarding understanding of issues and problems, to a more comprehensive understanding that takes the needs and interests of others more thoroughly into account. Processes of political community ought and sometimes do move people from a merely subjective to a more objective way of looking at problems and solutions. Sometimes the thinking of the participants in a public inclusive communicative process is enlarged: instead of understanding issues only from the point of view of my partial and parochial experience and interests, I move to a point of view capable of making a judgement of justice that places my interests among others.

Modern thought has often idealised objectivity as achieved by transcending particularities of social position and experience, abstracting from them to construct a standpoint outside and above them that is general rather than particular. Thus, most accounts of moral objectivity assume that a normatively objective concern for justice requires bracketing or transcending particular social location and adopting a 'view from nowhere'. There are at least two problems with such an interpretation of objectivity, however, especially when the inquiry involves assessment of social problems and rival proposals for addressing them fairly.

First, a monological method of bracketing or abstracting from the particularities of social position is notoriously unreliable. How can I and others be confident that I have not carried over assumptions and conclusions derived from my particular standpoint into the supposedly objective general standpoint? In making judgements about public or political action, how can I be sure that I have not given more weight to my own desires and interests than to the legitimate interests of others? Only the critical and differentiated perspectives of a plurality of others who discuss my claims and judgements can validate the objectivity of the latter.

Second, even if achieving a transparent impartial standpoint were possible, in political communication our goal is not to arrive at some generalities. Instead, we are looking for just solutions to particular problems embedded in a particular social context, not abstracted from it. The conclusions to political discussion and argument, that is, are particular judgements about what ought to be done. Appeals to principle have a place in such discussion, but they must be applied to particular situations in the context of particular social relationships. Thus participants in political discussion cannot transcend their particularity. If participants are to make objective judgements appropriate for their context, they must express their own particularity to others and learn of the particularity of those differently situated in the social world where they dwell together.

We thus need a different account of the distinction between a merely subjective or self-regarding point of view and an objective point of view. On this account, objectivity is an achievement of democratic communication that includes all differentiated social positions. Objectivity in political judgements, as I understand that term, does not consist in discovering some truth about politics or institutions independent of the awareness and action of social members. But it is also not simply some kind of sum of their differentiated viewpoints. An objective account of social relations and social problems, and an objective judgement of what policies and actions would address those problems, instead are accounts and judgements people construct for themselves from a critical, reflective and persuasive interaction among their diverse experiences and opinions.

Hilary Putnam offers one such theory of objectivity. Interpreting Dewey's understanding of intelligence and democracy as a method of solving social problems, Putnam argues that objectivity is a product of inclusive democratic communication. Without such inclusive discussion, privileged social positions are able to make judgements and take actions that suit themselves and rationalisations for them that go unchallenged.[3]

Feminist epistemologists offer a compatible account of objectivity as a product of what Donna Haraway calls 'situated knowledges' (see Haraway, 1991: 183–201). In socially differentiated societies, individuals have particular knowledge that arises from experience in their social positions, and those social positionings also influence the interests and assumptions they bring to inquiry. All positionings are partial with respect to the inquiry. Where there are structural differences of privilege and disadvantage, and where there have conditioned the discourses of received knowledge, the explicit voicing of the plurality of positions and their confirming or criticizing one another is necessary for objectivity.[4]

Especially where there are structural relations of privilege and disadvantage, then, explicit inclusion and recognition of differentiated social positions provides experiential and critical resources for democratic communication that aims to promote justice. Inclusion of differentiated groups is important not only as a means of demonstrating equal respect and to ensure that all legitimate interests in the polity receive expression, though these are fundamental reasons for democratic inclusion. Inclusion has two additional functions. First, it motivates participants in political debate to transform their claims from mere expressions of self-regarding interest to appeals to justice. Second, it maximises the social knowledge available to a democratic public, such that citizens are more likely to make just and wise decisions. I will elaborate each of these points.

Having to be accountable to people from diverse social positions with different needs, interests and experience helps transform discourse from self-regard to appeals to justice. Because others are not likely to accept 'I want this' or 'this policy is in my interest' as reasons to accept a proposal, the requirement that discussion participants try to make their claims understandable and persuasive to others means they must frame the proposals in terms of justice. Appealing to justice here does not necessarily mean that the others agree either with a person's or a group's principle or judgements of what justice requires. It means only that they frame their assertions to the others in terms of fairness or rights that they claim take others' interests into account and which others *ought* therefore to accept. Contrary to what some theorists of deliberative democracy suggest, policy proposals need not be expressed in terms of a common interest, an interest all can share. Indeed, some claims of justice are not likely to express an interest all can share, because they are claims that actions should be taken to reduce the privilege some people are perceived to have. Many other claims or proposals will not directly confront privilege, but will be multiple expressions of need and preference among which a polity must sort out relative moral legitimacy and relative priority. To make such claims participants in public discussion must generally recognise social difference.

Inclusion of and attention to socially differentiated positions in democratic discussion tend to correct biases and situate the partial perspective of participants in debate. Confrontation with different perspectives, interests and cultural meanings teaches each the partiality of their own and reveals to them their own experience as perspectival. Listening to those differently situated from myself and my close associates teaches me how my situation looks to them, what relation they think I stand to them. Such a contextualising of perspective is especially important for groups that have power, authority or privilege. Those in structurally superior positions not only take their experience, preferences and opinions to be general, uncontroversial, ordinary and even an expression of suffering or disadvantage, as we all do, but also have the power to represent these as general norms. Having to answer to others who speak from different, less privileged perspectives on their social relations exposes their partiality and relative blindness.[5] By including multiple perspectives and not simply two that might be in direct contention over an issue, we take a giant step towards enlarging thought. Where there are differences in interests, values or judgements between members of two interdependent but differently positioned groups, the fact that both must be accountable to differently situated others further removed from those relations can motivate each to reflect on fairness to all.[6] Where such exposure to the public judgement and criticism of multiply situated others does not lead them to shut down dialogue and instead leads some to try to force their preferences on policy, this process can lead to a better understanding of the requirements of justice.

By pointing out how the standpoint of those in less privileged positions can reveal otherwise unnoticed bias and partiality I do not mean to suggest, as have some standpoint theorists, that people in less advantaged social positions are 'epistemically privileged'. They too are liable to bias and self-regard in overstating the nature of situations, misunderstanding their causes, or laying blame in the wrong place. Some partialities and misunderstandings can best be exposed by discussion with differently situated others. Susan Wendell offers one example of how the experience and perspective of a structural social group can contribute to the social knowledge of everyone in order to promote more justice. When people with disabilities have the opportunity to express their perceptions of biases in the socially constructed environment or expectations of functions needed to perform tasks, then everyone learns how to see the social environment differently (Wendell, 1996: 66–9).

Aiming to promote social justice through public action requires more than framing debate in terms that appeal to justice. It requires an objective understanding of the society, a comprehensive account of its relations and structured processes, its material locations and environmental conditions, a detailed knowledge of events and conditions in different places and positions, and the ability to predict the likely consequences of actions and policies. Only pooling the situated knowledge of all social positions can positions produce such social knowledge.

Among the sorts of situated knowledge that people in differentiated social positions have are: (1) an understanding of their position, and how it stands in relation to other positions; (2) a social map of other salient positions, how they are defined, and the relation in which they stand to this position; (3) a point of view on the history of the society, (4) an interpretation of how the relations and processes of the whole society operate, especially as they affect one's own position; and (5) a position-specific experience and point of view on the natural and physical environment.

Norms of communicative democracy assume that differently situated individuals understand that they are nevertheless related in a world of interaction and internal effects that affects them all, but differently. If they aim to solve their collective problems, they must listen across their differences to understand how proposals and policies affect others differently situated. They learn what takes place in different social locations and how social processes appear to connect and conflict from different points of view. By internalising such a mediated understanding, participants in democratic discussion and decision-making gain a wider picture of social processes structuring their own partial experience. Such an enlarged view better enables them to arrive at wise and just solutions to collective problems to the extent that they are committed to doing so.

Paying specific attention to differentiated social groups in democratic discussion and encouraging public expression of their situated knowledge thus often makes it more possible than it would otherwise be for people to transform conflict and disagreement into agreement. Speaking across differences in a context of public accountability often reduces mutual ignorance about one another's situations, or misunderstanding of one another's values, intentions and perceptions and gives everyone the enlarged thought necessary to come to more reasonable and fairer solutions to problems. Complete agreement is rare, of course, even when people act in a cooperative spirit, for contingent reasons: there is not enough time, organising discussion is too difficult, people lose concentration and become frustrated, and so on. Procedures of majority rule and compromise are thus often necessary, and do not violate commitments to democratic legitimacy as long as persons and groups have reason to believe that they have had opportunity to influence the outcome.

Some disagreement may be endemic, however, on certain issues in the context of social structures differentiated by interdependent relations of privilege and disadvantage. Many contemporary political theorists conceptualise the sources of such deep disagreement in cultural differences or differences in basic world view and value framework; fundamental disagreements of that sort certainly do surface in most societies over some issues. Such attention to cultural pluralism, however, has diverted attention from a more common source of deep disagreement: structural conflict of interest. A basis of many disagreements about wage, trade or welfare policy within capitalist structural relations, for example, is neither illwill nor ignorance, nor difference in cultural meaning, but the structural fact that, at least sometimes, wages or public services provided for workers implies profit forgone for firms. One can argue that some disagreements over reproductive policy, the care of children, and the proper relationship of workplace to family responsibility reflect the structural inequalities of gender. By including diverse social positions in political discussion, we may not bring about agreed on solutions so much as reveal the structural conflicts of interest that would be obscured by discussion which successfully claimed that at bottom we have common interests. If in fact a society is structurally divided in this way, then deliberative processes ought to aim to reveal and confront such division, rather than exhort those who may have morally legitimate grievances to suppress them for the sake of some people's definition of a common good.

The claim that social difference provides a resource for democratic communication, then, does not necessarily imply that inclusion will make political communication easier, more efficient or better able to arrive at agreement. On the contrary, in some situations, greater inclusion may lead to greater complexity and difficulty in reaching decisions. This is an argument against attending to situated knowledge only if the political goal is to arrive at public decisions as quickly and with as little contest as possible. Public and private policy-makers often do have this goal, of course, but to reach it they often need to keep a process under tight and exclusive control. For many routine, trivial or administrative decisions such a goal may not be inappropriate, though it can be called democratic only if the decisions are embedded in a wider and more contestable public policy discussion. A primary goal of democratic discussion and decision-making ought to be to promote justice in solving problems, however, and I have argued that this goal requires inclusion even if it creates complexity and reveals conflicts of interest that can only be resolved by changing structural relations.

## Application: human rights dialogue

I have elaborated an ideal of democratic discussion in which the inclusion of all affected by an issue or decision is effected not simply by formal non-discrimination and principle of political equality, but more strongly by assuring that groups and social segments that stand in different positions in relation to one another and to the issues at stake are able to express the specificity of their perspective. They each bring partial and situated knowledge to the political discussion, which contributes to forming a more comprehensive and objective account for all of them when shared and examined through dialogue. I will conclude by offering an example of how the structuring of such a heterogeneous public might further progressive politics specifically in human rights debates.

Much contemporary disagreement about human rights today takes the following form. Many theorists and human rights activists assert that there is a finite set of universal principles that express basic respect for human dignity. Their universality derives from the fact that beneath our differences human beings have a common core of needs, desires and vulnerabilities to which correspond a set of universal values. Human beings also live out a vast diversity of practices, relations and cultural meanings that concretise and enrich these core values. If and when local authority and custom conflict with the universal rights, however, respect for human rights should trump local custom. Because they are universal and express core values of humanity, outsiders have the right and even the obligation to enforce human rights against those violating the rights of persons within their society.[7]

Some states, theorists and moral leaders of their people appear to disagree with these views. Often these dissenters from human rights discourse are from Asia or Africa, or speak from non-Western traditions within Western societies. There are, however, Western theorists who dissent from the account of human rights I referred to above, and there are many theorists and activists in Asia and Africa who endorse this sort of account. Dissenters rarely deny the general idea of human rights. Instead, they claim that the current discourse of human rights in international law and politics exhibits Western bias, in several respects. Western governments tend to privilege the principles that correspond to the individualist rights of property and economic and cultural rights that could be interpreted more collectively and which have more substance. Many take the philosophical bases for human rights principles as a fulfilment of Western Enlightenment ideals. Those who argue that contemporary human rights discourse express Western bias, finally, often suggest that outsiders to a society and culture do not understand the history and custom of societies in which they believe they see human rights violations enough to be justified in imposing their view of what should take place in those societies.[8]

Some people construct this sort of disagreement as a confrontation between moral universalism and moral relativism.[9] Those who question stated human rights principles or who defend the specificity of local custom against attempts to judge them believe that each culture has its own sense of right and wrong, and that each is different and incommensurate. Constructing human rights debates as a conflict between universalism and relativism, however, I think oversimplifies both the stance of advocates of and dissenters from certain human rights claims, and fails to take seriously enough the plea some voices makes for understanding the specificity of their situation and perspectives.

Nedelsky offers the useful suggestion that a concept of judgement can contribute to reframing this debate so that it has less exaggerated poles. As I discussed earlier, judgement designates the result of serious inquiry that claims objectivity, in at least two senses. The judges claim to be distant from their own partiality and immediate subjective point of view. The voicing of their judgement, furthermore, claims assent from others and the judgements are prepared to give reasons for their claims. The idea of judgement is different from the idea of universal moral principle, however, which claims to be a kind of moral knowledge that transcends situation and perspective. The moral point of view that generates universal principle is a 'view from nowhere', or the 'god's eye' view that Haraway criticises. From this point of view we arrive at universal claims by abstracting from or bracketing particular situated experience.

Understood as the result of judgement rather than the formulation of general principles, human rights claims are not the assertion of absolute principle to which everyone in the world can only say yeah or nay. Understood as judgements, the evaluation of particular actions or practices in terms of human rights is not a simply process of bring general standards from outside and seeing whether the practices measure up. Human rights claims and evaluations are better framed as seeking to acknowledge the specificity of local contexts while also adopting a critical perspective on them that attends to the position of the most vulnerable. The judgements are context-specific, but claim objectivity in the sense that they claim to offer reasons that anyone who understands the context ought to accept.

Many writers who comment on contemporary human rights debates assert that only genuine dialogue among people differently situated in the world can soften the positions and bring about more cooperation. Such calls for dialogue, however, are often rather vague and symbolic. The account of democratic discussion in which diverse groups and social positions are represented in the specificity of their experience and perspectives contribute to explicating the conditions of such a dialogue. Human rights should be thought of not as a settled set of finite universal principles brought to evaluate local context, but as a set of ideals whose meanings should be discussed among all the world's peoples in equal terms.

What does the inclusion of all the world's peoples in a dialogue on human rights on equal terms mean? Human rights politics today takes place largely among states only, and it usually presumes the hegemonic power politics among states today. This means that human rights discussions today are dominated by the interests and perspectives of the United States, Western Europe and their close economic and military allies. The achievement of open dialogue would mean first, enlarging the voices and perspectives of African, Asian and Latin American states.

States, however, are not necessarily the best representatives of the world's peoples in a dialogue on human rights, for at least two reasons. First, states and their representatives are often the agents under particular scrutiny in making human rights judgements. Second, many peoples do not find that they are adequately represented, or in some cases represented at all, by any existing nation states. Indigenous peoples, for example, properly refuse the representation of existing states in international politics. An open and equal human rights dialogue thus requires representation of cultural minorities over whom states now claim jurisdiction. A human rights dialogue ought not to involve only the perspectives of historic peoples or cultural groups, however, but other diverse social positions such as women, sexual minorities, factory workers, peasants, service industry works, and the like. Structurally and culturally differentiated groups that speak for positions and perspectives other than states are important in a human rights dialogue, both to situate and limit the perspectives of states on these issues, and to offer a store of situated knowledge and experience that fleshes out abstract ideas of need and dignity.

Assuming that publics exist or can be created that are inclusive and egalitarian in these sense, participants in a human rights dialogue should exhibit a commitment to openness of a sort now not always observable in human rights debates. On the one hand, no state, people or group should be able to claim that outsiders do not have a right to make judgements about what some of them claim are actions and practices relevant only to insiders. In a human rights dialogue, that is, no agent should be permitted to make a claim to sovereignty that amounts to an assertion that what we do is none of your business. Such an assertion is a refusal to enter into dialogue rather than a step in dialogue.

On the other hand, no agent or group should be able to say that they have the definitive list of human rights, or that they know which of a set of generally agreed principles have priority over others, challenges to which they are not open to hearing. Being open means that participants in dialogue are always willing to discuss the meaning and priorities of principles, ideals and practices that express basic human freedom, well-being and dignity. Odd as it may sound, if human rights ideals really are universal, then their formulation and application should always be revisable in response to the persuasive arguments of new or newly heard dialogue participants. Participants should also acknowledge that such moral and cultural tradition can potentially teach all the others about aspects or interpretations of these ideals.

The theory of a heterogeneous public explicitly attending to diverse positions and perspectives argues that the situated knowledges of each perspective can contribute to developing a more objective understanding for everyone. Applied to human rights dialogue this means that each participant comes to understand themselves as partial and that they have only a perspective on the global human condition. Some of the moves in contemporary human rights debates can be interpreted as an attempt to show to those who believe that they speak from a universal point of view that transcends any specific situation that they in fact have a perspective. The purposes of bringing up practices of breast implantation in a human rights dialogue about genital mutilation, for example, is not to excuse the latter practices, but rather to jar Westerners into seeing some of the practices they take for granted as strange and help them see that their social and cultural perspectives may contain biases and blindnesses (see Gunning, 1997).

Open and respectful human rights dialogue, moreover, recognises that there may be diverse global and local resources for understanding the meaning of human harms and the arguments that can be made to combat them. If human rights truly are universal, then it ought to be the case that every cultural tradition contains some ideas and elements that express commitment to human life and dignity in particular ways for particular circumstances, and which has the potential to enlarge the thinking of everyone.

## Notes

1. Melissa Williams (1999) argues that such forms of representation as recognition help re-establish trust when there has been a history of domination.
2. Elsewhere I interpret Arendt's notion of enlarged thought in a way that differs from other interpreters, account. Some people claim that the process of moving from understanding only one's own point of view to understanding a situation in a way that takes account of many points of view involves adopting the standpoints of all the others. I argue to the contrary that the enlargement of thought must take place from within my own position that listens across to others and learns from the expression of their standpoints without adopting it. See 'Asymmetrical Reciprocity: On Moral Respect, Wonder, and Enlarged Thought', in Young (1997).
3. Hilary Putnam (1990: 1671–97; 1996). See also Linda Alcoff's comment on Putnam in the same volume.
4. See Harding (1991); Barwell (1994: 63–78); Patricia Hill Collins develops the idea that there are specific social knowledges arising from social structural location in her account of an Afrocentric feminist epistemology; see *Black Feminist Thought* (1991, especially chapter 10 and 11); Alcoff (1996, especially chapter 3); Satya Mohanty has developed an account of social objectivity as arising from the interaction of ideas arising from social location. See Mohanty (1993: 41–80); Paula Moya has applied Mohanty's approach to the specific context of Latina feminism; see Moya (1997).
5. In the context of legal judgement and the responsibilities of judges, Martha Minow discusses the importance of multiple perspectives as a means of dislodging unstated assumptions about social relations and their consequences or assumptions about what is normal that are influenced by particular social positions; see Minow (1990, especially chapter 11).
6. Jodi Dean argues for a model of dialogic solidarity in which participants do not merely address one another but speak in the presence of a 'situated hypothetic third'. This appeal to the 'third' invokes the function of more distant third parties in motivating parties who either think they are allied or think they are in conflict to remember the interests and perspectives of those outside this relationship (Dean, 1996).
7. One example of a theorist with this strong universalist stance is Martha Nussbaum. See her *Sex and Social Justice* (1999, especially chapters 2 and 3).
8. For a useful discussion see the essays in Peter Van Ness, *Debating Human Rights: Critical Essays from the United States and Asia* (1999).
9. This is how Nussbaum understands at least certain human rights debates in her essay, 'Women and Cultural Universals', in *Sex and Social Justice* (1999).

# References

Alcoff, L.M. (1996). *Real Knowing: New Versions of Coherence Theory*. Ithaca, NY: Cornell University Press.

Barwell, I. (1994). 'Towards a Defence of Objectivity', in Kathleen Lennon and Margaret Whitford (eds.), *Knowing the Difference: Feminist Perspectives in Epistemology*. London: Routledge.

Collins, P.H. (1991). *Black Feminist Thought*. New York: Routledge.

Dean, J. (1996). *Solidarity of Strangers*. Berkeley: University of California Press.

Dewey, J. (1927). *The Public and its Problems*. Chicago: Swallow Press.

Gunning, I.R. (1997). 'Arrogant Perception, World Traveling, and Multicultural Feminism: The Case of Female Genital Surgeries', in A.K. Wing (ed.), *Critical Race Feminism*. New York: New York University Press.

Haraway, D. (1991). 'Situated Knowledges: The Science Question in Feminism and the Privilege of Partial Perspective', in *Simians, Cyborgs, and Women*. New York: Routledge.

Harding, S. (1991). *Whose Science? Which Knowledge? Thinking from Women's Lives*. Milton Keynes: Open University Press.

Honneth, A. (1998). 'Democracy as Reflexive Cooperation: John Dewey and the Theory of Democracy Today'. *Political Theory*, 26, 6.

Minow, M. (1990). *Making All the Difference*. Ithaca, NY: Cornell University Press.

Mohanty, S. (1993). 'The Epistemic Status of Cultural Identity'. *Cultural Critique*, Spring.

Moya, P. (1997). 'Postmodernism, "Realism" and the Politics of Identity: Cherrie Moraga and Chicana Feminism', in C.T. Mohanty and M.J. Alexander (eds.), *Feminist Genealogies, Colonial Legacies, Democratic Futures*. New York: Routledge.

Nussbaum, M. (1999). *Sex and Social Justice*. Oxford: Oxford University Press.

Phillips, A. (1995). *The Politics of Presence*. Oxford: Oxford University Press.

Putnam, H. (1990). 'A Reconsideration of Deweyan Democracy'. *Southern California Law Review*, 63, 6.

Putnam, H. (1995). 'Pragmatism and Moral Objectivity', in Martha Nussbaum and Jonathan Glover (eds.), *Women, Culture and Development*. Oxford: Oxford University Press.

Van Ness, P. (1999). *Debating Human Rights: Critical Essays from the United States and Asia*. New York: Routledge.

Wendell, S. (1996). *The Rejected Body*. New York: Routledge.

Williams, M. (1999). *Voice, Trust and Memory*. Princeton: Princeton University Press.

Young, I.M. (1997). *Intersecting Voices: Dilemmas of Gender, Political Philosophy and Policy*. Princeton: Princeton University Press.

Young, I.M. (2000). *Inclusion and Democracy*. Oxford: Oxford University Press.

# 3
# Identity Politics: Have We Now Had Enough?

*Anne Phillips*

For many of us today, identity politics is simultaneously what defines us and what we wish to distance ourselves from. In one sense, identity politics is now inescapable. It was always implausible to think of society as either a collection of discrete individuals or as the abstraction of 'nation' and 'people'; and these days, it is particularly difficult to accept an understanding of politics that abstracts from groupings by race, gender, ethnicity, sexuality, age, religion or class. Such understandings now appear elitist, in the sense that they speak for, rather than from, subordinated groups. They appear economistic, focusing at best on 'objective' markers of poverty, inequality or exploitation, but failing to register the additional injuries associated with the disparagement of minority characteristics or the stereotyping of identity groups. When wielded by those in power, they often strike us as deliberately obscurantist, pretending to a commonality of condition that is at odds with most people's experience. But even in the hands of social critics, they threaten to reinforce the very patterns of domination they otherwise claim to challenge, for in ignoring or promising to transcend differences of race, gender, ethnicity, etc., they treat difference as a problem – and those marked by them as a problem too.

The critique that underpins identity politics had its precursor in Marxism, which also took issue with the false abstractions of humanity on the one hand, and the Robinson Crusoe-like individual on the other, and focused attention on the class relations that framed the individual and undermined the generalising pretensions of humanity or nation. Marx, however, was only tangentially concerned with identity politics, for while he saw the development of a self-conscious proletarian identity as a key moment in the process of social transformation, he regarded this as a transitional stage that would ultimately leave such identities behind. In common with virtually all the modernising movements of the nineteenth and twentieth centuries, Marxism looked to a future in which people would put aside their partial identities of occupation, religion, locality, race or nation. Though it saw the formation of a specifically class identity as crucial to this (the movement from a 'class in itself' to a 'class for itself'), it believed this identity would itself become redundant in the transition to a better world. All other forms of group identity were already regarded as backward-looking, constraining, misguided (hence the difficulties Marxists had in accommodating what they continued to see as 'bourgeois' feminism); and the one legitimate form of group identification – by class – was only ever meant as a temporary phase.

Many now see this as mistaken, either because of a strong view about the importance of group identification to human well-being (I myself am agnostic on this), or more simply and politically, because of the way the critique of partial identities works to instal the authority of other identity groups. Exclusion operates, not just through the more tangible mechanisms of economic and social deprivation, but through denying people their specificity and voice: requiring women to set aside their trivial preoccupation with gender relations; appealing to members of an ethnic minority to look beyond their partial grievances; calling on those disadvantaged by disability or age to remember that there are bigger issues at stake. Even when driven by grand conceptions of a supposedly transcendent common interest, such appeals have the effect of silencing the most disadvantaged. In doing so, they leave the agenda to be set by people whose power has been so much taken for granted that they do not even think of themselves as a distinct social group.

Identity politics has exposed the universalist discourses that falsely proclaimed a unified 'we', and its role in breaking down those certainties has been crucial in reshaping the way people now think about democracy and power. Two key challenges in recent years illustrate this point. The first is the European-wide – not to say global – movement for the political representation of women as women, a movement that often talks in the relatively uncontentious terms of fairness and equality of opportunity, but always, in my view, refers back to notions of women as a identity group. The reason democracies need more women in politics is not simply to equalise the chances for women to compete for political office, nor to brighten up our parliaments, nor even to send a firmer message to female citizens that they too are part of the citizen body. There is nearly always an additional expectation that the policies pursued by a 'mixed' parliament (one, that is, in which women are equally represented alongside men) will take a different form from those pursued by a predominantly male assembly.

This expectation derives from the belief that political judgements are formed by life experiences, and that in societies ordered by gender, the life experiences associated with being male or female will generate different perspectives, priorities and goals. Women undoubtedly identify with their gender in different ways, not only because the experience of being a woman differs according to other dimensions such as race or class, but also because women vary in the political weight they attach to gender. The argument does not presume that women enter politics as advocates of a particular identity group or that they will define themselves explicitly through their gendered identity. But the case for more women in politics rests ultimately on the belief that it is impossible to escape the social processes that identify us (with or without our concurrence) with our gender. Politicians are no more disembodied than anyone else, and the idea that we should not worry if they all turn out to be male – or more implausibly, all turned out to be female – is either disingenuous or downright dishonest. This insistence on the pertinence of gender has been a relatively new argument in liberal democracies, and it draws its sustenance from identity politics.

The second illustration – also prominent in recent European debates – is the rejection of assimilationist models of citizenship as inappropriate to multicultural democracies. The population of most countries in Europe has been formed out of centuries of migration and displacement, but the process has speeded up enormously over the last fifty years, and no country can now pretend to ethnic or religious or cultural homogeneity. In the immediate postwar years, migrants often anticipated a rapid process of assimilation into their 'host' community: the West Indians who were recruited to meet the labour shortages in Britain, for example, usually saw themselves unequivocally as British; and with the appalling experience of the Jewish ghettoes still vivid in European memory, it was hardly a time for people to elaborate strategies of separation and difference. If assimilation had happened – if migrants *had* been offered the full and equal citizenship many of them so confidently expected – we might now be facing a different set of political concerns. But as patterns of economic and political disadvantage came to map so starkly onto divisions between majority and minority communities, there was an inevitable reassessment. Integration via assimilation came to appear as disingenuous as the presumption that sex is irrelevant to politics, and those who find themselves in the ethnic or religious minority have become more militant about their right to be different though equal.

Though both these developments reflect the emergence and growing importance of identity politics, it is notable that activists in both these fields have preferred to distance themselves from that label. Identity politics is in one sense inescapable: we cannot go back to naive (or dishonest) notions of a 'national' or a 'human' identity that swallows up and transcends all difference. But identity politics is also perceived as a dangerous dead-end, and even those most formed and shaped by its development often feel they have had enough. One of the most commonly expressed worries is that identity is more complex and shifting than is suggested by categorisations by race, gender, ethnicity, sexuality, disability, etc., for within each of these categories there is internal variation and contestation; and many identities are, moreover, hybrid and do not fall neatly into any one camp. The second commonly expressed worry is that the politicisation of identities can lead to such a proliferation of identity groups that it becomes impossible to forge sufficiently powerful alliances for change. We deconstruct humanity, for example, into women and men, but then find that women subdivide according to their race, age, class, sexuality and the ubiquitous, etc.; and each movement that forms around one of the subdivisions threatens to subdivide further into even smaller identity formations.

This fragmentation can be both exhausting and disabling. In the movements to make our democracies more inclusive, for example, it has proved difficult to replicate the relatively successful challenge to the political under-representation of women in the equally pressing area of ethnic under-representation. Part, at least, of the explanation for this is that in most parts of Europe, the non-white population is made up of a large variety of ethnic groups. We can appeal to the principles of identity politics to query the overwhelming dominance of 'white' politicians, but are immediately faced with the awkwardness of the category 'black', which lumps together groups with different cultures, different histories of migration and different experiences of racism, and suggests a more shared identity among non-white citizens than is usually the case. In Britain, there is certainly a consensus among Afro-Caribbean and Asian voters that non-white citizens are seriously under-represented in politics, but those who migrated from the Indian subcontinent would not necessarily see themselves as so much better represented by Afro-Caribbean representatives, nor, indeed, would Muslims who originated from Bangladesh or Pakistan necessarily see themselves as so much better represented by Hindus who originated from India. Many European parties have adopted some form of quota arrangement to raise the proportion of women representatives, but none so far has adopted a quota for ethnic minority representatives. Part of the reason for this is that there are many ethnic minorities, and it is hard in this context to develop a concerted campaign.

The fragmentation issue has been widely discussed, but I want in this chapter to turn to two other aspects of identity politics that continue to cause disquiet. The first relates to what Wendy Brown (1995) describes as its ressentiment and 'wounded attachments'; the second to the tensions Nancy Fraser has identified between a politics of recognition and a politics of redistribution (Fraser, 1997; 2000). In *States of Injury*, Brown talks of the 'wounded' character of much identity politics, the way that movements protesting against marginalisation or subordination become almost over-attached to their own conditions of exclusion, feed on their own sense of injury, become bound up in a politics of recrimination and rancour, want to be recognised precisely for their injuries, and in the process find it harder than ever to become free. There is a way of putting this that would end up with a simpler disparagement of identity politics: a calling on people to get things into better perspective, to see that the injuries that so preoccupy them are minor points in a catalogue of much larger oppressions; to pull up their socks and get on with the real business of the day. What is different about Brown's approach is, first, that she sees the proliferation and politicisation of identities as a constituent part of late modernity (and thus neither a failure to come to terms with modernity nor something best thought of as a moral or political *choice*); and second, that she shares with identity politics its critique of universalist discourses (and hence does not see its particularism as intrinsically misguided).

Brown suggests that 'identity politics may be partly configured by a peculiarly shaped and peculiarly disguised form of class resentment, a resentment that is displaced onto discourses of justice other than class, but a resentment, like all resentments, that retains the real or imagined holdings of its reviled subject as objects of desire' (Brown, 1995: 60). The reviled subject she has in mind is the middle class, but an idealised middle class that is viewed as already enjoying all the good things – job security, social recognition, freedom from harassment – that are denied to the marginalised 'others'. Without recourse to this ideal, she argues, identity groups 'would forfeit a good deal of their claims to injury and exclusion' (Brown, 1995: 61), but in measuring their loss against this other's gain, they both abandon themselves to the pain of their own exclusion and lose their capacity to mount a more sustained critique of capitalist power relations. It is an interesting argument, because we have tended to think of identity politics as breaking with the aspiration to sameness: we more commonly think of it as claiming equality through difference, as stressing the diversity of identity groups and the need to recognise this diversity rather than sublimating it in appeals to the common good. Brown's intuition – which strikes me as particularly forceful in the American context that is the explicit focus of her attention – is that identity politics remains trapped in its sense of what you have but I am denied. It looks backwards towards the injury rather than forwards to its own desires.

In this analysis, Brown sets out to rethink the relationship between an investment in identity politics and the re-legitimation of capitalism. She does not present identity politics as just a falling away from the 'real' issues (alienation, exploitation, economic inequality) that we ought to be addressing; and she recognises that identity politics is in many ways challenging the hegemony of dominant values, particularly through its critique of cultural assimilation (she addresses this last, only in a footnote, p. 59). She does, however, situate the emergence of identity politics within the demise of more far-reaching critiques of capitalism, and in her point about the middle class as the standard against which exclusion is measured, presents the politicisation of identities as part of a 'renaturalisation' of capitalism that forecloses more ambitious claims.

Fraser addresses a similar terrain in her discussion of the relationship between a politics of *recognition*, exemplified in claims for the recognition of sexual, cultural or ethnic difference, and a politics of *redistribution*, exemplified in claims for a more equitable distribution of resources and wealth. The first is closely associated with what we call identity politics, the second with socialism or social democracy, and while Fraser resists the either/or option that requires us to focus on only one or the other, she has become increasingly concerned by what she sees as a process of displacement. Despite (perhaps, as she says, even because of) the rapid exacerbation of economic inequality within and between nations, 'questions of recognition are serving less to supplement, complicate and enrich redistributive struggles than to marginalise, eclipse and displace them' (Fraser, 2000: 108).

In her view, this is partly because the politics of recognition has become too closely entwined with identity politics. When people respond to social subordination by calling for social recognition of their specific group identities – when they demand to be recognised not just as individuals or citizens, but as women or Muslims or lesbians or gay – they narrow down the injustices they have experienced to ones that can be dealt with through cultural measures alone. Obvious examples would be the (otherwise laudable) efforts made by many school authorities to challenge the stigmatising stereotypes children have imbibed of Roma or homosexuals or Blacks or Jews; or campaigns to challenge demeaning representations of minority groups in films or television. Useful as such initiatives may be, they cannot of themselves change the social structures that generate and re-create the stereotypes (the stereotype of young black men as more likely to be unemployed or imprisoned, for example, is not just stereotype but also a stark reflection of real racial disadvantage). An exclusive focus on recognising and revaluing different group identities may then displace attention from the institutions and structures through which the inequalities and injustices are sustained. Fraser argues instead that we should treat recognition as a question of social status: 'what requires recognition is not group-specific identity but the status of individual group members as full partners in social interaction' (Fraser, 2000: 113). The suppression or negation of different identities then appears as part of the problem, but the solutions should be pursued through equalising the status of the members of different groups.

Fraser's analysis, like Brown's, is very much derived from reflections on the current state of politics in the US. In both cases, we might be tempted to say that the identity politics that has developed in Europe has been more benign (though we would have to restrict ourselves to Western Europe in making any such claim); and that there has been neither such an obsession with past harms and injuries, nor such a detachment of issues of recognition from issues of redistribution. But in Europe too we face a marked retreat from economic egalitarianism, and a 'naturalisation' of economic inequality as just an inevitable part of the modern, globalised world. Poverty increasingly substitutes for inequality as the only problem of economic distribution we can hope to address: we will seek to ensure that no child grows up in poverty (currently the condition for one in five children in the UK), and that no adult falls below a humane minimum of resources; but as to the gap between rich and poor – who either hopes or feels the need to address this? What was earlier perceived as the crucial unfinished business of democracy is increasingly accepted as just a fact of life. Worrying about the gap between rich and poor is now redescribed as the politics of envy. Let us tackle poverty, of course, but not worry about more stringent conditions.

We cannot explain this seismic shift in social democratic politics by reference to the emergence of identity politics – though we might usefully follow Brown in referring some of the weaknesses of identity politics to its detachment from any larger critique of capitalist inequality

– but there are ways in which identity politics has contributed to this climate of retreat. I want to suggest that one element here is precisely the critique of assimilationism that has been such an important innovation. The other, sadly, is the notion of empowerment – otherwise such a significant part of current thinking about democracy and power.

What do I mean by these depressing claims? Looking back over centuries of contestation about the conditions for a full democracy, one of the recurrent debates has been about whether political equality means anything if it is not associated with economic and social equality: Rousseau's question, if you like, about whether you could talk of people as free and equal when one man was rich enough to buy the services of another and another so poor he had to sell himself into dependency. Political equality has often been celebrated as making it possible for people who are otherwise unequals none the less to be recognised as equal in the political domain. This is what Marx referred to (and criticised) in his essay 'On The Jewish Question', when he argued that the real meaning of political emancipation was the emancipation of civil society from the state: a *political* annulment of distinctions based on birth, rank, education, occupation or religion (much later than Marx's time, we can add in distinctions of sex and race) that freed these distinctions to do whatever they liked in the sphere of civil society. Hannah Arendt (1958) more positively described political equality as 'an equality of unequals who stand in need of being "equalised" in certain respects and for certain purposes'.

This understanding of political equality as a 'suspension' of the differences and inequalities that continue to rage through civil society has been recurrently contested; and most of those we think of as radical democrats (Arendt would be one notable exception) have taken the view that democratisation remains an empty promise unless it pushes on to address the power relations between rich and poor, white and black, women and men. Within this framework, it was frequently noted that the enjoyment of citizen rights is affected by economic conditions: that it is harder for the poor than the rich to secure redress through the law courts; that it is easier for the rich and well-educated to influence the course of a public inquiry; that middle-class citizens can make more of their equal right to participate in politics than citizens from the working class. Feminists added to this the argument that political equality was a hollow achievement if it was superimposed on subordination in the domestic sphere. For those who thought along these lines, economic and social inequalities were seen as blocking the full and equal exercise of democratic rights, and for most radical democrats, the solution was to reduce the range. Redistribution was then conceived as a political as well as an economic imperative. It was not just considerations of social justice that required us to equalise the distribution of resources and wealth; we also needed this equalisation to make good on the promise of democratic equality.

Convergence was a key part of this strategy: make people more politically equal by making their life conditions more the same. But as the analysis of inequality broadened out from the more exclusive emphasis on class to address further inequalities associated with gender, race, ethnicity (the categories, that is, associated with identity politics), it has made some aspects of the convergence model more suspect. We clearly cannot make equality of citizenship dependent on half the population undergoing a sex-change; we cannot make it depend on mass programmes of racial intermarriage that eliminate differences in skin colour; we cannot (or at least should not) make it conditional on convergence between the diverse cultural practices or religious beliefs that exist within the citizen body. To do so would be to treat difference as intrinsically a problem, as something that gets in the way; and experience suggests that it would always be the differences attached to minority or less powerful groups (never those associated with Brown's phantasmic middle class) that would be regarded in this light. As people have come to a clearer perception of the power dynamic implied in notions of convergence – a convergence that always seems to operate one-way – they have become more suspicious of an assimilationism that regards people as equals only when they become like one another in every conceivable way. In my view, this (entirely legitimate) critique of assimilationism then spills over into a lack of interest in economic convergence. New thinking on identity and difference then contributes to the current amnesia on economic concerns.

The point I am making here is rather different from the argument pursued by Fraser, for it is not just that the focus on identity issues leads people to 'forget' economic inequalities, or else reinterpret them as produced by inequalities in the cultural domain. The problem, rather, is that economic equalisation has come to seem a less compelling objective, and that one element aiding this process is that the preoccupation with convergence has become tainted by association with assimilationist goals. The right has never been convinced by the argument about political equality requiring economic equalisation. If the left has also evacuated this terrain, it is partly because of renewed interest in 'the political' as a realm unto itself, and partly because equality sounds like convergence, convergence sounds like sameness, and sameness is no

longer a fashionable goal. If sameness means all women remaking themselves in the image of men, or all citizens donning the same Mao jackets,
or all religions submerging their differences in some Esperanto-style
common beliefs, I imagine most of us will agree. But convergence is not
always such a bad objective, and in some aspects, remains central to the
project of democracy.

Democracy in its deeper sense is not just about equalising rights, or
even about equalising access to political influence and power; it also
raises the expectation that all citizens will be regarded as of equal standing and equal worth. It is hard, however, to sustain this strong sense of
equal worth when life experiences are fundamentally different – and all
too easy to fall back on self-serving justifications that present the poor
as less sensitive to hardship that the wealthy or women as more able to
cope with the repetitive tedium of semi-skilled work. The promise of
democratic equality continues to be subverted by stark differences in
access to income and wealth, and deep structural differences in positions in the social division of labour; and if we think of democracy not
just as a mechanism for generating governments but as a deeper claim
about the equality of citizens, there is necessarily a tension between the
universalism of political equality and the persistence of inequality and
domination in social and economic life. A narrowing of the income gap,
combined with greater convergence in occupations and responsibilities,
remains a crucial part of the project of political equality, but convergence is far less fashionable today. Part of the reason for this is that
discourses of difference have muddied the waters around equality, not
merely changing the balance between cultural and economic inequalities (Fraser's point), but directly affecting attitudes towards economic
equality.

Consider, as one example, current work on the gendered nature of
employment and care. Critiques of the male model of employment or
the Soviet-style institutionalisation of child care have cast doubt on
strategies that seek to equalise the position of women and men by
enabling women to mimic male experiences of work. As a result, there
is now more emphasis on 'family-friendly' policies (still very much
understood, however, as policies that will make it easier for *women* to
balance paid employment with their responsibilities for care), and more
emphasis on revaluing the work that is done by women. Sexual segregation *per se* is less frequently identified as a problem: it is not that we
need to get more women into fields of employment currently dominated by men, or more men into the caring occupations and activities
currently associated with women, but that we need to find new ways of

enabling the different priorities expressed by women. Though I share the critique of male models of employment, I remain attached to the notion that relations between the sexes would be less characterised by subordination and violence if men and women shared equally in occupations and care work and there were no longer distinct spheres of 'men's and 'women's' work. In the light of this attachment, I see current positions as edging too close to an accommodation of separate spheres: in this case, as in many others, an entirely appropriate critique of assimilation has generated a distinct lack of confidence in convergence.

My worries about empowerment follow a similar logic. I began with the comment that an understanding of politics that abstracts from differences of gender, race or ethnicity is now regarded as elitist: as speaking *for* rather than *from* subordinated groups. People are less willing to accept the 'substitutionism' that allows members of one social group to act as the mouthpiece of all others; do not put much faith in guardians from on high whose political wisdom will reveal to them the framework of a just society; and increasingly see justice as depending on the empowerment of all social groups, who must be enabled to participate as full and equal members in the processes of policy formation. I would not want to back away from this, any more than I would want to back away from the critique of assimilation, but here too the political initiatives can become detached from social and economic conditions, as if empowerment had no structural implications and were only a matter of political will.

The language of empowerment reflects two key insights. First, the development of fair and inclusive policies depends on the active involvement of groups that have previously been excluded from (or to be less conspiratorial, had minimal access to) the chambers of power. This draws on philosophical critiques that contest the pre-emptive claims of impartiality as the way to establish which policies are most just, stressing rather the partiality of all perspectives, and the necessity for genuinely inclusive dialogue in order to test competing claims. It also draws on historical and contemporary evidence about the way policies become skewed to the preoccupations of politically dominant groups. To put it at its simplest, when there is a heterogeneity of interests and experiences, people need to be involved as participants in policy formation, not just as recipients of the policies others design. The second insight is that people's political energy and imagination is not a simple function of their current standing in the social distribution of power. Poverty does not necessarily translate into passivity; subordination does not kill people's dreams; and some of the most innovative and transformative movements of our time have arisen among groups with minimal access to either economic or political power. (One might think here of the civil rights movement in the US, or the success of women's groups in India in making domestic violence a matter of national concern.)

Both insights stress the centrality of power relations: that power matters, and that power does not just follow the distribution of economic resources. Mostly, however, people have preferred to ignore the pessimistic implications of the first point, which casts deep shadows over current practices of policy formation, to dwell on the more optimistic implications of the second. We then end up with an understanding of empowerment as almost entirely a matter of political will. Think, in this context, of the extraordinary resonance in current policy circles (at both national and international level) of the notion of social capital, which I take to be the idea that what holds communities back is not so much the level of economic resources at their disposal but their ability to deploy social networks and thereby empower themselves. Why do some groups thrive and not others? Not, we are told, because some are richer or better educated or enjoy better social provision, but because some groups turn out to have more 'social capital' than others. I read this as a vulgarisation of the more radical notion of empowerment, and one that pushes to its limits the either/or between political and economic conditions. Of course, power is about more than money; of course groups empower themselves in all kinds of unexpected and imaginative ways. But when this is taken as a signal to abandon 'older' worries about economic and social dominance or outdated preoccupations with the distribution of resources, it turns too readily into an apologia for the status quo. Here, too, it seems that an entirely legitimate critique of an older paradigm – in this case, of the economism that attached too little weight to politics, or assumed that political activity was just a function of what people have – turns into a way of severing the relationship between democracy and social and economic power.

We are poised at a strange moment in the development of liberal democracies, when ideas of equality have become more pervasive and compelling than ever, but ideas of economic equality are largely off the political agenda. Both sexual and racial equality are taken more seriously than they were twenty years ago; countries in the European Union are now bound by gender equality Directives and are about to face a similar initiative around race; and it is widely accepted that democracies need to address in some way the political under-representation of women and people from ethnic and racial minorities. The idea that democracies should respect and accommodate minority cultures and practices has also come to be regarded (at least in some circles) as part of the meaning of equal citizenship in a multicultural world. Yet in some ways we seem to have travelled full circle, starting from an understanding of political equality as the equalisation of those who can otherwise remain unequal, passing through a century or so in which this was subjected to continuous critique, and now returning to an understanding of democratic equality as achievable through political measures alone. The retreat from economic equality as a condition for political equality reflects a larger movement away from redistributive economics, fuelled by a perception that nothing much can be done about economic equality (subtext: globalisation; collapse of socialism as a viable alternative), and justified by arguments about economic inequality being an entirely legitimate state of affairs (subtext: individuals are entitled to keep their own rewards). It also, I have argued, reflects a movement more internal to democracy itself, a movement away from the tension between political equality and economic inequality, and towards that further tension between invoking a universal subject (the abstract citizen much criticised by feminists) and recognising the specificity and diversity of constituent groups.

Identity politics has played a central role in this reformation. The most common objection to identity politics is that it gets the groupings wrong: that it boxes people into inappropriate identities, freezes identities that are hybrid and shifting, and somehow addresses people by the 'wrong' name. Since the key point about identity politics is that it flows from people's self-identifications, there is always something a bit puzzling about such claims. The further worry, addressed in this chapter, is that identity politics may be getting the problems wrong, that it may be misplacing the resentments, displacing the inequalities, and thereby encouraging us to sever political from economic power.

## References

Arendt, H. (1958). *The Human Condition*. Chicago: University of Chicago Press.
Brown, W. (1995). *States of Injury*. Princeton: Princeton University Press.
Fraser, N. (1997). *Justice Interruptus: Critical Reflections on the 'Post-Socialist' Condition*. London: Routledge.
Fraser, N. (2000). 'Rethinking Recognition'. *New Left Review*, May/June.

# 4
# Deliberative Democracy and Civil Society – An Expansion of Jürgen Habermas's Understanding of Civil Society

*Jens Ulrich*

## Introduction

Civil society has, with renewed vigour, announced its comeback within recent sociological and political theory. After some years in the shadows, civil society has come out of the mothballs, been dusted down and wheeled to the front of the theoretical stage. The hope is that the pressing need of modern society for democratisation can once again find its impetus in this sphere.

A glance at the history of ideas shows that with the centrality of Marxism in the 1970s, the theoretical focus was turned away from civil society to the state as the new arena for democratic strategies. With the neoliberal wave of the 1980s, the focus was transferred to the market as the new centre. The prevailing opinion was that democratic processes could only be strengthened by further focusing on free choice and that, therefore, a market rationale had to be brought into democratic processes. The market strategy has not necessarily been written out of history, but in the 1990s there were clear signs that civil society was being re-actualised as a basis for the increased demand for democratisation. The communitarian wave, which focuses on the family and traditions, is an excellent example of that movement. Political science's focus on governance in preference to government is another example. It is not possible to obtain a clear picture of whether the re-actualisation of civil society in this way is an expression of a reactionary wave or whether it leaves slope for new ideas. When Jürgen Habermas put civil society back on the agenda of democratic theory during the 1990s, it was often judged as a sign of reactionary thinking. In this chapter it is, however, my intention to show that Habermas's theory deserves more than to be sacrificed on the altar of reaction. At the same time, it is argued that a critical further development of his theories contains potential for new thinking in the theory of democracy.

## In the search for civil society

In critical theory and especially in Habermas's model, civil society has been ascribed two main functions. First, a social integrative function in which people's interaction and the experiences they gain from communicative actions mean that there can be potential for mutual appreciation and solidarity to emerge. Second, a democratising function where civil society is seen as the basis for securing the democratic process and legitimising the constitutional state. Civil society must be the site where political ideas and demands are fostered and at the same time the place where these political ideas pass their test of legitimacy. Civil society is seen as the guarantee that ensures that the political system receives input from ordinary citizens whilst helping the political system to legitimise itself – a double function and a double process where civil society is almost the glue that stabilises and binds together the democratic and political process.

The theoretical twists around civil society have not been about the import of civil society only, but about how civil society can, more concretely, be localised. If, therefore, we want to get away from thinking of civil society as a leftover category containing what is neither the state nor the market, then we must define more precisely what civil society actually encompasses. The triad of state, market and civil society is, therefore, not an exhaustive description of how civil society ought to be delimited. That in itself presents a huge theoretical unravelling task to determine the boundaries between civil society, the state and market respectively, a task that this representation wishes, casually to spring over. The following sections, on the other hand, will focus on the boundaries between civil society and the private domain or between the social and the political. Habermas, and for that matter many of his critics, maintain that such a dividing line is important. This primarily comes from the argument that one ought to make certain demands of the political sphere that cannot be made of the private and social sphere. With regard to the political activities that are played out in public and in civil society, one must be able to demand that the level of abstraction behind political activities transcends a simple, particular or egocentric horizon, a demand that cannot necessarily be made of activities that fall within the private or personal sphere. Habermas is confident that the dynamics the public possess guarantees that this transcending process can take place. The intention of this chapter is, however, to look more closely to determine whether this same dynamic can take place within other horizons than the one opened up by Habermas's understanding of civil society. Taking inspiration from the feminist Habermas reading it is, therefore, the intention of this chapter to show that expanding Habermas's understanding of the public sphere and at the same time toning down his focus on the institutional dimension of civil society can contribute constructively to a modern theory of democracy. But first let us turn to Habermas.

## Habermas's understanding of the public sphere and civil society

As suggested above there is a close link between the public sphere and civil society in Habermas's theoretical universe. As Habermas himself puts it, the public sphere has its societal foundation in civil society (Habermas, 1999: 74). In *Between Facts and Norms* [*Faktizität und Geltung*], where Habermas develops his theory of the modern constitutional state and deliberative democracy, civil society is defined in the following way:

> A civil society is composed of those more or less spontaneously emergent associations, organizations, and movements that, attuned to how societal problems resonate in the private life spheres, distill and transmit such reactions in amplified form to the public sphere.
>
> (Habermas, 1996: 367)

Thus civil society is made up of associations, organisations and movements that mirror problems rooted in the private sphere. It is in this way that we can talk of a perception of civil society that is bound in institutions, a perception that simultaneously isolates the private sphere and with it the modern family from civil society. The central point is to understand what characterises an actor in the private sphere and civil society respectively, or rather, what transforms a private actor into an actor in civil society. In this context Habermas brings to our attention that, as acting individuals, we occupy two roles, one as a private agent or member of society, the other as a citizen or subject. Often we occupy both roles simultaneously. As members of society we, for example, occupy roles as consumers, car drivers, patients, clients, tourists, and so on, all roles that create a set of interests and preferences. When something goes against our interests and expectations at this level –

negligence in hospital, for example – it brings about a series of demands and wishes which, initially, we come to terms with privately. We talk, for example, with family, friends and colleagues about how our expectations have not been realised. Habermas's point is that our social network is closely bound to the channels within the public sphere. Therefore, concrete, face-to-face relationships gradually dissipate in favour of more abstract perceptions of our situation. For example, it is a short step from bad treatment in hospital to becoming motivated to contact a patients' association. When private activities, in this way, are superseded by activities within an organisation in civil society, as with a patients' association, it is possible for the public sphere, civil society, to pass on private experiences of societal problems (Habermas, 1999: 73–4). The central point in understanding the transformation of a private action into civil action is that the participant himself comes forward into the public arena and hence into civil society. Before we return, in a critical sense, to this transformation it is important to look more closely at how the public stage is constituted and how it can be conceptualised into a broader democratic theoretical framework.

## A deliberative democratic theoretical framework

The deliberative democratic theory formulated within a critique of the liberal and classic republican democratic approach respectively is taken as the starting point in this chapter. The liberal approach to democracy is criticised for its faith that the common good can be realised through the simple aggregation of individual preferences whilst, at the same time, neglecting the political culture's potential for interest, value and moral formation. Whereas the classic republican approach to democracy is criticised for its essentialist understanding of the common good, in the republican tradition the function of democratic dialogue is not based on the creation of the common good. On the contrary, the dialogue should lead to a recognition of our insight into the common good. Within that, the deliberative approach tries to bridge the gap between an individually-oriented and an essentialist community-oriented foundation for perceiving democratic processes. It is the *autonomous* individuals' *creation* of *common* understandings and values through *communicative dialogue* that creates the core in the deliberative approach to democracy.

The responsibility for realising communicative dialogue is placed in the political democratic public sphere; or, as Habermas points out, the public sphere is the only guarantee of communicative action free from pressure and the colonising effect of strategic action (Habermas, 1996: 329–87). Claus Offe defines it in the following manner:

> The goal of argumentation is not the positive determination of the good but the negative elimination of particularistic prejudices, preoccupation with strategic interest, and cognitive narrowmindedness from practical discourse. (Offe, 1992: 68)

When the public sphere is given a central role in deliberative theory it is from the consideration that communicative dialogue can unfold democratically only if it occurs in the public sphere. The presence of a neutral person, functioning as a guarantor that the particularistic in the dialogue is eliminated, can happen only in the public sphere. Being present in the public sphere ensures that the individual agent can ignore his or her own perspective as well as that of the dialogue partner. The public sphere is, therefore, public only in the sense that the terms of communication as well as its development are displayed publicly (Habermas, 1996: 361), a public that, in the wording of Erik Oddvar Eriksen and Jarle Weigård, 'has the authority to decide what counts' (Eriksen and Weigård, 1999: 247; my translation).

Individuals' ability to judge, or democratic competence, therefore, can be realised only when the individual adopts the mantle of the citizen who has come of age and has entered the public arena. The construction of an ideal public, therefore, makes it possible for the autonomous citizen to develop democratic virtues, which makes him or her able to disregard particularistic interests. Such an action carried out in the public sphere can fulfil the criteria Offe advances as being a responsible action. Offe formulates it as follows:

> To act responsibly ... is for the agent to evaluate his or her own actions by methodically taking the critical perspectives, simultaneously an in the *futurum exactum*, of the expert, the generalized other, and of himself or herself. (Offe, 1992: 78)

In this way the democratic citizen emerges only when his or her action is executed, motivated and legitimised in public.

## The feministic critique of Habermas

The normative prioritising of the public sphere has been viewed highly critically from a feminist viewpoint. This critique centres on two themes, one concerned with the actual conception of the public sphere where the main objection has been that the construction of the public sphere favours men and excludes women; the other focused on the universalistic element in the rationale behind the deliberative thought and the public sphere theory. In brief this critique can be said to reflect the discourse ethic's relationship to the care ethic.

In relation to the actual conception of the public sphere it has been argued that the public sphere Habermas portrays as the ideal is reserved for male citizens (see, for example, Fleming's critique of Habermas's early understanding of the public sphere (1995)). In practice the public sphere has been reserved for male citizens as gender inequality has meant that women have not had free access to the public sphere prescribed as ideal. In its way the critique is fair enough. Habermas's early perception of the public sphere was characterised by an understanding that the public sphere was seen as singular and whose foundations should be sought in institutions within civil society (Habermas, 1962). Habermas has since revised this monistic access to the public sphere (to which we will return later). Seen empirically, the critique of such an understanding of the public sphere is obvious. Men have traditionally had privileged access to the public sphere. But whether this historical practice means that one ought to reconsider the normative prioritising of the public sphere is, however, a different matter. A specious argument, in this context, would be that the normative prioritising of the public sphere is precisely an argument for changing the practice and not the practice changing the normative point of origin. An objection typical of the period is that this historical development (at least in the Nordic welfare states, but perhaps also in other Western countries) has overtaken this discussion. Has gender equality not reached the point where men no longer have privileged access to the public sphere? Or is it still a sign of segregation and exclusion when one can see a difference in the way the two genders are represented?

Parallel to the critique of the normative prioritising of the public sphere, feminists have also questioned Habermas's sharp separation between the private and public sphere (see, for example, Benhabib, 1992: 89–120; Young, 1990: 96–121). As there is no doubt that Habermas insists on such a separation, the question is how we should interpret it. Is the separation necessarily as sharp as certain feminist theorists claim? Habermas's roots in the liberal tradition are very clear here. There ought to be a place where the private sphere cannot be held accountable to the demands of public discussion and legitimisation – a private place, where making up one's mind about ethical matters and personal relations is shielded from outside influence. The ethical questions will first be a matter of moral evaluation when they are judged as having relevance to society and not until then are they moved from the private to the public sphere (Habermas, 1996: 366).

When we talk about the separation between the private and the public sphere, the question arises: how do we constitute this separation? Is it universally founded or decided contextually? Radical feminists' critique has taken as its starting point that Habermas's segregation in itself creates a thematic separation in relation to what naturally relates to either one or the other sphere, the point being that the actual construction of the public sphere takes account of universal male values and ignores female caring values (Pateman, 1988; Benhabib, 1992: 148–77). However, Habermas refutes this critique on the grounds that it is the historical circumstances and not the nature of the public sphere that has caused this imbalance. It is the historical development that has decided what has been made the object of the public's reasoning. That women, historically, have been more or less excluded from the democratic public sphere is not a result of the universal character of the public sphere. On the contrary, Habermas points out that women, through their hard-won political rights, possess an historically created potential to change the patriarchal character of the public sphere (Habermas, 1992: 427–9). The essence of the public sphere is not decided from outstanding structures which *a priori* determine what kind of question should be included and what kind of question excluded from public discourse. The character of the public sphere is always a contextual mirroring of the pluralistic character of the private sphere (Habermas, 1996: 365–6). Or put another way, the key issue in the separation of the private sphere and the public sphere is not a question of *what* is debated but *how* one debates it. Therefore, when Harriet Bjerrum Nielsen says that, by definition, Habermas rejects the body, feelings and desires as matters of public reasoning, it is a good example of how he is often misinterpreted (Nielsen, 1995: 17).

Despite the fact that historical developments compensate for the feminist critique of the public sphere, there are still problems related to Habermas's early concept of the public sphere. To keep to a view of the public sphere as a homogeneous entity verges on a theoretical simplification and an idealising of the tenets of the traditional bourgeois society. In a dynamic and differentiated world, such an ideal is neither realistic nor desirable, something Habermas acknowledges in his later work (Habermas, 1992; 1996). Here Habermas extends his perception of the public sphere to include a myriad of public spheres, which are given the same democratic potential as that expressed in the earlier monistic approach. The common factor for these semi-public spheres remains that in Habermas's perception they have to be aimed at the parliamentary complex (Habermas, 1996: 359). Habermas's focus on a parliamentary understanding of politics thus makes him incapable of capturing the potential of the modern perception of politics. When, for example, Ulrich Beck, arguing from the concept of subpolitics, attempts to capture political processes, which are not aimed at parliament but which, for example, are between citizens and the economic system directly (Beck, 1994), Habermas cannot see the positive democratic potential of this approach.

When Habermas insists that the public spheres necessarily have to be aimed at the parliamentary complex, it is in conjunction with his view of the constitutional state as the answer of modern society to the in-stitutionalisation of the common good (Habermas, 1996; 1994). Habermas's basic concern that the common good is marginalised to the advantage of particular interests as the leading light for opinion and will formation, makes him blind to, for example, the democratic potential of subpolitical processes. In another context he expresses the fear, in many ways substantiated, that an understanding of democracy which is system-theoretical and where autonomous subsystems lose the common inter-subjective world understanding, can result in the collapse of successful communication (Habermas, 1996: 346). In this way, Habermas expresses an antipathy towards system-theoretical democratic understanding, which means that he looks on all forms of non-parliamentary understanding of the public sphere very sceptically, a scepticism that also affects the value he places on subpolitical processes.

It is, however, not necessarily the case that an understanding of politics which, for example, includes subpolitical arenas cannot keep an inter-subjective world understanding of it breaks free from the parliamentary complex. If one does not focus exclusively on the common good in its institutionalised form as the overriding framework for judging the democratic value of the public sphere one can easily capture new democratic possibilities. Instead, one can value the democratic value of concrete dialogues' orientation towards the common good. If the dialogue is carried out with the common good as the overall discursive framework, it will be less important if it is focused on the parliamentary complex. Democratic dialogue and democratic value and will formation ought, therefore, primarily to be valued for their manifestation and realisation within the horizon of the common good. When the common good is regarded as the overriding discursive framework, or as the boundary of democratic dialogue, we are not talking about a wide-ranging perception of the common good. The common good is not universally based. On the contrary, the common good should be regarded as a project defined by the process and not by the substantial goals of the process. In this way neither the need for intersubjectivity nor the communicative dialogue is surrendered as a condition of the democratic process. On the contrary, the way is open for a greater possibility of valuing the democratic potentials by political identities, which do not necessarily orient themselves towards the parliamentary complex. Once again it is a question of *how* the discussion is carried out rather than *what* is discussed or *where* it is discussed.

Over and above the critique of the perception of the public sphere, a critique of Habermas's universalistic approach has also been central to the critical feminist reading of Habermas. The question is whether the dissimilarities are overlooked in favour of similarities when the public sphere is seen as the only guarantee of the deliberation with the common good as the horizon. The critique is, in a sense, motivated by the same sceptical view of the public sphere as that which produced the critique of the separation of the private and public spheres. The starting point is that the public sphere is an expression of a patriarchal structure. But rather than focusing on the nature of the separation, this critique focuses on the universalistic nature of the public sphere.

Iris Marion Young is one of the theorists who, in the strongest terms, have elaborated this critique, and as the title of her work *Justice and the Politics of Difference* indicates, it is the differences that are the focus. The central point is that we, in conjunction with our identification with a given social group, possess a series of different interests, which should not be subjected to universalisation. Young expresses this very radically when she criticises the citizenship tradition being unfolded within the theme: 'Citizenship for everyone, and everyone the same *qua* citizen' (Young, 1998: 401). A slightly sarcastic critique, which, in the first instance, has a broader aim than Habermas's position but, which at the same time, unproblematically, can be focused on the role one ought to take in Habermas's opinion when entering the public sphere. In the above, the role of spectator has been portrayed as central in connection with transcending egocentric interests in one's role as citizen. Intrinsically, it is this spectator role that Young puts under the microscope.

In respect of the dissimilarities as a starting point it is Young's view that Habermas thinks of the public sphere as possessing an impartial perspective, a perspective that mediates dissimilarities in such a way that heterogeneity is abandoned in favour of universality in the search for the common best or the universal. Young disputes the possibility of such an impartial position. In her definition such an approach means that you take a position from where you can see the whole and from where, from a neutral viewpoint, you can judge between right and wrong. Only by virtue of an impartial position should it be possible to transcend particular interests (Young, 1998: 424). Young obviously feels that such a position is illusory, and, with reference to Michael Sandel, points out that if one were to take such a position it would involve such a degree of self-abstraction that one would have to go beyond what it is to have a history, delete what it is to be a member of society, and go beyond what it is to be dependent on a physical form. Or to put it another way, self-abstraction in the direction of possessing the abilities of an nonexistent person must be the paradoxical aim if such an impartial position is taken (Young, 1998: 425; see also Sandel, 1982).

Taken exclusively from the view that such a position is illusory one can, on the face of it, agree with Young's critique of Habermas's apparent insistence on impartiality. But if you look at it in a more nuanced manner, in terms of the problems projected by Young, then Habermas's approach is not necessarily wrong. First, it must be made clear that Habermas does not think that the individual casts aside his motives when he or she enters the public arena. On the contrary the public sphere must function as a catalyst for how the individual handles his or her particular motives. In this regard Young agrees with Habermas; we are motivated by particular interests. Her critique comes into play when Habermas insists that it is possible to view one's interests from another angle when they are subjected to the rationale of the public sphere. Young finds fault when she equates what it is to transcend particular interests with having a position from where you can view the whole. Such a reversed anthropomorphic approach, where the individual by virtue of his or her role as citizen is omniscient, is obviously implausible. Jodi Dean castigates such a misinterpretation when she says:

> Habermas' use of the observer perspective as a perspective within a moral dialogue thus should not be confused with a 'view from nowhere' or with the equation of a moral point of view with the privileged standpoint of an ideal spectator.                    (Dean, 1996: 169)

The presence of an observer in itself is not automatically what decides that the communicative dialogue within the public sphere ends in consensus whereby all particularistic traces are eliminated. It is not the observer himself or herself but the awareness of the presence of an observer that demands a communicative dialogue in the public sphere. As a con-sequence of this Dean points out that 'the term "neutral" conceals the fact that the observer is a context-bound judge' (Dean, 1996: 169), which, in her views, puts her in total agreement with Habermas's approach.

Where the critique, of which Young is an exponent, goes fundamentally wrong is in its failure to acknowledge a level displacement between the ethical and the moral levels. The moral level, which is characterised by its focus on procedures, has to be viewed separately from the ethical level, which is made up of values and attitudes. When Habermas expounds the universalistic approach it is entirely on the moral level. The procedures, which we can agree should form our framework for any discussion of ethical questions, ought to have universal character, but the values and perceptions prevalent in relation to our view of the good life should not be a matter for universal thinking. Therefore, when Young and others think that this universalism, of which Habermas is a spokesman, is an expression of a wish for homogeneity, they fail to appreciate Habermas's distinction between the moral and the ethical, and with it his whole universalism concept.

## Habermas bought or sold?

Where does this critique lead us? Or how, in practice, should we expand the theory if the intention is to realise an extended view of civil society? A short summary of the above discussions would be a good approach, partly because there are aspects of Habermas's view of civil society and the public sphere which are worth retaining, and partly because there are aspects which can profitably be developed.

In the above we have mentioned two critiques, which in themselves do not give occasion for a revision of Habermas's theory. The first is that the critique levelled by the feminist side which has been levelled at Habermas's perception of universalism does not seem to be plausible as an immanent theoretical critique. Of course, one could dispute the normative starting point, which is inherent in Habermas's insistence that norms for social action ought to have a universalistic character – any modern system theorist would do so. It is, however, unfair from such a divergence from the normative starting point to claim that Habermas *a priori* excludes certain themes from the public debate. Moral questions should be weighed on universal scales, whilst ethical questions are always contextually and subjectivistically decided.

The other point, which in itself ought not to give cause for revision of the theory, lies in a continuation of the dispute concerning universalism; that is, the question of Habermas's view of the nature of the public sphere. As we have seen, it has been stated in these critiques that the organisation of the public sphere has prioritised male admission to moral discussions – a critique which, on an empirical level, is or perhaps more accurately used to be justified, but which on the normative level has the character of a defensive and reactionary view of the possibilities for women in late modern society.

Habermas's view of the universal and his understanding of the public ideal cannot, in this way, form a basis for demanding a revision of the theory. It is, however, different when we investigate his view of politics. In the above it has been argued that Habermas's perception of politics is far too narrow. Late modern society generates other forms of political action than the one aimed directly at the parliamentary system. This critique also has indirect implications for the understanding of the public sphere and, with it, for Habermas's perception of civil society. The observer role is a central issue in Habermas's perception of civil society. In the next section we shall argue that a constructive critique of this observer role can bring about a perspective of civil society which Habermas's theory cannot accommodate.

## The observer, the generalised other and the hypothetical third

Despite the fact that Habermas extends his perception of the public sphere to contain a series of semi-public spheres, these are still preconditional on the recognition of an observer role. There has to be a third party in the public dialogue to guarantee that one transcends particular and egocentric interests and values in favour of a position which has the common good as its horizon. The question, however, is whether this observer can guarantee this and whether the establishment of the common good as a goal could be achieved in another way. Dean points out that this observer, this judge, will always be context-bound, which means that he or she cannot plead any form of neutrality. The observer cannot be the spokesman of the common good. The challenge lies, therefore, in keeping a perspective on the public sphere or civil society, where the common good as a superior discursive frame can be kept within a horizon where one abandons the illusions of a neutral observer and the possibility of going beyond the context.

Seyla Benhabib is one of the feminist theorists who have placed a big question mark over Habermas's perception of the public sphere. Her starting point is that we ought to revise our perception of the public sphere where the common good forms the centre of the rationale. With reference to the debate between Lawrence Kohlberg and Carol Gilligan, Benhabib points out that when Habermas holds to the idea that the public dialogue has to be aimed at the common good it is an expression of male rationality (Benhabib, 1992). According to Benhabib, Habermas neglects the female form of rationality, a form of rationality which is largely geared towards caring rather than towards justice. When Habermas, inspired by Mead, glorifies the abstract other as a result of the presence of the observer in the public sphere, Benhabib argues that the concrete other, and with it female rationality, is driven out of the public sphere. Without entering further into the psychological basis for the separation between a female and a male form of rationality, the argument will be that it is still constructive and possible to think of the public sphere as a place where the common good is seen as the overall discursive framework. When Benhabib points out that there can be problems with the perception of the abstract other, that in itself is not sufficient to abandon the concept of the universal.

In line with this, Dean points out that just because we acknowledge that the observer cannot be a guarantee for realising the interests of the common good it does not necessarily mean that we must give up the thought of something universal, which is what Benhabib concludes (Dean, 1996: chapter 5). That the abstract other is always context-bound does not mean that we must refer to this other in its concrete form: 'By articulating the situatedness we can reinterpret the third-person perspective as that of situated, hypothetical third' (Dean, 1996: 171). When Dean introduces the concept of the hypothetical third, the point is to make the abstract concrete. This concretisation must not be mistaken for the concrete other, but by making the abstract concrete, we open up the possibility that we in the public dialogue can 'strive to see from the prospective of myriad others' (Dean, 1996: 171). With this perspective, Dean manages to maintain a perception of the universal. This cannot be reduced to a generalisation and thought of in abstractions but, instead, will find a foothold in a hypothetical attitude taken to an endless and unlimited plurality of 'otherness'.

Our entrance onto the public stage is, therefore, not determined by a third person, who can be a guarantor for the observer and judge role, but by the dynamics of the public sphere which should be sought in the possibility of allowing the perspective of the hypothetical third to come into play. Dean points out, through her development of a concept like reflexive solidarity, that our willingness to take on board this perspective is fostered through the experiences we have had in communicative togetherness (Dean, 1995; 1996: chapter 1). Communicative communities can exist only if they are based on the recognition of the free and autonomous qualities of the other participants. By entering into such communities we gain practical experience that all others, in principle, could participate in such dialogues. We acknowledge and experience that the attitudes, values and opinions of others should be taken seriously, an acknowledgement of plurality which requires the viewpoint of the hypothetical third. This acknowledgement, therefore, means that the public dialogue can unfold without Habermas's observer role and this, of course, always within a horizon of common character.

If we put this together with the argument about the expansion of the concept of politics, a different picture of civil society emerges. In Habermas's universe, the family, for example, has not been seen as a part of civil society. When civil society is seen as society's expression of the public, then the family, which is private and not public, cannot be included in civil society. However, the point is that when the demand to have an observer is substituted by the possibility of taking the perspective of the hypothetical third, then the demand on the public can be reduced to a matter of perspective on the respective dialogue. Or, to put it another way, it is not crucial to the common character of the dialogue if it takes place in the public sphere or, for example, in the family, the decisive point being whether the common good constitutes the overall discursive framework. If, therefore, we want to look to where communicative dialogue can take place, as a dialogue with politically democratic dimensions, it is no longer necessary to maintain a view of civil society as being limited to associations, organisations and movements. The family, like the patients' associations mentioned earlier, can be included in civil societies. Communicative dialogue, with the common good as its horizon, can easily take place at the dinner table. And the demands and wishes that can come from such a dialogue can easily be a matter of community when political questions, in respect of the extended understanding of politics, do not necessarily need to be channelled through the parliamentary system.

# References

Beck, U. (1994). 'The Reinvention of Politics', in U. Beck, A. Giddens and S. Lash (eds.), *Reflexive Modernization*. Cambridge: Polity Press.

Benhabib, S. (1992). *Situating the Self: Gender, Community and Postmodernism in Contemporary Ethics*. Cambridge: Polity Press.

Dean, J. (1995). 'Reflective Solidarity'. *Constellations*, 2, 1.

Dean, J. (1996). *Solidarity of Strangers: Feminism after Identity Politics*. Berkeley: University of California Press.

Eriksen, E.O. and J. Weigård (1999). *Kommunikativ handling og deliberativt demokrati* [Communicative Action and Deliberative Democracy]. Bergen: Fagboklaget.

Fleming, M. (1995). 'Women and the "Public Use of Reason" ', in J. Meehan (ed.), *Feminists Read Habermas: Gendering the Subject of Discource*. New York: Routledge.

Habermas, J. (1962). *Strukturwandel der Öffentlichkeit*. Neuwied: Hermann Luchterland Verlag.

Habermas, J. (1992). 'Futher Reflections on the Public Sphere', in C. Calhoun (ed.), *Habermas and the Public Sphere*. Cambridge, Mass.: MIT Press.

Habermas, J. (1996). *Between Facts and Norms*. Cambridge: Polity Press.

Habermas, J. (1999). 'Det sivile samfunn og rettsstaten' [Civil Society and the Constitutional State], in J. Habermas, *Kraften i de bedre argumenter* [The Force in the Better Argument]. Selection by Ragnvald Kalleberg, Oslo: Ad Notam Gyldendal.

Nielsen, H.B. (1995). 'Kjønn som irratasjonsmoment i det moderne' [Gender as a Source of Irritation in the Modern Society ]. *Grus*, 47, 16.

Offe, C. (1992). 'Bindings, Shackles, Brakes: On Self-Limitation Strategies', in A. Honneth et al. (eds.), *Cultural-Political Interventions in the Unfinished Project of Enlightenment*. Cambridge, Mass.: MIT Press.

Pateman, C. (1988). 'The Fraternal Social Contract', in J. Keane (ed.), *Civil Society and the State*. London: Verso.

Sandel, M.J. (1982). *Liberalism and the Limits of Justice*. Cambridge: Cambridge University Press.

Young, I.M. (1990). *Justice and the Politics of Difference*. Princeton: Princeton University Press.

Young, I.M. (1998). 'Impartiality and the Civic Public: Some Implications of Feminist Critiques of Moral and Political Theory', in J.B. Landes (ed.), *Feminism, the Public and the Private*. Oxford: Oxford University Press.

Young, I.M. (1998). 'Polity and Group Difference: A Critique of the Ideal of Universal Citizenship', in A. Phillips (ed.), *Feminism and Politics*. Oxford: Oxford University Press.

# 5
## Globalisation, Democracy and Participation – The Dilemmas of the Danish Citizenship Model[1]

*Birte Siim*

### Introduction

In modern democracies the new feminist movement has contributed to place women's concerns and interests on the national political agenda, and the international women's movement has in some cases succeeded in influencing the international agenda to be more sensitive to women's rights, for example the case of women's rights as human rights (Ackerly and Okin, 1999: 137). Globalisation has created new problems to expand democracy beyond the nation state and to deepen democracy by including women and marginalised social groups. This chapter looks at the gendered challenges of linking the politics of everyday life[2] with transnational politics and on the interconnection between the inclusion of women and ethnic minority groups (Christensen and Siim, 2001).

Feminist scholars have analysed women's citizenship and have constructed new conceptual frameworks in order to include women and marginalised social groups in the democratic dialogue. Two paradigmatic examples are Iris Marion Young's notion of 'a politics of difference' (1990) and Anne Phillips' notion of 'a politics of presence' (1995). Young is concerned with the participation and representation of oppressed groups through 'a voice and a vote' and with the transformation of politics 'from below'. Phillips' influential work is concerned with the inclusion of women and marginalised social groups in politics 'from above' through new principles of representation. Women's political inclusion in the Nordic countries[3] has been interpreted as a citizenship model that links the two forms of inclusion in democracy with women's *agency* at the core (Siim, 2000; Skjeie and Siim, 2000; Christensen and Siim, 2001). Today it is debated whether this model can be applied in other countries and whether it can be applied to different groups of women, especially immigrant women (Borchorst and Siim, 2002).

The object of this chapter is to discuss the gendered challenges to democracy presented by the double challenge of globalisation and immigration on the basis of the Danish case. I suggest that the Danish case can illustrate the dilemma of the active model of citizenship with a high degree of equality in times of globalisation and Europeanisation. On the one hand, women are concerned about the contrast between the democratic inclusion of women in Denmark and their political marginalisation in transnational governance, for example, in EU institutions.[4] On the other, there is tension between the inclusion of women in democracy and the political marginalisation of ethnic minority groups. In this chapter the gendered challenges to democracy thus address two related questions: (1) How is it possible to mobilise citizens around global issues, responsibilities and solidarity? and (2) To what extent is the citizenship model used to include women in democracy fruitful for ethnic minority groups?

The first section looks at the paradox of globalisation on the basis of sociological theories of modernity and discusses the potential and problems with Anthony Giddens' vision of dialogue democracy on the basis of the Danish model of citizenship. The gendered problems combining the local, national and global levels of politics are discussed on the basis of the recent study of citizenship in Denmark. The study illustrates the potential of democracy 'from below' based on the participation of citizens in relation to local democracy and in voluntary associations (Torpe, 2003). It also shows the tension between local, national and global politics that is at the same time a gender difference in political identities, defined as interests, competence and orientation with different levels of politics (Goul Andersen, Andersen and Torpe, 2000: 15).

The second section discusses the implications of immigration by focusing on the tension between the inclusion of women and ethnic minority groups. The Danish case illustrates the dilemma between equality and diversity, and it challenges basic beliefs in feminist political theory about the relation between gender, difference and diversity. One question is whether it is possible to use the same models and strategies to include women and marginalised social groups through a 'politics of difference' (Young, 1990) or a 'politics of presence' (Phillips, 1995).

The conclusion discusses the proposals to expand democracy beyond the nation state centred on cosmopolitan democracy (Giddens, 1994;

Held, 1995), and develop a feminist universalism based on new forms of solidarity and global responsibilities (Benhabib, 1996; Dean, 1996; Young, 2000) and a global civil society[5] (Ackerly and Okin, 1999; Dryzek, 1999). From a gender perspective the debate raises two sets of questions: How do we stimulate the political identities and activities of women citizens – now directed towards the local and national level – to be concerned with global issues and responsibilities? And to what extent is it possible for transnational governance 'from above' to include women and marginalised social groups, for example in the governance of the European Union?

## The paradox of globalisation

Anthony Giddens has discussed 'the paradox of globalisation' and the relation between globalisation, democracy and the transformation of everyday life. He argues that globalisation, with its attendant transformation of everyday life, is behind the pressures towards democratisation, and at the same time discloses the limits of the democratic structures, parliamentary democracy (Giddens, 1994: 110; 1999). The German sociologist Ulrich Beck makes a similar analysis of the tendency towards individualisation and changes in family and gender relations in post-traditional risk societies (Beck, 1994). The sociological theories of modernity connect globalisation with everyday life politics and their concepts of 'life politics' and 'subpolitics' challenge fundamental beliefs in political science about who the key actors in politics are, about where the centre of democracy is, and about what the new political issues are (Siim, 1999).

In Giddens' framework globalisation challenges the understanding of democracy and politics rooted in industrial society (Giddens, 1991; 1994). According to Giddens there are four areas where globalisation and institutional reflexivity have created new potentials to expand democracy outside formal politics: (1) Politics is increasingly about 'personal life' problems, for example, sexual relations, marriage and issues in family life; (2) social movements and self-help groups open up new areas for public debate for example about reproductive technologies; (3) there are new possibilities to expand democracy to corporations through decentralisation and more flexible management strategies; and (4) finally, there are new potentials for expansion of democracy to the global order and for creating new forms of transnational political institutions both through formal and informal politics (Giddens, 1994: 117–24). Here the focus is on the link between everyday life politics concerned with personal problems and global politics.

Giddens' influential work points towards parallel tendencies for a new individual reflexivity in post-traditional societies and for an expansion of democracy from parliament to the whole society. Dialogue democracy presumes that there are new local and global actors willing and able to connect the different arenas as well as linking formal and informal politics. It is not about rights or representation of interests, but it concerns the furthering of what he calls cultural cosmopolitanism defined as 'a global generalisation of civil associations', and it is a crucial link between individual autonomy and solidarity (Giddens, 1994: 130).

The concept of dialogue democracy rests on a direct conversation between individuals and a 'life-political' agenda that places moral and existential questions on the political agenda. Ulrich Beck has developed a similar notion called 'sub-politics' that expresses a renewal of political subjectivity within and outside political institutions with citizens, not politicians, as the central actors. It is Beck's thesis that we move from an industrial society to a global 'risk society' that refers to the situation where economic, political and individual risks increasingly escape the institutions with the objective to govern society and protect individuals (Beck, 1994: 17). According to Beck subpolitics is a renewal of politics that represents an alternative to the classical perception of politics in political science on three aspects: (1) the institutional aspect of the political community (polity); (2) the content of political programmes (policy); and (3) the political process about distribution of power and values (politics). This indicates that politics during the 1980s has moved to new arenas outside parliaments, that there are new political actors, especially active citizen groups, and that there is a struggle to create a new dimension in politics, for example, in relation to ecological and moral problems.

Subpolitics is a vision about a society created 'from below' with new political agents at the centre of democratic politics. It is an expansion of democracy in the sense that it gives social groups that have not been involved with elite politics 'a voice and a share', for example, grassroots, citizen groups, group of workers and expert groups. Subpolitics is a conceptualisation of new conditions and challenges for democracy after the fall of the Berlin Wall, and it indicates that politics tends to transcend Left and Right as well as the public/private split. There is a tendency towards a 'reinvention of politics', that is 'to create new rules', instead of just 'following rules'. According to Beck, the fundamental questions have become 'life-political', for example, the attitudes of individuals to risks/uncertainties, attitudes towards strangers and attitudes to creation of society (Beck, 1994: 42).

The paradigms of Giddens and Beck are interesting from a gender perspective, because they draw attention to a new dimension in politics that at least potentially connects global politics with everyday life issues as well as to the direct participation of citizens outside the classical political institutions (Beck, Giddens and Lasch, 1994). This approach resembles the feminist emphasis on new forms of politics that are able to engage women citizens directly in the democratic dialogue based on issues in everyday life.

The paradox of globalisation and the dilemma connected to the notions of life-politics and subpolitics can be illustrated from the Danish context. Danish democracy since the 1970s has emphasised an active citizenship model with social movements and voluntary organisations as key actors and an interconnection between parliamentary politics and everyday life politics. During the 1990s the limits of this model have become visible. It is a problem how to link the participation of citizens in local and national democracy with concerns for European and global issues and how to create new forms of solidarity that include diversity based not only on gender, but also on the recognition of diversity and difference. In the following the dilemma of dialogue democracy to link global and everyday life politics through citizens' activities in the era of globalisation and immigration will be discussed on the basis of the Danish case.

### The Danish model of democratic citizenship

Danish political culture has emphasised a participatory model of citizenship and a vision of democracy from below that rests on active citizens engaged in the problems of everyday life (Siim, 2000; Torpe and Goul Andersen, 2000). The Danish model of democracy was redesigned 'from below' during the 1970s and 1980s to include new actors and new forms of grass-roots politics from young well-educated men and women organised in the social movements. New issues were placed at the political agenda and the meaning of politics changed in order to deal with issues like peace, the environment and gender quality (Christensen and Siim, 2001).

The vision of democracy 'as a way of life' (H. Koch, 1961) is one expression of the active model of citizenship rooted in Danish political history and institutions. The notion was introduced after the Second World War in a debate about democracy between the Grundtvigean-inspired clergyman Hal Koch and the Professor of Law Alf Ross. Koch argued that democracy is a goal in itself and he conceptualised the key aspect of democracy as 'a way of life' (H. Koch, 1961), while Ross argued that the key aspect of democracy was 'a method of government' (Ross, 1967). According to Hal Koch the *dialogue between people* was at the centre, and he argued that democracy as 'a way of life' is basically about relations between people – including relations in the family and the neighbourhood as well as between social groups and between nations. From this perspective the true meaning of democracy is discussion and dialogue, and citizens need to learn democracy, especially in voluntary organisations and popular social movements. According to Alf Ross's more conventional understanding, political democracy is a form of governance and representative institutions with the civil rights of citizens at the centre (Christensen and Siim, 2001). Looking back, we can see that the two did indeed share many ideas about the importance of people's democratic mentalities and of social equality as a precondition for democracy.[6]

Hal Koch emphasised the participatory aspect of democracy and saw voluntary organisations as 'schools in democracy'. According to Koch the 'people' are made up of all oppressed social groups that should organise in order to develop democratic competence, efficacy, self-confidence and capabilities to participate in the governing of the national community with their specific social perspective on life and politics. Koch perceived women as an oppressed social group that needed to develop their organisational skills, but he was critical of women's organisations that he found lacked the will to influence the public debate and contribute to 'the common good' (Christensen and Siim, 2001: 73). Bodil Koch, Hal Koch's wife, who was Minister of Religious Affairs in the Social Democratic governments between 1950 and 1962, had a more positive perception of how to develop women's democratic responsibilities through a new grass roots organisation, 'Folke-virke', directed towards women. Her vision of a female perspective on democracy was based on women's active citizenship and a perception of democracy rooted in the family, and she wanted to connect women's activities in the family with their participation on the public arena (Christensen and Siim, 2001: 77–83).

Alf Ross and Hal Koch agreed about the extension of fundamental rights, including social rights, as a precondition for a well-functioning democracy, but Ross emphasised the liberal-constitutional and Koch the republican aspect of democracy. Alf Ross's version became the dominant model of democracy during the 1950s, but during the 1960s there was a revival of democracy, and the social movements, including the strong women's movement, reformulated the practice of participatory citizenship 'from below' (Christensen and Siim, 2001). Since the 1970s, the

Danish model of democracy has been based on the active participation of citizens.

The Danish case illuminates the link between the two perceptions of democracy, and today the Danish model of democratic citizenship 'from below' includes:

- participation of citizens in the formulation and implementation of politics;
- organisation of oppressed social groups as political actors in order to form democratic identities and learn democratic competence; and
- social equality and redistributive politics as a precondition for democracy.

From a Nordic comparative perspective the Danish gender model has been described as a 'movement-oriented' democracy, where the women's movement, the peace and the environmental movements have since the 1970s and 1980s succeeded in influencing politics and changing the norms and practices of everyday life (Bergqvist et al., 1999). The Danish model which combines participatory citizenship with an emphasis on social equality and redistributive politics has both potentials and problems for women (Siim, 2000). We argue that 'movement dependency' has potential, because it enables women's agency to influence politics, and problems because it is dependent on an active women's movement able to place gender issues on the political agenda (Christensen and Siim, 2001). During the 1990s, immigration exposed the dilemma of the model to include diversity and difference. Recently, it has been criticised, because the homogeneous notion of culture does not recognise diversity and difference, but expects citizens to conform to the same 'Danish way of life' (Christensen and Siim, 2001; Schwartz, 2002).

Globalisation, Europeanisation and immigration represent new challenges to the Danish model of democracy. First, the Danish vision of democracy has been interpreted as a barrier against expanding democracy beyond the nation state. Danish citizens have generally been negative towards a deepening of political co-operation in the EU, and Denmark has adopted four exceptions to further European co-operation as a result of the referendum about Mastricht.[7] Scholars[8] have noted that Danish citizens and politicians often use the ideal vision about Danish democracy, especially as a participatory open and responsive democracy, as a contrast to the democratic deficit and bureaucracy of the European Union (Kelstrup, 1999: 12–14). Second, it is debated whether the Danish perception of democracy[9] rooted in a highly homogeneous culture may be a specific barrier to the political inclusion of immigrants and refugees groups (Schwartz, 2002). Arguably, the political marginalisation of immigrant groups is a serious problem in the Danish model of democracy based on a vision of active citizenship and democratic governance where all members of society are expected to participate in the formulation of politics (Togeby, 1999: 134).

In the next section the potentials and problems for Danish democracy posed by globalisation and Europeanisation will be explored on the basis of Danish research with a focus upon two related questions: (1) the differentiation of the participation, interests and identities of citizens in relation to different political arenas; and (2) the relation between the models and strategies to include women and immigrant and refugee groups.

## The gendered dilemma of participatory democracy

The study of Democracy from Below[10] can illustrate the dilemma of the participatory Danish model and the differentiation of Danish citizens' political identities and practices in relation to different levels of politics. The overall picture is a relatively high degree of participation and feeling of efficacy of citizens in relation to local democracy and everyday life politics (Goul Andersen et al., 2000: 151; Torpe and Goul Andersen, 2000b: 179–80). There is a high degree of gender equality in the political participation in relation to three key areas: (1) local democracy; (2) membership and activities in associations; and (3) institutions related to everyday life, for example, in schools and child care institutions (Christensen and Siim, 2001: 136). The study also indicates that there are gender differences in women's and men's political identities (Christensen and Siim, 2001: 150).

The survey confirms many specific characteristics of Danish democracy. It shows first that a large majority of Danish citizens (78 per cent) support the normative ideal of participatory democracy where citizens should be able to influence decisions between elections, and less than 10 per cent support the elite version of democracy (Christensen and Siim, 2001: 164). Second, it shows an increase in the participation of Danish citizens in voluntary associations between 1990 and 1998, and in contrast to Norway there is no longer a gender difference in participation or in the gender profiles of associations (Christensen and Siim, 2001: 130). Third, it shows that there has also been an increase in the participation of both women and men 'as users' – or as 'citizen-parents' – in public service institutions, especially in relation to schools and child care institutions,[11] although women are still more active than men (Christensen and Siim, 2001: 139). On this basis Lars Torpe and Jørgen Goul Andersen conclude that Denmark can be considered as a participatory democracy, at least if we talk about politics on the local level (Torpe and Goul Andersen, 2000: 180).

The study indicates that in spite of the high degree of gender equality in political participation, women and men have different political identities, defined as political interest, political competence and political orientations (Goul Andersen, 2000b: 15). Women are generally more interested in and feel more empowered by local democracy and tend to identify with the politics of everyday life, while men are more interested in national politics and tend to identify with larger political issues (Christensen and Siim, 2001). The level of political interest in Denmark is comparatively high (almost 80 per cent are very or somewhat interested in politics), and the gender difference in political interest has fallen from 20 to 10 per cent between 1990 and 1998 (78 per cent of men and 68 per cent of women are very or somewhat interested in politics), but there are gender differences in the political interest of citizens in relation to different levels of politics. Men are more interested than women in national politics (10 per cent difference) and women are more interested in local politics than men (2 per cent difference). The gender difference in political interest has increased in questions regarding the relation between Denmark and the EU and foreign policy issues (Christensen and Siim, 2001: 146). The results illustrate a general dilemma for democracy: citizens feel a relatively high degree of empowerment in relation to local democracy, and the feeling of political competence decreases if we move from the local to the national level and decrease even more at the European level (Goul Andersen, 2000b: 151; Torpe and Goul Andersen, 2000: 179).

Inspired by these results scholars involved in the Danish study of Democracy from Below have introduced the term 'everyday maker' as the symbol of a new political figure (Bang et al., 2000). The everyday maker is constructed as an ideal type that expresses a new political identity with democratic potentials inspired by Giddens' notions about dialog democracy and life-politics. The figure is described in the following way:

> She relates directly to the problems in everyday life, at work, in the home, in voluntary organisations, in the service institutions and other places where you meet problems that need common solution.
> (Bang and Sørensen, 1997: 24)

The political identity of the everyday maker is different from members of political parties and members of grass-roots movements. 'She' is primarily concerned with *ad hoc* politics and the politics of everyday life is presently directed towards the local welfare state, for example, child care issues, environmental politics and care of the elderly. It has been noticed that this identity resembles women's political profile as local activists, and the everyday maker is described as if she were a woman. According to Bang and Sørensen the everyday maker, however, expresses a new identity rooted in the network society that is different from the previous political activists engaged in social movements as well as from activists in Leftist organisations.

From a perspective of deliberative democracy it has been noticed that the emphasis on daily life tends to reproduce a problematic split between small and big politics – between experts and citizens as well as between participation and power (Ulrich, 2001). From a gender perspective it has been noticed that the everyday maker is the expression of a problematic split between small and big democracy that hides a differentiation between the political participation, identities and power of men and women (Christensen and Siim, 2001). It is also a problem that the everyday maker tends to be active primarily in local issues and to be ambivalent towards issues connected with European governance and trans-national politics. The everyday maker has potential, for example to act as a political consumer, and it is possible for there to be a spillover effect from local issues to the concerns with global issues like the environment that also have local effects. In Denmark there is a close institutional connection between local and national democracy around the organisation of everyday life issues, like childcare, elderly care and health care and citizens are interested in national politics. The study of Democracy from Below indicates, however, that the political identities of citizens in terms of interest, orientation and identification is still closely related to local and national levels of politics. This is paradoxical since the influence of European politics and the power of the European parliament is increasing. Researchers, therefore, debate how to stimulate the political identities of citizens, especially in relation to the EU (Goul Andersen, 2000a).

## The Danish gender model and the inclusion of ethnic minority groups

The Danish gender model is based on women's participation in voluntary organisations and their representation in political institutions, and as a result there is a high degree of gender equality in political partici-pation 'from below'. Today there are new challenges to democracy for the Danish gender model based on 'movement politics', because there is no longer an organised women's movement that speaks with one voice (Christensen and Siim, 2001). The dilemma to link the politics of everyday life to global politics is a gendered dilemma.

Multiculturalism is another challenge to the Danish model of citi-zenship as well as to the gender model that has revealed the dilemma between equality and diversity. One of the assumptions in feminist theory has been the close connection between theories, models and strategies to include women and marginalised social groups. This premise has been inspired by gender models in countries like the US and Britain, where affirmative action was first adopted to integrate Blacks in the labour market and later extended to women. Arguably it is the other way round in Scandinavia. In Denmark gender quotas were adopted in 1986 in the Social Democratic and Socialist Party in order to include women in political parties and increase their number in parliament. They were never popular, and they were abolished in 1996 (see Ann-Dorte Christensen, this volume, chapter 6), and there have been no political arguments in favour of quotas for immigrant groups or attempts by political parties and feminist politics to link the inclu-sion of women to the inclusion of immigrant groups.

Feminist scholars have emphasised that one of the potentials of Scan-dinavian democracy has been 'an empowerment model' based on the interconnection between grass-roots politics and representative politics (Skjeie and Siim, 2000). During the 1990s there has been a growing frag-mentation of the social movements, including the organised women's movement, but at the same time Danish women have, as noted above, increased their participation in associations and in the social service institutions (Christensen and Siim, 2001). As a result there is a growing tension between the political empowerment of Danish women and the political marginalisation and disempowerment of immigrant and refugee groups, especially ethnic minority women (Siim, 2003; Togeby, 2003). The public debate has constructed a conflict between gender equality and multiculturalism, and the extreme right has used gender equality as an argument against the cultural recognition of immigrant groups.

Immigration is a relatively new phenomenon in Denmark and dates back to the 1960s. Until the 1980s immigrants were perceived primar-ily as workers. The cultural, economic and political integration of ethnic minorities is thus a relatively new problem, and the debate about how to combat political marginalisation was sparked by reports produced by the power commission in the late 1990s (Togeby, 1999). The democratic problems with the political inclusion of immigrant groups have become more visible during the 1990s, because immigrants are demanding 'a voice and a vote' (Hussain, 1999; Schwartz, 2002).

I suggest that the Danish case questions basic premises in feminist democratic theory about the meaning of the politics of difference and the politics of presence. As noted above, the 'empowerment model' has included Danish women in politics, but this has not made political institutions more open to marginalised groups or changed social policies in the interests of marginalised social groups. Arguably the populist Right has taken over the agenda for 'the politics of everyday life' connected to the nation state with the objective of restricting immigration and reserving social, civil and political rights for Danish citizens. One implication is that the political inclusion of women is increasingly at odds with the political marginalisation of immigrant groups, and the acceptance of gender equality in politics is at odds with the resistance of Danish citizens towards the political influence of immigrant groups (Togeby, 1999; Christensen and Siim, 2001). This indicates that there is no automatic link between the inclusion of women and marginalised social groups in democracy. From a gender perspective one question is whether ethnic minority women can use the same citizenship strategy as Danish majority women or whether it is necessary to use other means to integrate ethnic minorities in political institutions.

### The political marginalisation of ethnic minorities

One of the new challenges to the participatory model of democracy is the differentiation between Danish citizens and ethnic minority groups. Today there is a political struggle about the principles of citizenship that to some extent transcends the classical conflict between Left and Right. The populist Right wants to close the borders to immigrants and limit social rights to Danish citizens who are 'like us', while the Left wants to have more open borders and equal social rights for all individuals living in Denmark. The Social Democratic Party, as well as feminists, have been divided on the issue of immigration as well as on the relation to the EU.

Lise Togeby's study of the political participation of immigrants in Denmark shows that there is a serious democratic problem with their integration as citizens. They do not have an effective 'voice or vote', and they do not participate in the democratic dialogue to the same extent as Danish citizens. Immigrants have basically the same formal social and political rights as Danish citizens. Only Danish citizens can vote in national elections, but foreign citizens have gained the right to vote in local and regional elections after being in the country for three years (Togeby, 1999: 140). One of the problems is that immigrant groups have lower political participation than Danes do. First, they do not exercise the right to vote to the same extent as Danish citizens. Second, there is a lower percentage of immigrants and refugees organised in national associations or associations for ethnic minorities compared to Danish citizens (Togeby, 1999: 143). The study concludes that immigrant and refugee groups represent a double challenge to Danish democracy. First, it is a challenge to give them real opportunities to use their democratic rights to the same extent as Danish citizens; and second, it is a challenge to change the attitudes of Danes to accord immigrants the right to influence political decisions (Togeby, 1999: 150).

The issue of immigration is politically controversial and illustrates the dilemma of the politics of everyday life that has increasingly been taken over by the populist Right which wants to limit immigration and reserve social rights to Danish citizens. During the 1990s, conflicts and controversies around the social and political integration of immigrant and refugee groups have increasingly dominated the Danish public debate, and there has been a growing trend towards assimilation policies. In Denmark multiculturalism is controversial, and there have been heated discussions about diversity, for example, about 'forced marriages' and the right of Muslim girls to wear the chador in the labour market. A new integration law[12] was adopted in 1998, and in November 2001 a Liberal-Conservative government replaced the old Social Democratic-Centre government with the support of the Far Right. The new government has adopted more restrictive rules for immigrants and adopted a number of controversial measures – for example, lower social benefits for immigrants than for Danish citizens, and Danish citizens cannot marry a foreign citizen until they reach the age of 24 (Fenger-Grøn et al., 2003).

Danish researchers do not agree about the explanations of the high degree of political marginalisation of immigrant groups. Some emphasise the barriers in immigrant cultures, others the barriers in Danish political culture (Schwartz, 2002), and some focus on discrimination in political institutions (Hussain, 2000). Lise Togeby has recently compared the Danish 'ethnicity regime' with other regimes on the basis of two dimensions: a cultural and civil/political dimension. She notes that, culturally, there is a mix between an open democratic culture and informal trends towards assimilation. In terms of political rights Denmark has had quite generous formal rules (Togeby, 2003: 56–9). The conclusion is that Denmark is less pluralistic than Britain, the Netherlands and Sweden and has, during the 1990s, moved closer to the cultural assimilation pole and to a more closed system of citizenship with stronger barriers to become citizens.

The American sociologist Allan Wolfe and the Danish-American political scientist Jytte Klausen have suggested that there may be a trade-off between a solidarity that underpins welfare states and multiculturalism, because, even though equality and solidarity are both desirable objectives, they may often conflict (Wolfe and Klausen, 2000: 28). They note that national pride and fragile bonds of citizenship must be taken seriously, because it is easier to feel solidarity with those who broadly share your values and way of life. On the basis of a study of official reports they claim that Danes and Swedes have reasserted national values and that the Swedes have rejected multiculturalism, but accepted diversity, and that the Danes have rejected multiculturalism and barely accepted diversity. Their main point is that the welfare state is not morally neutral between different conceptions of the family, and immigrants must often abandon cultural beliefs and practices that violate the norms of Scandinavian solidarity.

The Danish model has similarities with communitarian forms of democracy, and it can illustrate Iris Marion Young's dilemma between the inclusion of citizens from either a 'particular' or 'universal' perspective. The politics of everyday life can be interpreted as a particularistic perspective which is indeed combined with the universal social rights of the welfare state. Danish citizens score high on empowerment, social trust and social capital (Torpe, 2003), and Denmark also scores high on foreign aid to poor Third World countries. The problem is that many Danish citizens want to restrict the universal perspective to Danish citizens who also behave 'like Danes'. This illustrates the dilemma of the participatory model of citizenship between social equality and recognition of diversity. The model does not by itself stimulate the formation of political identities that include universal solidarity with 'the other' which is different from the Danish majority and recognise the different culture, language and religion of the minority.

I find that the Danish model illuminates Nancy Fraser's 'equality/ recognition' dilemma between redistributive politics based on social equality and the politics of recognition based on recognition of cultural difference (1997). In contrast to the Anglo-American model, the Danish citizenship model is based on social equality and a high degree of political participation of citizens. And in contrast to the marginalisation of American women, Danish women have been included in democracy, and gender equality has been accepted as a part of social equality. Arguably, women no longer represent difference and diversity, but have become 'one of us'; however, this has not solved the problem of recognising other kinds of difference and diversity. The political marginalisation of ethnic minority groups illustrates the need to include recognition of diversity in the Danish citizenship model. It also indicates that there may be different logics associated with the inclusion of ethnicity and gender. I conclude that the Danish case illustrates the dilemma of the participatory perception democracy between universal social rights and recognition of diversity of ethnic minority groups. Arguably, the Danish model of democracy has been good for women citizens, but there is no guarantee that it is also good for ethnic minority groups. One question is whether this gender model can also be useful for ethnic minority women; another is how to link the different logic connected to gender and ethnicity (Siim, 2003).

## Cosmopolitanism and a global feminist theory and politics

Globalisation and Europeanisation pose new challenges to democratic theory and politics, and this chapter has emphasised the gendered challenges to democracy on the basis of the Danish case. The chapter has discussed the dilemma of participatory democracy and has identified two sets of problems: to expand the political identities of (women) citizens from the local to global responsibilities and to expand the model of citizenship to include recognition of diversity.

Theories about cosmopolitan democracy have been at the centre of recent debates about new paradigms and visions that address the problems of globalisation. Giddens suggests that we need to develop global cosmopolitanism on the basis of universal values of solidarity (Giddens, 1994: 252–3), and feminist scholars have suggested that we need a new form of feminist universalism that transcends the nation state and is based on a global responsibility (Benhabib, 1996; Dean, 1996). Young suggests that it is possible to develop a vision of local and cultural autonomy in the context of global regulatory regimes (Young, 2000: 236). The argument is that commitments to justice begin with local and particularistic relationships and that feelings of solidarities are not timeless and natural but constructed, and that transnational sentiments of solidarity ought to be constructed to correspond to transnational obligations (Young, 2000: 242–3).

The Danish case illustrates the limitations connected with feelings of local identification and cultural affinity, and indicates that it is both a theoretical and an empirical challenge to stimulate citizens' concerns for global issues and develop their responsibilities that transcend the nation state. It confirms that there are limitations connected to equality and solidarity confined to citizenship in the nation that cannot easily be extended to marginalised minority groups, especially ethnic minorities. Both sets of questions emphasise the important role of political agency and the political identities of citizens for the expansion of democracy beyond the nation state.

Feminist theory and politics face new challenges about how to construct a global feminist theory and politics. The feminist strategy to empower women and marginalised social groups by giving them 'a voice and a vote' is a fruitful starting point, but it needs to be reformulated in the global context. The Danish case indicates that there is no automatic link between strategies to include women and ethnic minority groups or between local and global responsibilities. One of the new challenges is to mobilise women as political actors with responsibilities for common concerns beyond the nation state, to reinvent a politics able to link local and global problems and develop new forms of solidarities with marginalised social groups. This new vision of democracy should be based upon equality and solidarity with marginalised groups and should include recognition of diversity and difference.

## Notes

1. This essay was first presented at the GEP International Conference, Vilvorde, August 2000, and is based on results published in *Køn, demokrati og modernitet – mod nye politiske identiteter* [Gender, Democracy and Modernity] with Ann-Dorte Christensen (2001). I want to thank Lars Torpe and Ann-Dorte Christensen for constructive comments.
2. Political scientists have used many different concepts to describe political issues connected with people's daily lives that are often contrasted with larger political issues connected with the nation or with international relations, for example 'high' and 'low' politics. In this chapter 'the politics of everyday life' is defined as political issues concerned with problems closely related to people's daily lives, for example, child care, primary education, health care, elderly care, healthy livelihood, urban planning and environmental issues. The politics of everyday life is rooted in civil society and can be connected to the local as well as to the national level. In the Danish investigation of citizenship we distinguished between activities in relation to institutions in the everyday life of citizens, for example the family, the workplace, the service institutions of the welfare state and the local community, called 'nærdemokratiske' forms of participation, and activities in relation to the big democracy, for example political parties, elections, voluntary organisations (Andersen et al., 1993). This differentiation is close to the distinction in the

Swedish investigation of citizenship between 'small' democracy, defined as citizens' activities to influence their own life-situation in the family, at the workplace and as users in public service institutions, and 'big' democracy, defined as citizens' activities to influence the political community (Petersson et al., 1989).

3. There are both commonalities and differences in the citizenship model and gender profiles in the five Nordic countries; see Berqvist et al. (1999).

4. The issue of Danish citizens' attitudes towards the European Union is controversial, because of the Danish referendums about the EU treaties. The Danish population voted No to the Maastricht Treaty in 1992, but as a result of the adoption of four reservations the No was changes to a Yes in 1993. In 2000 the Danish population again voted No to the Euro in a referendum. Women tend to be more critical of European integration and feel more disempowered by the EU than men (Goul Andersen, 2000: 136).

5. The globalised economy has inspired a global citizens' movement against the negative effects of the free market with the objective to regulate the global market by democratic forces (see Pianta, 2001). Women tend to be invisible in the leadership of the globalisation movement and gender issues has also been absent from the discourse of the movements (Eschle, 2003).

6. Ross agreed with Koch that democracy is also a way of life, but he emphasised that democracy is first and foremost a method of government concerned with a set of procedures of 'how' and not 'what' to organise. He also agreed that increasing social equality may be a precondition for the survival of democracy, but he argued that economic, social and cultural equality does not automatic follow from political equality (Christensen and Siim, 2001).

7. The exceptions to further European cooperation concern: (1) European citizenship; (2) membership of the Euro; (3) participation in legal cooperation; and (4) participation in a European army (Goul Andersen, 2000).

8. The democratic deficit has also been described as a democratic dilemma between a strong national democracy based on either a weak European parliament, and a strong European parliament that will weaken the national democracies (Kelstrup, 2000).

9. The Nordic countries have historically been based on a high degree of homogeneity in relation to religion, culture and ethnicity (Østergaard, 1992). Danes have been described as a 'tribe' who tend to assume that people living in Denmark have the same values and the same legal citizen rights. This is a problematic assumption today with a growing number of refugees and immigrants who cannot get Danish citizenship, and a growing number with foreign citizenship or who are born outside Denmark of parents who are not Danish citizens.

10. Democracy from Below is a representative Danish survey from 1998 which repeats many of the questions from the 1990 citizenship study. This enables us to compare the development in the political participation and identities of citizens between 1990 and 1998 (Goul Andersen, 2000).

11. In 1994 Danish citizens gained new rights in relation to education, sabbatical leave and parental leave. Parental leave has been the most popular and most controversial of the three. It gives parents new citizen rights to participate in decisions in relation to child care institutions and schools. The investigation of citizenship in Denmark found that there is a high degree of

gender equality in the participation of women and men as citizen-parents in relation to schools and child care institutions (see Siim, 1994). The investigation of citizenship from 1998 shows that the participation of citizens as users increased during the 1990s and that there is a tendency for women's participation to increase more than men's (Christensen and Siim, 2001).

12. The Danish integration law of 1998 is controversial. The objective is to integrate immigrants in the labour market, in politics, and socially and culturally. It is directed at all foreigners defined as immigrants and refugees living legally in Denmark and who are not citizens of the Nordic countries or of member states of the EU. The law is part of the new active social and labour market policy for Danish citizens. The purpose of the law is, through integration, to contribute to newly arrived foreigners are given the opportunity to participate equally with other citizens in society's political, economic, working, social, religious and cultural life, Chapter 1, §1, 1998 (www.indenrigs.dk).

# References

Ackerly, B. and S.M. Okin (1999). 'Feminist Social Criticism and the International Movement for Women's Rights as Human Rights', in I. Shapiro and C. Hacker-Cordón (eds.), *Democracy's Edge*. Cambridge: Cambridge University Press.

Andersen, J., A.-D. Christensen, K. Langberg, B. Siim and L. Torpe (1993). *Medborgerskab. Demokrati og politisk deltagelse* [Citizenship, Democracy and Political Participation]. Herning: Systime.

Bang, H. and E. Sørensen (1997). 'The Everyday Maker: a New Challenge to Democratic Governance'. ECPR paper to the 26th Joint Sessions of Workshops, 25–28 March 1998. *Working Paper*, Department of Economics, Politics and Public Administration, Aalborg University. 1998: 2.

Bang, P.H., A.D. Hansen and J. Hoff (eds.) (2000). *Demokrati fra neden. Casestudier fra en dansk kommune* [Democracy from Below. Case Studies from a Danish Locality]. Copenhagen: DJØF Forlag.

Beck, U. (1994). 'The Reinvention of Politics: Towards a Theory of Reflexive Modernization', in U. Beck, A. Giddens and S. Lash (eds.), *Reflexive Modernization. Politics, Tradition and Aesthetics in the Modern Social Order*. London: Polity Press.

Beck, U., A. Giddens and S. Lash (eds.) (1994). *Reflexive Modernization. Politics, Tradition and Aesthetics in the Modern Social Order*. London: Polity Press.

Benhabib, S. (1999). 'Citizens, Residents, and Aliens in a Changing World. Political Membership in the Global Era', in U. Hedetoft and M. Hjort (eds.), *The Postnational Self. Belonging and Identity*. Minneapolis: University of Minnesota Press.

Bergqvist C., A. Borchorst, A.-D. Christensen, N. Raaum, V. Ramnstedt-Silén and A. Styrkasdottir (eds.) (1999). *Equal Democracies? Gender and Politics in the Nordic Countries*. Oslo: University of Oslo Press.

Borchorst, A. and B. Siim (2002). 'The Women-Friendly Welfare State Revisited'. *NORA, Nordic Journal of Women's Studies*, 10, 2.

Christensen, A.-D. and B. Siim (2001). *Køn, demokrati og modernitet – mod nye politiske identiteter* [Gender, Democracy and Modernity – Towards New Political Identities]. Copenhagen: Hans Reitzels Press.

Clinell, B. (2001). *ATTAC. Græsrøddernes oprør mod markedet* [The Revolt of the Grass Roots against the Market]. Frederiksberg: Indroit Publishers.

Dean, J. (1996). *Solidarity of Strangers. Feminism after Identity Politics.* Berkeley: California University Press.

Dryzeck, J. (2000). *Deliberative Democracy and Beyond. Liberals, Critics and Contestations.* Oxford: Oxford University Press.

Eschle, C. (2003). ' "Skeleton Women": Feminism and Social Movement Resistance to Corporate Power and Neoliberalism'. Paper prepared for the International Studies Association annual conference, Portland, Oregon, 25–28 February.

Fenger-Grøn, C., K. Qureshi and T. Seidenfaden (eds.) (2003). *Når du strammer garnet – et opgør med mobning af mindretal og ansvarsløs asylpolitik.* Aarhus: Aarhus Universitets forlag.

Fraser, N. (1989). *Unruly Practices. Power and Discourse in Contemporary Social Theory.* Minneapolis: University of Minnesota Press.

Fraser, N. (1997). *Justice Interruptions. Critical Reflections on the 'Postsocialist' Condition.* London: Routledge.

Giddens, A. (1994). *Beyond Left and Right, The Future of Radical Politics.* London: Polity Press.

Giddens, A. (1999). *Runaway World. How Globalisation is Reshaping our Lives.* London: Profile Books.

Goul Andersen, J. (2000a). 'ØMU og demokratiet – aspekter af det demokratiske underskud i EU' [The Euro and Democracy – Aspects of the Democratic Deficit in the EU], in S. Dosenrode (ed.), *Danmark of ØMUEN – politiske aspekter.* Århus: Systime.

Goul Andersen, J. (2000b). 'Magt og afmagt: Nyt perspektiv på "political efficacy" ', pp 123–52, in J. Goul Andersen, L. Torpe and J. Andersen, *Hvad folket magter. Demokrati, magt og afmagt [The Empowerment of Citizens. Democracy, Power and Disempowerment].* Copenhagen: DJØF Forlag.

Goul Andersen, J., L. Torpe and J. Andersen (2000). *Hvad folket magter? Demokrati, magt og afmagt [The Empowerment of Citizens. Democracy, Power and Disempowerment].* Copenhagen: DJØF Forlag.

Gundelach, P. and L. Torpe (1999). 'Befolkningens fornemmelser for demokrati: foreninger, politisk engagement og demokratisk kultur' [The Population's Sense of Democracy: Associations, Political Engagement and Democratic Culture], in J. Goul Andersen et al. (eds.), *Den demokratiske udfordring* [The Democratic Challenge]. Copenhagen, Hans Reitzels Press.

Held, D. (1995). *Democracy and the Global Order.* London: Polity Press.

Hussain, M. (2002). 'Etniske minoriteters organisering i Danmark' [The Organisation of Ethnic Minorities in Denmark], in F. Mikkelsen (ed.). *Bevægelser i demokrati. Foreninger og kollektive aktioner i Danmark.* Århus: Aarhus University Press.

Kelstrup, M. (2000). 'Demokrati, EU og ØMU' [Democracy, the EU and the Euro], in S. Dosenrode (ed.), *Danmark og ØMUen – politiske aspekter.* Århus: Systime.

Koch, B. (1947). 'Skal kvinderne have særopgaver i politik?' [Should Women Have Special Tasks in Politics?]. *Verdens Gang,* 2.

Koch, H. (1961). *Hvad er demokrati?* [What is Democracy?]. Copenhagen: Gyldendal (first published in 1945).

Lister, R. (2003). *Citizenship. Feminist Perspectives.* London: Macmillan (2nd edn).

Østergaard, Uffe (1992). *Europas ansigter. Nationale stater i en ny og gammel verden* [The Faces of Europe. Nation States in a New and Old World]. Copenhagen: Rosinante.

Petersson, O., Westholm, A. and Blomberg, G. (1989). *Medborgernas Makt* [The Power of Citizens]. Stockholm: Carlssons.

Phillips, A. (1993). *Democracy and Difference.* London: Polity Press.

Phillips, A. (1995). *The Politics of Presence.* London: Polity Press.

Pianta, M. (2001). 'Parallel Summits of Global Civil Society', in *Global Civil Society.* Oxford: Oxford University Press.

Ross, A. (1967). *Hvorfor demokrati?* [Why Democracy?]. Copenhagen, Nyt Nordisk Forlag (first published 1946).

Schwartz, J. (ed.) (2002). *Medborgerskabets mange stemmer* [The Many Voices of Citizenship]. Århus: Magtudredningen.

Siim, B. (1994). 'Engendering Democracy – the Interplay between Citizenship and Political Participation'. *Social Politics. International Studies in Gender, State and Society,* 1, 3.

Siim, B. (1999). 'Feministiske perspektiver på demokrati og medborgerskab' [Feminist Perspectives on Democracy and Citizenship], in E. Amnå (ed.), *Demokrati och medborgerskabp. Demokratiutredningens forskarvolum II,* SOU 1999: 77.

Siim, B. (2000). *Gender and Citizenship. Politics and Agency in France, Britain and Denmark,* Cambridge: Cambridge University Press.

Siim, B. (2003). *Medborgerskabets udfordringer. Etniske minoritetskvinders politiske myndiggørelse.* Århus: Aarhus University Press.

Skjeie, H. and B. Siim (2000). 'Scandinavian Feminist Debates'. *International Political Science Review,* 21, 4.

Togeby, L. (1999). 'Et demokrati, som omfatter alle, der bor i Danmark?' [A Democracy that Includes Everybody who Lives in Denmark?], in J. Goul Andersen et al. (eds.), *Den demokratiske udfordring* [The Democratic Challenge]. Copenhagen: Hans Reitzels Press.

Togeby, L. (2003). *Fra fremmedarbejdere til etniske minoriteter* [From Immigrant Workers to Ethnic Minorities]. Århus: Aarhus University Press.

Torpe, L. (2003). 'Social Capital in Denmark. A Deviant Case?'. *Scandinavian Political Studies,* 26, 1.

Torpe, L. and J. Goul Andersen (2000). 'Tilskuerdemokrati eller elitedemokrati' [Spectator Democracy or Elite Democracy], in *Hvad folket magter. Demokrati, magt og afmagt* [The Empowerment of Citizens. Democracy, Power and Disempowerment]. Copenhagen: DJØF Forlag.

Ulrich, J. (2001). 'Hverdagsmageren og det myndige alternativ' [The Everydaymaker and the Democratic Alternative], in A.-D. Christensen and B. Siim (eds.), *Køn, demokrati og modernitet – mod nye politiske identiteter* [Gender, Democracy and Modernity – Towards New Political Identities]. Copenhagen: Hans Reitzels Press.

Wolfe, A. and J. Klausen (2000). 'Other People'. *Prospect,* December.

Young, I.M. (1990). *Justice and the Political Difference.* Princeton: Princeton University Press.

Young, I.M. (2000). *Inclusion and Democracy.* Oxford: Oxford University Press.

# 6
# The Danish Gender Model: Between Movement Politics and Representative Politics

*Ann-Dorte Christensen*

## Introduction

In Denmark, as in the other Nordic countries, we have witnessed a number of changes over the past couple of decades or so in feminist analysis, from focusing on women's exclusion to highlighting women's inclusion in modern democracy (Bergqvist et al., 1999; Siim, 2000; Christensen and Siim, 2001). The inclusionist perspective will be one of the focal points of this chapter. In particular, I shall focus on the discussion surrounding various types of political strategies evolved by women as elements in their collective mobilisation in Denmark over the past 30 years.

The key concepts will be the Danish gender model (Christensen and Siim, 2001; see also Birte Siim, this volume, chapter 5), the impact of which is closely related to the intersection between movement politics and representative politics. By the term *movement politics* we mean political activities that take place primarily within social movements or voluntary organisations. By the term *representative politics* we refer to political activities that are institutionalised in connection with the formal, political institutions in the political system or in relation to formal organisations in civil society. This distinction is often referred to as a distinction between 'from below' and 'from above'.

Nevertheless, it is important to stress that one of the special characteristics in the Danish gender model is the close interaction and interplay between movement arenas and the arena constituted by the political institutions (Kaare Nielsen, 1991; Bergqvist et al., 1999; Siim, 2000; Christensen and Siim, 2001). Within movement studies, the connection to the political institutions has also been highlighted. Dieter Rucht, for instance, contends that it is often difficult in practice to draw a precise line between the various arenas (Rucht, 1996). In addition, Solveig Bergman's analysis of the new social movements in the Nordic countries shows that movements have tended to orient themselves more towards the political system – through the establishment of new institutions and by exerting influence on existing ones (Bergman, 1999: 116).

One of the main themes in my own research is the wide-ranging mobilisation in the new social movements spanning the late 1960s to the late 1980s. Despite the fact that both the movements and the capacity to mobilise have lost some of their original potency, they did have considerable influence on political life in that period. This is key to understanding the development of modern democracy, not least from a gender point of view.

In a *democracy perspective*, the social movements symbolise both tradition and the renewal of the particular Danish features. *Tradition*, because the movements are both an extension of and are based on one of the specific aspects of the Danish gender model, which is the close mutual association between movement politics and representative politics. *Renewal*, because the movements introduce novel questions to the political agenda thanks to the new actors entering entered the arena and the new organisational forms that have evolved (Togeby, 1994). So, even though the new social movements are based on the unique features of Danish political culture, it is my thesis that they also challenge the balance between 'movement politics' and 'representative politics'.

The new social movements are also interesting from a *gender perspective*. Even though mobilisation in most of the movements embraced both sexes, they had a special impact on the mobilisation of women and on the continued integration of women into democratic life. First, and especially by dint of the movement arena, gender equality in political participation grew compared to earlier. Second, because attention in a number of areas was directed especially towards questions related to women's politics. This occurred primarily within the new women's movement, of course, but such questions were also addressed in environmental and peace movements. Third, because new gender strategies were developed through the movements, the effect of which was not restricted to the movements themselves, but reached the political institutions as well.

## Context and outline

The early 1960s was the first time in Denmark after the war that a broad mass mobilisation of women took place. Here, the political medium of expression was demonstrations and marches. The catalyst was the Campaign Against Nuclear Weapons, which will be particularly remembered for its Easter marches in 1961–62 which attracted between 5,000 and 35,000 activists. The main goal was to show the strength of the opposition against the nuclear arms build-up and to prevent the deployment of nuclear weapons on Danish soil. However, the campaign had another effect, namely (re)invigorating the tradition of mass demonstrations and mass participation in Denmark, which, in the postwar period, had been seen only in connection with labour disputes. In addition, this campaign marked a breakthrough for a significant generational shift where the young and well-educated groups were the prime moving forces (Gundelach, 1986; Christensen and Siim, 2001).

Thus, the Campaign Against Nuclear Weapons represents a milestone in the development of Danish democracy. It marks a continuity, on the one hand, in which, after several decades of relative political passivity, a return was made to the great social movements and the wide participation that had characterised a century of Danish political culture. On the other hand, the campaign marks the start of something new – a national effort on behalf of new political values and organisational forms, which came together in the new social movements during the subsequent three decades.

From the anti-nuclear campaign there are *two main channels* which are essential for understanding the process through which Danish women were included in modern democracy. The first and most important went through the new social movements where not only the new women's movement, but also the environmental movement and the peace movement were important contexts for mass mobilisation and for women's mobilisation too. The second channel went through the political institutions, the political parties in particular. A number of women who were active in the anti-nuclear power campaign entered elite politics (mainly the Social Democratic Party); other women chose both to remain in the movements and to work within the political parties.

Focusing on these two channels, I will look at *differences in women's political identities and strategies* which have been essential to the development of the Danish gender model.[1] I examine two cases: (1) the 'movement channel' with a focus mainly on the involvement of different groups of women in the new peace movement; and (2) the 'institution channel' with an emphasis on the Socialist People's Party (SPP) and the gender quota debate. In both cases, the connections between the political strategies and women's political identities will be analysed.

My main focus will thus be on extended changes in Danish political culture, with a specific focus on women's mobilisation in the 1970s and 1980s. In the last section of the chapter, I will discuss this development in relation to current changes and challenges to the Danish gender model due to new forms of mobilisation/demobilisation as well as new generations and new political identities in women's agency.

## Women's political strategies in movement politics

The new women's movement in Denmark (particularly the Redstockings) emerged in the wake of the youth uprising and found further inspiration in other Western countries, especially the US. The movement started in Denmark in 1970 and attracted mainly middle-class women, often with a connection to the universities. In her analysis of the Redstockings, Drude Dahlerup captures the four most important factors in her definition of the movement as 'a radical, left-wing women's movement with women's community and women's struggle as its main strategy and the basis group as the main organisational principle' (Dahlerup, 1998, I: 155).

The *radical feminist* viewpoint was expressed in the form of a basic demand for an end to the oppression of women, which, in their opinion, permeated the public as well as the private sphere. The *leftist viewpoint* was something the Redstockings brought with them from the critique of the capitalist society set out by the rest of the political left wing. The link between the leftist and the radical feminist can be illustrated by the slogan 'No women's struggle without class struggle, and no class struggle without women's struggle'. The uniqueness of the ideas that evolved within women's liberation feminism is to be found in, for example, the combination of a leftist anti-capitalist critique with radical feminism, and their formulation in opposition to the equal opportunity feminism of the old women's movement (Dahlerup, 1998, I: 155–6).

The feminist project in the 1970s and 1980s was not concerned with stressing differences between women; the main issue was women's community in autonomous women's organisations. According to Dahlerup, this constitution of women as a group did not come about through a focus on experiences common to women in general (as mothers, for instance, or the traditional woman's role), or through the assertion that all women are alike. It was rather the awareness that all women – irrespective of their social class – were oppressed in relation to men of the same social class. Inequality, discrimination and oppression were considered to affect all women alike, and, therefore, also were the principal justification for an autonomous organisation of women and for the confrontational stance vis-à-vis patriarchal society (Dahlerup, 1998, II: 399).

## The women's peace movement

In the 1980s, more or less at the same time as mobilisation within the new women's movement was declining, the peace movement was going through a process of renewal – not only in Denmark, but in a number of Western European countries.[2] In Denmark, the ongoing political mobilisation roused the old peace organisations from their slumber at the same time as a number of new peace organisations saw the light of day. The most important new movement organisations were Women for Peace, which admitted women only, and No to Nuclear Weapons, which was open to both sexes. Another significant difference between the two movement organisations was that while members of No to Nuclear Weapons were typically students, the members of Women for Peace were generally middle-aged, often mothers, and a relatively large proportion were part-time workers and women who worked solely in the home (Christensen, 1991).

A comparison of the two movement organisations shows that the differences in political strategies were quite wide. While No to Nuclear Weapons was relatively instrumentalist in its attempts to influence political decision-making processes, by, for instance, building up a stock of alternative, progressive expertise, Women for Peace tended to base their arguments on the moral and ethical dimension. The differences were evident organisationally and in the way in which Women for Peace maintained a far more decentralised and localised structure than No to Nuclear Weapons, which leant far more towards a national organisation model. If we compare the two different strategies, emphasising either the local or the national aspect, the interesting finding is that the strategies of the peace movement were not expressed in opposition to one another, as could be seen in the Green Movement, but far more by means of *supplementary* or *complementary strategies*. To take an example, participants in Women for Peace expressed a profound respect for the alternative progressive expertise built up by No to Nuclear Weapons and the ability of the latter to influence political decision-making processes. But they also emphasised that they preferred to work along alternative lines and in relation to different target groups. This comprehensiveness, however, was considered an advantage for peace work as such.

Despite the fact that Women for Peace was an autonomous women's movement, contact with the new women's movement was limited.

Activists within Women for Peace were not mobilised on the basis of a radical feminism, but rather on women's traditional experiences with family life and motherhood. This was particularly evident in the symbolic and cultural forms of expression employed by the movement. For instance, the local groups were designated 'kitchen groups', the national periodical the 'Kitchen Roll' and the local Aalborg bulletin the 'Potholder'. Many analogous symbols were employed with reference to their other activities, like 'hanging out the washing' ceremonies. In Women for Peace, the autonomous women's organisation is not considered an end in itself, more as a means to create a space for women (including the politically unschooled) to become active.

Apart from the women in Women for Peace and No to Nuclear Weapons, there was group of young, radical feminists in the women's peace movement in the 1980s. These women identified with the liberation feminism of the new women's movement, but felt drawn to the peace movement. For this group, the violence and oppression represented by the military was inextricably bound up with society's patriarchal structures. Similarly, peace and freedom were inextricably bound up with the end of women's oppression.

The considerable differences within the women's movement came together in a common political practice at the Women's Peace Camp at Ravnstrup, 1984–85. Here the women pitched their tents and built a camp, much as the women at Greenham Common in England did, and launched protests against the construction of a NATO bunker by means of a range of non-violent actions. Within the women's peace camp, the various groups of women were more or less as one with regard to their political demands, goals and strategies for peace. In contrast, contention was rife concerning the connection between women's politics and peace politics. These disagreements were manifested in attitudes towards women's community, among other things. Should the camp be an arena for the cultivation of a feminist counter-culture, or should it provide a framework for more restricted activities concentrating on peace politics, thus maintaining an appeal to a wider section of women?

The (young) radical feminists represented the former viewpoint, the women from No to Nuclear Weapons and Women for Peace the latter. The intense polarity that emerged during the camp's final phase has some interest, of course, but it is equally important to draw attention to the fact that for more than a year it was possible for a number of very diverse groups to unite in the particularly cramped conditions imposed on them by the quite radical actions they initiated and everyday life in the camp itself.

It is clear, then, that the new peace movement consisted of several different groups of women who had all constructed political identities based on their specific connection to everyday life as well as to political goals and visions. The characteristics of the three groups can be summarised as follows (cf. also Christensen, 1991):

- A group of women who, like men, are intent on influencing the political decision-making process and developing an alternative, progressive expertise. The groups set great store by influencing opinion in general and establishing contact with politicians and experts. Women and men work side by side in the same organisations. These women are organised in particular in No to Nuclear Weapons.
- A humanitarian, ethically focused group, predominantly mobilised around women's traditional experiences of the family. They want to create a space for the mobilisation of many women on their own terms. Their political strategy is an autonomous women's community – not to evolve a feminist counter-culture, but to find room for as many women as possible. These women joined forces in Women for Peace.
- A radical feminist group that views peace and liberty as inseparable from women's suppression, which is ideologically close to feminist perspectives in the new women's movement, but in the 1980s the prevailing practice in the peace movement is primarily the non-violence network. Their strategy is an autonomous women's community through which a feminist counter-culture and an alternative political practice related to peace issues can develop.

These political strategies and forms of identity are both grounded in major differences between the actors' everyday lives and life course, in contrast to goals and strategies within peace politics and the goals of women's politics. This diversity in political identities and political strategies are of central importance for an understanding of the democratic challenges created by the mobilisation of women and the new social movements. I will briefly discuss what I believe to be crucial in our understanding of the movements' impact from a democratic point of view.

## The new social movements and the democratic challenges

The new women's movement, by virtue of its radical and left-wing feminism, found it hard to see how improvements could be made by going through the political institutions. It was therefore not surprising that the movement avoided relating to parties *directly*. On the other hand, because of the wide mobilisation, the movement had a wide *indirect* effect on political institutions and politics (Dahlerup, 1998, II: 406). The distinguishing feature of the peace movement was, as we have seen, the multifarious ways in which the movement's organisations related to the political institutions. But it is also the case that among themselves, they recognised the political benefit of this diversity of strategies in the work for peace. The peace movement as a whole thus embraced several complementary strategies and, in addition, was characterised by a high level of pluralism.

If we look at the two autonomous women's organisations in the peace movement, it is clear that the young, radical feminists inherited the new women's movement's lack of belief in the possibility of improvements via political institutions. On the other hand, Women for Peace had an entirely different reason for not working in a focused manner in relation to the political system; namely, that it would be inconsistent with the political comprehensiveness that represents the movement's foremost quality. This is not to say that no weight is given to dialogue with the institutions. On the contrary, it is a great acknowledgement of, for instance, the political work done by No to Nuclear Weapons to construct an alternative fund of progressive expertise in the effort to influence political decision-making processes.

In general it appears that women are more supportive of non-hierarchical and decentralised structures than men. This can be seen in the high degree of decentralisation and correspondingly low level of country-wide coordination and policy formation (for instance, the difference between Women for Peace and No to Nuclear Weapons, as well as the importance of the basis groups as the structural unit in the Redstocking movement). If we take the environmental movement, it is apparent that women in their political vision value decentralisation and the dismantling of hierarchies far more than their male counterparts.

As we have seen, the movements devised a variety of strategies for women's inclusion in democracy. This is true in relation to both the substance and the form of the policies. If we first examine the political content, the feminism of the Redstocking movement made up the pivotal point, with a special emphasis on combining radical feminism with leftist anti-capitalism. This was the movement's great strength, but it also presented the movement with a number of dilemmas. In reality, it was tension between the movement's class struggle theory on the one hand, and the theory and practice of women's struggle on the other, that undermined the movement's strategy and stood in the way of the establishment of permanent alliances with others. Within the women's peace movement, although women's politics had less potency, the political basis was more inclusive. There was a great deal of open-mindedness towards the diversity of views and strategies in the peace effort, though, in contrast, dissension arose concerning the connection between the work for peace and feminism (Christensen and Siim, 2001).

In terms of form, what is groundbreaking is that the autonomous women's organisation becomes a key element in the mobilisation of women. However, the justifications for the autonomous organisation of women differ significantly. For some groups, it represents an end in itself and a move towards a feminist counter-culture. Women's groups are perceived by others as a means to secure breadth of participation. There is also an important difference in the political identities behind the community of women, which for some groups are based on the collective oppression of women and discrimination, for others on the shared experiences of women, especially in connection with the traditional woman's role. Beyond the similarities and differences of the movements, the above is evidence of a temporal change. I will return to this aspect in the last section.

## Women's political strategies in representative politics

The second channel created by the mobilisation of women in the 1970s and 1980s leads to the political parties. I will focus on one party only, the Socialist People's Party (SPP). Of all the Danish parties, the SPP is referred to as 'the party of movements'; it is also the party with the closest links between actors in the new women's movement and in a political party. It is therefore no coincidence that the SPP was the party that articulated and advanced the demands of the new women's movement. According to Drude Dahlerup, the SPP helped to absolve the Red-stocking movement from any obligation to conduct itself according to the ground rules of the formal political institutions. The movement was therefore exempt from having to act in line with the institutionalised political system (Dahlerup, 1998, II: 196ff).

But the political standpoints and organisational forms of the new women's movement came to exert a significant impact on SPP itself. There was talk of an offensive feminist strategy, based on the combination of a radical feminism and a leftist, class-based political ideology. As a socialist party, the class aspect represented a fundamental part of the SPP's collective identity, but the association to feminism was not taken equally for granted.

It is the debate concerning feminist strategies in the SPP and their adoption that have been my point of departure in a discursive analysis in which I compare the debates in the SPP on gender quotas with those that took place in the Social Democratic Party and the Socialist Left Party (Christensen, 2000).[3]

The main conclusions of this analysis are as follows. The SPP was founded in 1959, but it was not until the early 1970s that women's politics appeared as a serious item on the agenda. This, in turn, was sparked by the anti-EEC campaign of 1971–72. With the subsequent success of the pro-membership side in the referendum, a group of Redstockings decided collectively to apply for membership in the party stating as their reason their wish to break the patriarchal public sphere (Søgård, 1984).

Once in the party they formed autonomous women's groups, as in the movement, which became the foundation of the party's work in the field of women's politics over the following decades. The women's groups survived for 17 years (1971–88). Their impact was considerable, and during the 1970s the SPP evolved from a relatively male-dominated party to the Danish party with the most distinct profile on women's issues. Naturally, this was not a smooth and harmonious process. The introduction of gender quotas was a principal demand of the SPP's women's groups. The party has had quotas in the following periods:[4]

| | |
|---|---|
| Party quotas | 1977–96 |
| Candidate quotas (EU) | 1983– |
| Candidate quotas (Parliament/local councils) | 1988–90 |

The gender quota debate in SPP revolved around one point in particular, the question of women's place in the party's internal democracy. The distinguishing feature of the debate in SPP was the large number – including supporters of party quotas – that opposed candidate quotas because they were perceived as inconsistent with the SPP's stance on democracy (in the representative democracy) and the popular socialist basis. The debate was also characterised by the strong link forged between the gender quota issue and the justification of the women's groups within the party.

If we first look at *the 1970s gender quota debate in SPP*, we see that the impact of the new women's movement was considerable. The analysis shows that the argument in favour of gender quotas was put forward in the form of a combined identity and discrimination argument. The identity argument stressed the existence of certain values and experiences common to women, which distinguish women from men and which sanction solidarity between women as a political strategy. The discrimination argument is associated with male dominance and women's repression in the party and in society at large. Further, the analysis shows that this method of *combining identity and discrimination arguments* succeeded. The identity argument highlights the need for a special form of solidarity between women – that women have different experiences and perceptions of reality than men; that women will gain in strength if they group together with tighter bonds as a basis. The discrimination argument addresses mainly the male dominance prevailing within the party, but with more than a passing reference to the oppression of women in society in general.

Despite the generally high level of acceptance of the strategies of the women's groups in the 1970s, counter-arguments were also voiced. One type of counter-argument comes from a group of women within the party, a group that refuses to identify itself with the idea of women's community and who are not members of the women's groups. They dismiss gender quotas, which they consider to be inconsistent with their own views with regard to both politics in general and women's issues in particular, and they distance themselves from the identity argument and the discourse on women's solidarity. They support, on the other hand, the discrimination argument, but disagree with the prevailing strategy within women's politics because they identify with the autonomous organisation of women. The second batch of counter-arguments come largely from a group of men in the party. In their opinion, the women's groups and gender quotas are at distinct odds with both the socialist and the democratic ideal. They consider the arguments that special women's values exist and that there is a need for a particular form of solidarity between women, to be sectarian and positively harmful to a socialist party.

From the mid-1980s we see in the SPP – as in the rest of society – a decline in activity in the field of women's politics. The women's groups disband after a period of 17 years and many women leave the SPP; it proves difficult to recruit new women members.

In the *gender quota debate in the 1990s*, new actors took their place on the stage. A new generation of women made their mark on SPP, and quite a lot of them established themselves in opposition to the frontline feminists from the women's movement. In particular, they dissociated themselves from a special focus on 'women' and the oppression of women. Now the issues are gender and equality for both sexes and, in extension of this position, the new actors assert that the gender quota argument lacks credibility. The arguments against gender quotas confront head on the idea of women's community and the argument that women have certain values and experiences in common. They also reject the idea of a special kind of discrimination against women in the party. The problem is no longer tied to women or to gender, but to generations – the men are tired of politics too. 'In places where mothers of small children have never actually set foot in a town council chamber, the fathers of small children are probably in the process of backing out of the same chambers' (Antorini, 1993).

There is a stress on the claim that while women once fought for a better life in the women's movement, today young women and men are fighting shoulder to shoulder to get their everyday lives to work. Gender quotas are no longer an issue for young women. They do not want to be chosen because of their biological sex, and see no justification for a community of women.

By way of an alternative, the *diversity argument* is set out. In this argument, rather than emphasising similarities between women, differences are highlighted. For instance, attention is directed towards common experiences within generations and the problems faced by young families in the political area. The road ahead is therefore no longer one of autonomous women's groups or gender quotas, but of finding new ways to work politically that take account of women and men.

We see, then, a marked shift in women's strategies in the SPP. While the emphasis in the 1970s when justifying the introduction of gender quotas was on women's groups and the community of women, the new generation of women of the 1990s actively distanced itself from this idea of fellowship. The political identity of female party members is no longer linked to women's communities or discrimination. Instead, new political identities are fashioned out of the new communities based on women's (and men's) everyday lives. The old strategies with their stress on autonomous women's organisations and gender quotas no longer fit the bill.

## New challenges to the Danish gender model

The mobilisation of women in the social movements in the 1970s had a great impact on the formation of the Danish gender model. More women were included as active citizens, and more political attention was drawn to gender political issues in society. The analysis has shown that women's political identities have undergone major changes over the past 30 years. While the women's movement in the 1970s was characterised by its combination of radical feminism and a leftist political stance, several complementary women's strategies coexisted in the women's peace movement in the 1980s, and the 1990s saw the young women in the SPP press for a break with strategies based on women's community and autonomous women's organisations, putting in their place diversity and differences related not only to women, but also to women's overlapping gender identities with men, for instance as parents.

The analysis shows that rather than one overriding strategy for women's inclusion in democracy, complementary and competing strategies have existed side by side. Some of them were closely associated with movement politics, others with representative politics. However, the important point here is that there are two crucial and interrelated elements in the formation of the Danish gender model: (1) the interconnection between movement politics and representative politics, which is a special characteristic of Danish political culture. We are not talking about two (distinct) models (a movement model and a representative model), but of several models, each based on a combination of politics 'from above' and 'from below'; and (2) the intersection between different political identities among active women, and most of all the dynamics and interaction between a radical feminism on the one hand and a broad thematisation of gender political issues on the other.

One of the main conclusions in Christensen and Siim (2001) is that in Denmark the democratic model and the gender model are interrelated. As we have seen, the Danish democratic model has been a good foundation for creating a broad dialogue that includes new groups in the democratic community and for democratic policy that puts everyday concerns on the political agenda. However, we have also emphasised that the Danish political culture is most responsive to changes and new ideas when they come about as a combination of pressure 'from above' and 'from below'. Without active movements and other political communities in civil society that can challenge and interact with elite politics, the Danish model weakens (Christensen and Siim, 2001: 242).

We have seen this weakness since the beginning of the 1990s because it was a demobilised as well as a turbulent decade as basic social, political and cultural conditions changed along with phenomena like globalisation and growing immigration.

One challenge to women's democratic inclusion is related to the differentiation between Danish citizens and ethnic minorities where it seems that the high degree of cultural homogeneity makes it difficult to integrate the diversity that refugees and immigrants represent (see Birte Siim this volume, chapter 5).

Another challenge is related to the democratic profile that young citizens have developed. It is remarkable that political participation has generally decreased among young people, especially among young women. This lack of involvement, particularly in political institutions, among 20–25-year-old women, has been a main theme in my study for the Danish Democracy and Power Study (Christensen, 2003). I find that neither young women without active citizenship nor young women who are actively involved in the radical anti-globalisation movement relate to the political institutions. It seems as if the political institutions, for example the political parties, have sharply declined as a potential arena for political influence or political practice for the young women. For those who are not active, the political institutions have no meaning or importance in their political identities. In other words, they take them for granted, but they do not use them in their construction of political identities. The young women who are active in the radical anti-globalisation movements express great resistance towards the political institutions. Rather than identifying with the institutions, it seems as if dis-identification with what Ulrich Beck has called 'grandpa's mega-organisations' (Beck, 1998) plays a crucial role in their individualisation and political identity- making.

I will argue that both challenges call for a fundamental renewal of the Danish gender model. The model must be able to integrate diversities, not only among Danish women, but also the diversity represented by ethnic minority women. Equality and solidarity are still cornerstones in democracy as well as in feminism. At the same time the model must be able to cope with new political identities among young women. The interaction between movement politics and representative politics appears to have changed. However, for the Danish democracy model as well as for the Danish gender model it is very important to maintain the dynamic between these two elements. This depends on the ability to renew the political institutions so that they can play an important role in the continued inclusion of women in democracy and in the making of political identities among not only elderly and middle-aged citizens, but also among young citizens of today.

## Notes

1. When I use the term *political strategies*, I want to emphasise the overriding aims and visions as well as the more concrete means (and organisational forms) used by certain groups to accomplish social change. When I use the term *political identities*, I stress motivations and reasons that fuel specific political practices and linkages both with the actors' biographies and every-

day lives, and the political learning that took place in the movements and political institutions (see also Peterson, 1988; Christensen, 1991; 2003).
2. The actual spark was NATO's decision in 1979 to deploy 572 tactical nuclear warheads in Western Europe starting December 1982. This would be effected unless disarmament negotiations with the Warsaw Pact countries rendered it superfluous.
3. I stress in my reading of the concept of *discourse* in the analysis of the party debates the interconnection between discourses and social practice. Discourses are not viewed simply as representations of social reality, but also as social practice (Fairclough, 1992). Specifically, this means that I stress, among other things, the historical context in which the debates were embedded.
4. I distinguish between candidate quotas and party quotas. Candidate quotas are designed for public elections and the representative democracy. Party quotas are intended for use within the party organisation alone (Christensen, 2000).

# References

Antorini, C. (1993). 'Farvel til kvindepolitik' [Goodbye to Women's Political Issues], *Det Fri Aktuelt*, 9 December.
Beck, U. (1998). *Democracy without Enemies*. Cambridge: Polity Press.
Bergman, S. (1999). 'Women in New Social Movements', in C. Bergqvist et al. (eds.), *Equal Democracies? Gender and Politics in the Nordic Countries*. Oslo: Scandinavian University Press.
Bergqvist, C., A. Borchorst, A.-D. Christensen, V. Ramsted-Silén and A. Styrkasdottir (eds.) (1999). *Equal Democracies? Gender and Politics in the Nordic Countries'*. Oslo: Scandinavian University Press.
Christensen, A.-D. (1991). 'Women in the New Peace Movement in Denmark: Empowerment and Political Identity', in T. Andreasen et al. (eds.), *Moving On. New Perspectives on the Women's Movement*. Acta Jutlandica, Humanities Series 66, Aarhus University Press.
Christensen, A.-D. (1999). 'Women in Political Parties', in C. Bergqvist et al. (eds.), *Equal Democracies? Gender and Politics in the Nordic Countries*. Oslo: Scandinavian University Press,
Christensen, A.-D. (2000). *Debatterne om kønskvotering i de politiske partier i Danmark* [Debates on Gender Quotas in the Danish Political Parties]. Research Report, Aalborg University.
Christensen, A.-D. (2003). *Fortællinger om identitet og magt. Unge kvinder i senmoderniteten* [Narratives on Identity and Power. Young Women in Late Modernity]. Århus: Magtudredningen.
Christensen, A.-D. and B. Siim (2001). *Køn, demokrati og modernitet – mod nye politiske identiteter* [Gender, Democracy and Modernity – Towards New Political Identities]. Copenhagen: Hans Reitzels Press.
Dahlerup, D. (1986). 'Is the New Women's Movement Dead? Decline or Change of the Danish Movement', in D. Dahlerup (ed.), *The New Women's Movement. Feminism and Political Power in Europe and the USA*. London: Sage.
Dahlerup, D. (1998). *Rødstrømperne. Den danske Rødstrømpebevægelses udvikling,*

*nytænkning og gennomslag 1970–1985* [Redstockings, The Danish Women's Liberation Movement, 1970–1985]. Vols 1–2. Copenhagen: Gyldendal.

Dean, J. (1996). *Solidarity of Strangers. Feminism after Identity Politics*. Berkeley: University of California Press.

Fairclough, N. (1992). *Discourse and Social Change*. Cambridge: Polity Press.

Gundelach, P. (1988). *Sociale bevægelsor og samfundsændringer* [Social Morements and Social Changes]. Århus: Politica.

Kaare Nielsen, H. (1991). *Demokrati i bevægelse* [Democracy in Movement]. Århus: Aarhus Universitetsforlag.

Peterson, A. (1988). *Women in Political 'Movement'*. Monograph from the Department of Socioly, University of Gothenburg, No. 37.

Phillips, A. (1995). *The Politics of Presence*. Oxford: Clarendon Press.

Rucht, D. (1996). 'The Impact of National Contexts on Social Movement Structures', in McAdam et al. (eds.), *Comparative Perspectives on Social Movements. Political Opportunities. Mobilizing Structures*. Cambridge: Cambridge University Press.

Siim, B. (2000). *Gender and Citizenship. Politics and Agency in France, Britain and Denmark*. Cambridge: Cambridge University Press.

Søgà6rd, S. (1984). 'Da kvinderne blev synlige' [When Women Became Visible], in *Socialisme pà6 dansk – SF gennem 25 à6r*. Århus: SP Forlag, pp. 100–12.

Togeby, L. (1994). *Fra tilskuere til deltagere. Den kollektive politiske mobilisering af kvinder i Danmark* [From Spectators to Participants], Århus: Politica.

Young, I.M. (1990). *Justice and the Political Difference*. Princeton: Princeton University Press.

# 7
## Gendered Citizenship: A Model for European Citizenship? Considerations against the German Background

*Ute Gerhard*

As is often emphasised, citizenship is a very broad, multifaceted and amorphous concept. It offers a frame of reference for different political trends and theoretical approaches: for the political Left as well as for neoliberals; for civic-republican theorists as for communitarians, and last but not least for feminists. (For an overview, see Lister, 1997.) Especially fruitful for feminist theorising was T.H. Marshall's concept of citizenship as not only a legal, but a social status, historically developed and consisting of three elements: civil, political and social citizenship rights (Marshall, 1950). Whereas the German tradition of legal and social policy still tends to limit the idea of social rights in its minimal definition to social security issues, Marshall's concept includes 'the right to share to the full in the social and to live the life of a civilized being according to the standards prevailing in the society' (Marshall, 1950: 10–11), or, as Ruth Lister puts it: 'To be a citizen in the legal and sociological sense, means to enjoy the rights of citizenship necessary for agency and social and political participation. To act as a citizen involves fulfilling the full potential of the status' (Lister, 1997: 41).

Apart from the exclusive argument with regard to gender and other disadvantaged groups in every society, the varied vocabulary shows that it has not yet been possible to define citizenship as a universal and abstract category. Instead, it is necessary to consider the distinctive historical background and to deconstruct or construct citizenship by contextualising its definition.

I will, therefore, start by recapitulating the particular meanings and ambiguities of the German concept of citizenship. Then, against this historical background, I will discuss the gender of citizenship and examine whether women's historical experiences with the exclusionary character of citizenship and citizenship rights might prepare the ground for post-national citizenship the status and range of which must be negotiated. Since Article 61 of the 1997 Amsterdam Treaty promises a new 'space of freedom, security and the rule of law', the motivating question in the third section will be whether the European Union, although to date is has been characterised by a lack of democratic rules and transparency, might also offer a political opportunity structure for the empowerment of women.

## The ambiguity of citizenship as a concept in Germany

Modern citizenship is tightly connected to the emergence and development of the nation state, which means that it is and was exclusive with regard to a culturally and legally constructed nationality, and it was always tied to a particular territory and authority. The exclusiveness was legitimised by the principles *jus soli* or *jus sanguinis*. Citizenship characterised a new and immediate relationship among and between the individuals and the state. During the transition from a feudal system to civil society, this relationship replaced a variety of corporate layers, which were connected with particular privileges or disadvantages and formed a hierarchicy of only indirect or diversely mediated relations between the sovereign and the people. In European history, the forerunner of the citizen – besides the model for citizenship in the cities of the Middle Ages – was the subject (in the sense of being subjected). The subject was created in the period of absolutism by absolute rulers who were opposed to traditional, ascribed entitlements in the estate system (see Koselleck, 1975: 52f). Thus, the normative universalism of the absolutist state is both an achievement and a problematic heritage of the modern state. In any case, because of the varying processes in history, we have to be aware of different stories and asynchronous developments.

The German concept of the citizen (translated as *Bürger* and *Staatsbürger*) is both ambiguous and vague due to its varied political history (see Riedel, 1979: 672ff). Its different meanings reveal a particular sociohistorical context and societal as well as political structure (see Kocka, 1995: 24). With the demise of the Holy Roman Empire of German Nations at the beginning of nineteenth century, the political order was characterised by the individual character of small states (39 states joined in the German Alliance in addition to Prussia and Austria), and a variety of legal sources and traditions in the so-called 'common law', besides local statutes and as important codifications as the Prussian General Code (ALR 1794), the French Code Civil of 1804, and the Austrian Civil

Code (AGBG 1811). Combined, they made up the patchwork of what defined the legal position. Since then – an era of social and political transformation into a society called civil and/or bourgeois – the concept of citizen/*Bürger* has had multiple meanings: it distinguished a citizen in the city (*Stadtbürger*) from a mere inhabitant and from a so-called charge (*Schutzverwandte*, a person without legal status, but under the protection of an authority); it meant belonging to a particular class, namely the bourgeoisie, as distinct from peasantry and nobility; and with the demise of feudalism, the citizen displaced the vassal or subject and thus embodied a new, unmediated relationship between individual and state: that of the *citoyen*.

A consequence of the delay in the formation of a nation state and a common civil and public law in Germany was the uncertainty of citizenship rights. (For a comparison with France, see Brubaker, 1992; for a critical angle, see Gosewinkel, 2001.) However, the great debate in the course of political and social reforms after 1815 (especially in the context of the Prussian administrative reform of the state, named after von Stein and Hardenberg) generally distinguished strictly between inhabitants and citizens. Even inhabitants were divided into at least two categories: those who were entitled to stay, marry, earn a living, acquire property and become landowners, and the rest, who were tolerated, but excluded from all entitlements, particularly from social support in old age or sickness. In the process of industrialisation and in the face of poverty, which was a consequence of radical social changes and cleavages, these restrictions and rules (the so-called *Heimatrechte*) derived from the responsibility of the local communities and small cities to take care of 'their' inhabitants with subsistence-level welfare benefits.

The delay in the nation-building process may also explain why philosophy and legal theory were so relevant in the German context and had such an impact on the legal development and the formation of a state governed by the rule of law. Thus, the distinction between the *Stadtbürger* (bourgeois or citizen) and *Staatsbürger* (*citoyen*) governed jurisprudence throughout the nineteenth century. It was the distinction between the citizen or bourgeois as a private person, entitled to civil (that is, private rights) on the one hand, and the *citoyen*, entitled to political rights to take part in government and sovereignty on the other. This distinction mirrored the separation of public from private spheres as well as the systematic differentiation between public and private legal rights, a systematic division according to Roman law.

In his legal theory, Kant mapped the territory with a definition already containing these oppositions and contradictions of civil society:

The only qualification for being a citizen is being fit to vote. But being fit to vote presupposes the independence of someone . . . This quality of being independent, however, requires a distinction between active and passive citizens, though the concept of a passive citizen [as Kant himself has to admit] seems to contradict the concept of a citizen as such.                    (Kant, 1797/1996: 458)

In the following sentence, this definition contains the often quoted statement about the difficulties women encountered in being active citizens:

all women and, in general, whose preservation in existence (his being fed and protected) depends not on his management of his own business but on arrangements made by another (except the state). All these people lack civil personality . . .        (Kant, 1797/1996: 458)

Hegel had a similar impact as theorist of civil society and the state with his three-part framework consisting of family, civil society and the state (Hegel, 1955, addition to §182). In this conceptualisation, the family – and this meant specifically women's place and destination – was explicitly excluded from civil society, legitimised by an understanding of marriage as an institution without individual civil rights for the one partner, that is the woman (Hegel, 1955, §158ff; see also Cohen and Arato, 1995: 91ff).

Marx, in his critique of Hegel's 'Philosophy of Right', again makes the distinction between *citoyen* and bourgeois. It is the starting point for his theoretical and polemical critique of the bourgeois society: here 'modern social conflict' was unmasked as class conflict (Dahrendorf, 1992: 54). In his early utopian writings, the distinction between the 'bourgeois' (the owner of private property and member of a class) and the *citoyen* (a person born equal and free, with human rights and a right to equal participation in the public sphere, regardless of nationality or race) in a principally demanding way marked how the status quo of bourgeois society had to be transcended. The 'truly individual human' is defined as a citizen of the world or cosmopolitan. Interestingly, Marx elaborated these reflections in his essays under the title 'On the Jewish Question' (Marx, 1975: 347ff). In the neo-Marxist debate of the 1960s and 1970s, this critical approach to civil society as a bourgeois society (in German, *bürgerliche Gesellschaft*) continued to burden the understanding.

The 'difficulty the German language has with the concept of the citizen', Ralf Dahrendorf writes, 'in comparison to the English *citizen* and *citizenship'*, is determined by a number of distinctions, oppositions and inequalities. These include the temporal distance between the state and its democratic constitution, between the founding of the state and nation-building, as well as the delay in general citizenship rights, which in Germany 'bind the citizen by law to the state instead of protecting him or her from the state'. In contrast, *citizenship* 'describes the individual precisely in so far as he or she is NOT merely a part of the nation. The relationship between citizen and state has to be specifically absent from the definition of the citizen. Here freedom is essential' (Dahrendorf, 1992: 54–5).[1] As accurate as this characterisation may be, Dahrendorf also expresses a liberal understanding of the law and state which emphasises freedom to the detriment of principles of social justice and equality.

Until recently the differentiation between citizens and merely tolerated residents structured German citizenship rights, although the regulations for acquiring the right to become a German national, the *Staatsangehörigkeitsgesetz* ('New Citizenship and Nationality Law'), changed on 1 January 2000. Whereas the former law (the *Reichs- und Staatsangehörigkeitsgesetz* of 1913) asserted the claim to citizenship through descent, the new law offers full citizenship rights to children of immigrants whose parents have lived in Germany for more than eight years. This highly contested reform also includes the partial introduction of a *jus soli* for all children of immigrants born in Germany. They can opt for dual citizenship, but have to decide by the age of 23 which nationality they want to retain. Further those who did not aquire citizenship by birth now have a right to naturalisation after being resident for more than eight years.

## Gendered citizenship: the women's case

The women's case in the history of citizenship is a different and even more complex story. Despite many similarities internationally in the exclusion of women from the public sphere and from participation in decision-making, the reasons and arguments against equal citizenship for women have varied depending on place and time. They were subject to change, and were contradictory and diverse (see Siim, 2000). My contribution will be limited to catchwords because this subject has been extensively covered by feminist scholars and gender studies in terms of political history, social theory and philosophy. Our knowledge seems more limited when it comes to legal history and the practice or implementation of the law (see Gerhard, 1997).

Let me summarise the findings I want to discuss. The broken promise of freedom and equality for women ever since the French Revolution and the Declaration of Human Rights, as well as the systematic exclusion of women from the public sphere and their confinement to the private realm were neither coincidental nor a hangover from the past, but were constitutive of the way civil society functioned. The public/private divide as a main plank of liberal civil society maintained the inequality of women in and because of the family as an immanent contradiction. As the dual foundation or hidden base of civil society, the family (see Hegel, 1972), was regulated by a contract – the 'sexual contract' (Pateman, 1988; 1989) or marriage contract (Gerhard, 1990/2001: 22ff, 154) – and legitimised by 'customs' (see Wolff, 1754/1980) and private law, especially family law. In addition, their exclusion from citizenship was regulated by a broad range of political measures in public law.

These legal measures and political interventions, which were intended to hinder women's participation in power and sovereignty, are multifaceted and tell us a story of a democratisation process that not only excluded women, but took place at their expense. The story refers not only to their disenfranchisement, but also to all the implicit and explicit prohibitions and gender-related discrimination that have accompanied the history of women's movements for 200 years and provoked mobilisation and numerous initiatives and policies. For instance, the rights of women from the privileged classes to represent and vote in communities and corporations were abolished in the nineteenth century. As soon as democratisation converted these corporate privileges and property rights into rights of political representation, the adjective 'male' was appended to the right to vote. This was not only the case in the English Reform Act of 1832, but in all revisions of the ordinances in cities and communities of the German Alliance, especially in Austria and Prussia throughout the nineteenth century. (For more details, see Frevert, 1995: 62ff; Gerhard, 1997: 515ff).

Finally, bans on women's political associations or participation in political assemblies (see, for example, the association laws in Germany and Austria after the failed revolution of 1848 which remained in force until 1908 and 1918 respectively) explicitly excluded women from participation in the public sphere and from political representation. These barriers were all the more serious in so far as bourgeois society drew its democratic legitimacy from this new 'type of social organisation', from associations and voluntary organisations (see Nipperdey, 1972; Dann, 1976). It is interesting to note how eagerly lawyers and political theorists justified this exclusion at the end of the nineteenth century. This was not only about maintaining the gender division of labour or roles, or the stress on protecting the family, but also about the idea that 'the written law, as well as customs have always opposed the admission of women to political power and still do' (according to a legal thesis by M. Ostrogorski in 1897, which received a diploma from the law school in Paris; see Gerhard, 1997: 526).

The 1850 ban in the German Alliance hit women and the women's movement at the core of their civil rights and shows that the exclusion of women from a new political public realm was not only staged in terms of a bourgeois-patriarchal right of marriage or through the denial of the right to vote, but before that through the legalities of assembly rights. This exclusion was clearly a reaction to the political mobilisation of women and to the founding of 'democratic women's associations' during the 1848 revolution. Today it may seem astonishing how dangerous these activities must have appeared to the authorities at the time. The rigidity is unique in the 'civilised countries' of Europe and the world. The political muzzle was repeatedly affirmed through supreme court decisions and implemented by the everyday reality of police violence and harassment. This muzzle hindered the organisation of women's interests and the activities of bourgeois as well as proletarian women's associations on a daily basis and influenced them in their accommodation to these circumstances. The laws of association became a farce only after the various directions the women's movement was taking around the turn of the century became an undeniable feature of public life, by way of mass protests and petitions, educational initiatives, self-help projects, charitable organisations and their commitment to social reform and the professional praxis of their social work. Yet not until 1908 was a Reichs association law passed, which no longer discriminated by gender. From the activists' point of view, this step to recognise the 'female citizen' even before the right to vote was gained was a milestone in the history of women's rights. 'The path has been cleared for the political and public life of women!' reads a title in the magazine *Die Frauenbewegung* (The Women's Movement), although Minna Cauer's commentary emphatically attacked the new exclusion in the Law of Association, the so-called language paragraph, which targeted citizens of Polish descent and allowed the right of assembly only in the German language (Cauer, 1908: 65).

Historical research on citizens' rights in the context of gender and

concepts like 'citizenship' reveals a multitude of spheres where participation and cooperation occur within civic society. The research also
shows how women – primarily because they had no other choice – used
less formal relationships, means of social service and their 'female
destiny' for civil rights activism and thus transcended the narrow limits
of their private sphere to enter public life 'through the back door', so
to speak: 'But the relation of women's emancipation to social science
does not only spring from a common origin; it is more direct: through
humanitarian interests which formed the starting-point of social
research, and practical social work itself, actually provided the back-door
through which women slipped into public life' (Klein, 1971: 17).

By overcoming the obstacles, women's movements in different
nations and phases have frequently demonstrated an aptitude for
political action with different arguments, strategies and social practices.
Initially, and for the most part, they argued for the equality of all people,
yet they also emphasised the diversity, the different lifestyles and experience of women. The bourgeois women rights activists of the turn of
the century legitimised their programme as 'organised motherhood',
which 'sends women not only to day care centers, kindergartens and
schools, but also to parliaments' (Zahn-Harnack, 1928: 77; cf. Sarvasy,
1994: 306f). This was a strong point in the face of patriarchal means of
domination across the world. At other times, criticism was based on the
shortcomings of policies in terms of solidarity and social awareness,
policies that lack the element of care for others, which is why feminists
even today argue for a reconceptualised notion of 'democracy as the
practice of care' (Tronto, 2000: 25f). The eventual success of these movements in the twentieth century must be seen as a highly dynamic and
open-ended process that permanently extended and changed the political space. Yet the objective of this struggle for self-determination and
political participation has not been and is not to become like men or
to achieve the same status as men, let alone to produce sameness. The
objective rather is to make freedom possible for different human beings
and to validate the relevance of experiences of injustice. Meanwhile it
is emphasised again and again that the theoretical as well as the practical process of 're-gendering citizenship' is about the transcendence of
false dichotomies: 'Beyond equality versus difference' and 'beyond an
ethic of justice versus an ethic of care' (Lister, 1997: 91f). Since categories of gender alongside those of class, age, nationality or ethnicity
and other differences that are recognised as fundamental cannot be the
only focal point of political mobilisation, however, the unfinished
history of equal rights for women may possibly be a proto-process that

can serve as a model for new multiple (see Mouffe, 1992; Meehan, 1993) and dynamically conceptualised forms of citizenship.

The emphasis in feminist approaches to civil rights theory varies considerably, so let me summarise them with respect to European civil rights. All feminists agree that the right to act as a 'female citizen' presupposes the inclusion of care in the conceptualisation of citizenship; that is care for others in the private as well as the public sphere, 'so that the rights of time to care and to receive care are protected' (Knijn and Kremer, 1997: 357). Some maintain theories of difference to argue this necessary new conception, and emphasise a gendered, dual model of civil rights (cf. Elshtain, 1981; Pateman, 1989); others criticise this model of citizenship for its fixation on a certain female identity. In the face of migratory movements and various memberships, they prefer pluralist and post-national models (Soysal, 1996: 181f). Iris Marion Young's concept of 'different citizen rights for different groups', which proposes a political voice, recognition and the right to participate for all previously excluded social groups in society beyond class, race and gender or nationality, has frequently been criticised (cf. Kymlicka and Norman, 1994: 370). Chantal Mouffe, among others, fears that such a policy of difference may increase the discrimination of certain groups, rather than abolish it. In her 'radically democratic conception of citizenship', Mouffe argues for a pluralist, multiple and dynamic model, which assumes that everybody is tied in to many social relationships, or an ensemble of 'subject positions'. Her point of departure is the actors of social movements: women, workers, blacks and others who 'identify' with certain democratic aims and whose identity is forged by certain discourses and is subject to change. Yet she insists that a radically democratic project cannot acknowledge all differences. Rather, its goals and norms have to secure the implementation of democratic principles of freedom and equality, 'for the recognition of plurality [has] not to lead to a complete indifferentiation and indifference, criteria must exist to decide between what is admissible and what is not' (Mouffe, 1992: 13; cf. pp. 225–39). Civil rights are thus subject to ongoing renegotiation and acquisition. Like other rights, they should not be understood in terms of property or possession, but as an expression of and rule for social relations and relationships with other people. Or in the words of Iris Young: 'Rights refer to doing more than having, to social relationships that enable or constrain action' (Young, 1990: 25).

The question remains what kind of framework or normative, spatial or actual boundary citizenship needs with regard to the globalisation processes and 'postnational constellations' (Habermas, 1989), for it makes no sense to resolve citizenship in abstract or as a form of utopia for a future world citizenship, since it has to meet the needs of citizens in concrete historical contexts and is still about the rights of and justice for women.

## European citizenship – an option for women?

Against the background of women's legislative history it seems appropriate to draw a parallel between the process of creating more equality for women and ideas about European citizenship. It is debatable, however, whether women need or should apply for European citizenship, and if so whether a common European identity would be a prerequisite. According to Kymlicka and Norman, citizenship is 'not just a certain status . . . It is also an identity, an expression of one's membership in a political community' (1994: 369). From a feminist point of view, Scandinavian women are asking whether European citizenship is desirable, considering the comparatively well-developed, 'woman-friendly' Scandinavian welfare states.

Since its foundation more than 40 years ago, The European Community (since 1992 the European Union or EU), has evolved into a community of law, guaranteed by various institutions. Even though its codes of law are very complex and rarely transparent, they increasingly determine the everyday lives of all EU citizens. Indeed, 'Citizen of the Union' became a legal term in the Maastricht Treaty of 1992. It was confirmed and extended in the Amsterdam Treaty of 1997. The Amsterdam Treaty says that a 'citizen of the Union is anyone who is citizen of any of the member states'. Listed as rights are the freedom to live where one likes, local rights to vote and be elected, diplomatic as well as consular protection, and the right to petition the European Parliament (Arts 18–21 of the Amsterdam Treaty). This is indeed not a trifling matter for all those who are citizens of a EU nation. The definition of union citizenship by law, however, does not entail citizenship in a European state in the sense of a people or sovereign. Thus the problem in the fact that the European Union rests on the will of the people or on how Union citizens are represented in the institution of the EU is not yet democratically resolved. So far, European citizenship appears to be a 'top-down' order; it is not an intrinsic concern of the citizens. At least the status of citizen is now agreed by a treaty and articulated in legal terms. It explicitly addresses not only the 'Peoples of Europe', but also individual rights and obligations. The citizens' concerns have thus found their place on the political agenda.

The literature on and debates about European citizenship and a European constitution are too extensive to be included here (but see, for example, Evers, 1994; Grimm, 1995; Pierson, 1996; Böckenförde, 1997; Wiener, 1998; Lemke, 1999), but let me note that on the one hand, the democratic deficit in the European institutions, insufficient democratic control within the bureaucracy and the prevailing focus on economic goals – in short, the absence of politics – have been rightfully regretted; and, on the other, it cannot be denied that European integration has unfurled a dynamic process that will determine the future not only of citizens and inhabitants, but also of immigrants and the community of states. From the perspective of gender, important gains in terms of equal rights can be discerned. They were introduced in Article 119 of the European Economic Community (EEC) Treaty on equal pay and advanced by guidelines from the European Commission on equal treatment and by the jurisdiction of the European High Court. Feminist critics have nevertheless complained that the gains in equal rights are geared towards working women only, and that they follow a skewed economic logic of adapting male standards. One concern is whether it will be possible 'to establish a genuinely democratic political project side by side with the dominant economic project of liberalized markets'. Christiane Lemke takes this question to the heart of her argument that Europe should be understood as 'a space for political design' to 'provide a democratic foundation for the conflicts that are entailed by processes of economic and socio-political change' (Lemke, 1999: 1–14).

However, political scientists who have observed and analysed the dynamics of European integration, have discovered alongside a new community of law ('integration through law') a parallel process of integration by means of formal and informal civic rights practices (integration through citizenship) (Wiener, 1999: 272). In her comprehensive study 'European Citizenship Practice: Building Institutions of a Non-State' (1998), Antje Wiener critically examines historical phases of European integration to find out when and in which contexts the idea of a 'Europe for Citizens' was first raised. She identifies the conferences in Paris and Copenhagen in the early 1970s as the settings where the explicit desideratum of a political union was added to the purely economic orientation. Without idealising the situation, the author describes political discourses and practices that follow as changes in the so-called *acquis communautaire*, a technical term also used in the text of the treaties, which signifies the active property of rules, court decisions, agreements and forms of collaboration (formal as well as informal) opinions and practices (cf. Article of the 2 Treaty of the European Union, common regulations). Wiener also emphasises informal practices and civil rights discourses, social movements and diverse expressions of European identity:

> Crossing internal borders as economically active citizens, carrying burgundy coloured passports across external EU borders as travellers, exchanging knowledge as scholars and students, voting commonly for European Parliament and sharing municipal governance as Union citizens were aspects of this process. Emerging patterns of belongingness were generated step by step, area by area, and group by group. Union citizenship does not supersede national identities. Instead, it has evoked multiple identities. (Wiener, 1999: 286)

Once the subject of European civil rights is raised, the question of European identity is never far away. There is the argument that the multiplicity of languages is an obstacle not only to Europeanwide communication but also to the formation of a European public sphere and a European political discourse (Grimm, 1994: 46). Yet, do we need a collective identity first? Do we need it to lay the foundation for European civil rights? I don't think so and assume, like Erhard Denninger, 'that neither the common language nor the unity of a "people" in the pattern of a nation state [is] the *sine qua non* for the formation of a European consciousness of belonging together' (Denninger, 2000: 150). This does not exclude the possibility that a notion of belonging and responsibility – 'Europeanness' – may arise from the further development of consensus on the constitution of Europe, from a consensus on basic rights and a federal structure and from the contribution of new members. What we can 'learn from Europe' and in Europe is to feel at ease with multiplicity and divergence, especially in its history of economic, legal and cultural developments. The history of European modernisation is, after all, marked by asynchronicities, interdependencies and processes of 'retrieved development' which produced a specific dynamic of development (Senghaas, 1982: 25f). In view of the history of European law, Europe's current architecture is often compared to the 'Holy Roman Empire of German Nations', which lasted from the beginning of the eleventh century until 1806. Advocates of enlightenment had scorned it for its multi-layered forms of authority, corporate power balances and interwoven legal institutions as a 'monster that is similar to a body of state', or a hybrid monarchy-federation (Wesel, 1997: 352). It nevertheless secured the Empire, apart from territorial changes, by means of its legal institutions and supreme institutions 'despite all shortcomings an uncontested legitimacy that lasted several centuries' (Evers, 1994: 123). This comparison between a construction of a post-national order of states with a pre-national form is interesting not for its intent at restoration, but for its reference to a multi-layered structure of authority and the form of multiple or dual legitimisation, which may possibly express 'a form of representation that is closer to reality and in this sense "more modern" than an exclusively valid authority of the state that is brought about by national identity' (Evers, 1994: 123). However, a strong and permanent trait in European culture seems to be interaction between a multiplicity of cultures, including non-European ones. Europe's violent history of wars and colonisation is so profoundly ambivalent, since it also produced the intellectual principle of dialogue and discourses that mark the culminating points of European culture, for example the *Querelles des femmes*, as the genuine European debate about gender is called, the long-lasting processes of Roman law (Koschaker, 1947) and the idea of human rights.

This cultural tradition produced the concept of 'active citizenship', which Elisabeth Meehan describes in her vision of European citizens' rights:

> It is that a new kind of citizenship is emerging that is neither national nor cosmopolitan but that is multiple in the sense that identities, rights, and obligations, associated . . . with citizenship, are expressed through an increasingly complex configuration of Common Community institutions, states, national and transnational voluntary associations, regions and alliances of regions.   (Meehan, 1993: 1)

These considerations are relevant because they reject the exclusiveness of the traditional concept of citizenship, which was based on nationality and territoriality, and recognise an important prerequisite for democratising Europe in the development of a multi-layered system of rights, obligations and loyalties (see Lemke, 1999: 11). For this reason it is referred to as post-state (Wiener, 1998) or post-national, which does not mean substituting the state relationship, but is intended as a compensation for the loss of the exclusiveness of a nation state, or as Preuß concludes: 'The status of citizenship does not rest with an abstract equality resulting from equal membership of a composite state, but is founded on the multiplicity of social realms that, according to this concept of democracy, must be present in the sphere of articulating politics' (Preuß, 1999: 167).

The European Union as a democratic project would thus be a trial run for civil society activities and a political structure of empowerment for women. In Europe, the women's movements bring in political and historic experiences that are indispensable for developing European civil rights. They have put new standards of justice on the European agenda, which intervene into the so far untouched private sphere, and they have fought for their recognition. There is no doubt that new forms of intervention and new forms of coalition-building are necessary, which transcend national limits and do not refrain from acting on the multiple levels of European politics. In my opinion, the ultimate test for a successful status of 'active' citizenship will be how we treat asylum seekers and migrants from non-EU countries. It will be an issue of how we deal with the exclusivity of the new status of community, and whether we really want to construct a 'Fortress Europe' by means of a common foreign and security policy. In this respect the Amsterdam Treaty is well worth taking seriously. On the issue of asylum and migration, the Treaty admonishes 'the preservation and further development of the Union as a space for freedom, security and the rule of law' (see Article 2 of the EU Treaty and article 61 of the Amsterdam Treaty).

## Note

1. My translation from German. This passage is not part of the English edition of the 1988 book.

## References

Böckenförde, E.-W. (1997). *Welchen Weg geht Europa?* München: Carl-Friedrich-von-Siemens-Stiftung.

Brubaker, R. (1992). *Citizenship and Nationhood in France and Germany.* Cambridge, Mass. and London: Harvard University Press.

Cauer, M. (1908). 'Freie Bahn'. *Die Frauenbewegung,* XIV. Jg., 9.

Cohen, J.L. and A. Arato (1992). *Civil Society and Political Theory.* Cambridge, Mass: MIT Press.

Cott, N.F. (1998). 'Marriage and Women's Citizenship in the United States, 1830–1934', in *The American Historical Review/American Historical Association.*

Dahrendorf, R. (1992). *Der moderne soziale Konflikt.* Stuttgart: Deutsche Verlagsanstalt.

Dann, O. (1976). 'Die Anfänge politischer Vereinsbildung in Deutschland', in U. Engelhardt u.a. (Hg.), *Soziale Bewegung und politische Verfassung. Beiträge zur Geschichte der modernen Welt.* Stuttgart: Klett.

Denninger, E. (2000). 'Anmerkungen zur Diskussion um Europäische Grundrechte'. *Kritische Vierteljahresschrift für Gesetzgebung und Rechtswissenschaft,* H. 2.

Elshtain, J.B. (1981). *Public Man, Private Woman. Woman in Social and Political Thought.* Princeton: Princeton University Press.

Evers, T. (1994). 'Supranationale Staatlichkeit am Beispiel der Europäischen Union'. *Leviathan*, 22.

Frevert, U. (1995). 'Mann und Weib und Weib und Mann'. *Geschlechterdifferenzen in der Moderne*. München: C.H. Beck.

Gerhard, U. (1997). 'Grenzziehungen und Überschreitungen. Die Rechte der Frauen auf dem Weg in die politische Öffentlichkeit', in U. Gerhard (Hg.). *Frauen in der Geschichte des Rechts. Von der Frühen Neuzeit bis zur Gegenwart*. München: C.H. Beck.

Gerhard, U. (2001). *Debating Women's Equality. Towards a Feminist Theory of Law from a European Perspective*. New Brunswick: Rutgers University Press. (German 1990: *Gleichheit ohne Angleichung. Frauen im Recht*. München: C.H. Beck).

Gosewinkel, D. (2001). *Einbürgern und Ausschließen. Die Nationalisierung der Staatsangehörigkeit vom Deutschen Bund zur Bundesrepublik Deutschland*. Göttingen: Vandenhoeck & Ruprecht.

Grimm, D. (1995). *Braucht Europa eine Verfassung?* München: Carl-Friedrich-von Siemens-Stiftung.

Habermas, J. (1989). *The Structural Transformation of the Public Sphere: An Inquiry into a Category of Bourgeois Society*. Cambridge, Mass.: MIT Press.

Habermas, J. (1992). *Faktizität und Geltung. Beiträge zur Diskurstheorie des Rechts und des demokratischen Rechtsstaates*. Frankfurt/M: Suhrkamp.

Hegel, G.W.F. (1972). *Grundlinien der Philosophie des Rechts. Hrsg. von Johannes Hoffmeister*. Hamburg: Meiner.

Kant, I. (1996). 'The Metaphysics of Morals' [1797], in M. Gregor (ed.), *Cambridge Texts in the History of Philosophy*. Cambridge: Cambridge University Press.

Klein, V. (1971). *The Feminine Character. History of an Ideology* [1946]. London: Routledge.

Knijn, T. and M. Kremer (1997). 'Gender and the Caring Dimension of Welfare States: Toward Inclusive Citizenship'. *Social Politics: International Studies in Gender, State, and Society*, 1.

Kocka, J. (1995). *Bürgertum im 19. Jahrhundert. Deutschland im europäischen Vergleich*. Göttingen: Vandenhoeck & Ruprecht.

Koschaker, P. (1947). *Europa und das römische Recht*. München: Biederstein.

Koselleck, R. (1975). *Preußen zwischen Reform und Revolution. Allgemeines Landrecht, Verwaltung und soziale Bewegung von 1791–1848*. Stuttgart: Klett.

Kymlicka, W. and W. Norman (1994). 'Return of the Citizen: a Survey of Recent Work on Citizenship Theory'. *Ethics* (January).

Lemke, C. (1999). 'Europa als politischer Raum. Konzeptionelle Überlegungen zur aktiven Bürgerschaft und zur Demokratie in der europäischen Union'. *Kritische Justiz*, 1.

Lister, R. (1997). *Citizenship: Feminist Perspectives*. Basingstoke: Macmillan.

Marshall, T.H. (1950). *Citizenship and Social Class*. Cambridge: Cambridge University Press.

Marx, K. (1975). *On The Jewish Question. Collected Works, Vol. 3*. Moscow: Progress Publishers.

Meehan, E. (1993). *Citizenship and European Community*. London: Sage.

Mouffe, C. (1992). 'Feminism, Citizenship and Radical Democratic Politics', in J. Butler and J.W. Scott (eds.), *Feminist Theorize the Political*. New York and London: Routledge.

Nipperdey, T. (1972). 'Verein als soziale Struktur in Deutschland im späten 18.

und frühen 19. Jahrhundert', in *Geschichtswissenschaft und Vereinswesen im 19. Jahrhundert. Beiträge zur Geschichte historischer Forschung*. Göttingen: Vandenhoeck & Ruprecht.

Ostner, I. and J. Lewis (1995). 'Gender and the Evolution of European Social Policies', in S. Leibfried and P. Pierson (eds.), *European Social Policy, between Fragmentation an Integration*. Washington, DC: The Brookings Institution.

Ostrogorskij, M.J. (1897). *Die Frau im öffentlichen Recht. Eine vergleichende Untersuchung der Geschichte und Gesetzgebung der civilisierten Länder*. Leipzig: Wigand.

Pateman, C. (1988). *The Sexual Contract*. Cambridge, and Oxford: Stanford University Press.

Pateman, C. (1989). *The Disorder of Women. Democracy, Feminism and Political Theory*. Cambridge and Oxford: Polity Press.

Pierson, P. (1996). 'The Path to European Integration. A Historical Institutional Analysis'. *Comparative Political Studies*, 29.

Preuß, U.K. (1999). 'Auf der Suche nach Europas Verfassung: Europa hat noch keine Verfassung'. *Transit*, 17.

Riedel, M. (1979). 'Bürger, Staatsbürger, Bürgertum', in Brunner, Conze and Koselleck (Hg.). *Geschichtliche Grundbegriffe, Bd. 1*. Stuttgart: Klett-Cotta.

Sarvasy, W. (1994). 'From Man and Philanthropic Service to Feminist Social Citizenship'. *Social Politics: International Studies in Gender, State, and Society*, 1.

Senghaas, D. (1982). *Von Europa lernen. Entwicklungsgeschichtliche Betrachtungen*. Frankfurt/M: Suhrkamp.

Siim, B. (2000). *Gender and Citizenship. Politics and Agency in France, Britain and Denmark*. Cambridge: Cambridge University Press.

Soysal, Y.N. (1994). *The Limits of Citizenship: Migrants and Postnational Membership in Europe*. Chicago: University of Chicago Press.

Soysal, Y.N. (1996). 'Staatsbürgerschaft im Wandel. Postnationale Mitgliedschaft und Nationalstaat in Europa', *Berliner Journal für Soziologie*, vol. 6, 181–9.

Tronto, J. (2000). 'Demokratie als fürsorgliche Praxis'. *Feministische Studien extra*, Jg. 18.

Wesel, U. (1997). *Geschichte des Rechts. Von den Frühformen bis zum Vertrag von Maastricht*. München: C.H. Beck.

Wiener, A. (1998). *'European' Citizenship Practice: Building Institutions of a Non-State*. Boulder, col.: Westview Press.

Wiener, A. (1999). 'The Constructive Potential of Citizenship: Building European Union'. *Policy & Politics*, 27, 3.

Wolff, C. (1980). *Grundsätze des Natur- und Völkerrechts, worin alle Verbindlichkeiten und alle Rechte aus der Natur des Menschen in einem beständigen Zusammenhang hergeleitet werden können* [zuerst Halle: Renger, 1754]. Königstein: Scriptor.

Young, I.M. (1989). 'Humanismus, Gynozentrismus und feministische Kritik', in E. List and H. Studer (Hg.). *Denkverhältnisse. Feminismus und Kritik*. Frankfurt/M: Suhrkamp.

Young, I.M. (1990). *Justice and the Politics of Difference*. Princeton, NJ: Princeton University Press.

Zahn-Harnack, A. von (1928). *Die Frauenbewegung. Geschichte, Probleme, Ziele*. Berlin: Deutsche Buch-Gemeinschaft.

# 8

# A Politics of Recognition and Respect: Involving People with Experience of Poverty in Decision-Making that Affects their Lives[1]

*Ruth Lister*

## Introduction

People living in poverty and their organisations should be empowered by involving them fully in the setting of targets, and in the design, implementation, monitoring and assessment of national strategies and programmes for poverty eradication and community-based development, and ensuring that such programmes reflect their priorities.

Five years ago, over 100 countries signed up to this statement in the Copenhagen Declaration and Programme of Action at the UN World Summit for Social Development. In the UK, the Summit provided the catalyst for the establishment of the UK Coalition against Poverty (UKCAP), which now has around 160 members. Its mission was the inclusion of people with direct experience of poverty in partnership with local, national and international organisations, working towards ending poverty and campaigning for the national anti-poverty programme to which governments signed up at the Summit.

Towards this end, the Coalition raised money for the *Voices for Change* project, a key element of which was the establishment of an independent Commission on Poverty, Participation and Power, of which I was a member. The second section of this chapter describes the work of this Commission, together with a number of other initiatives in the UK, which reflect the spirit of the Copenhagen Declaration. It considers the position of the UK government and points to lessons to be learnt from the experience of the southern hemisphere.

The first section of the chapter attempts to put such practical initiatives in a theoretical context. Using the concepts of exclusion, citizenship, democracy, recognition and empowerment, it makes a normative case for the involvement of people in poverty in decision-making that affects their lives. It argues that such involvement should be seen as a central element in a 'politics of empowerment and inclusion'.

## Theoretical perspectives

The politics of poverty is increasingly being couched in a non-materialist discourse of human and citizenship rights, democracy, inclusion and respect.[2] This does not represent a denial of the material conditions that lie at the heart of poverty. What it does do is offer an opportunity to transform the politics of poverty into one that addresses questions of power as well as material resources. At the same time, it integrates the concerns of those in poverty into wider debates about citizenship and democracy, rather than treating them as separate (Lister, 2004). This section represents an initial attempt to develop an analytical framework in which this emergent politics of poverty can be both understood and forged. It does so through the application of a number of, at times overlapping, concepts in social and political theory.

### Social exclusion

Social exclusion has become an increasingly fashionable concept in many parts of Europe, including New Labour's Britain. Graham Room has suggested that, whereas the notion of poverty primarily concerns the distribution of material resources, that of social exclusion focuses 'primarily on relational issues, in other words, inadequate social participation, lack of social integration and lack of power' (Room, 1995: 5).[3] The last element points to the political as well as social nature of exclusion.

In the same volume, Jos Berghman identifies as helpful the breadth and dynamic nature of the notion of social exclusion. Breadth, in his exposition, refers to failure in a number of different systems of integration: economic (through the labour market), welfare, interpersonal (through family/community) and civic (through the democratic and legal systems). This approach, he suggests, points to the conceptualisation of social exclusion as 'the denial – or non-realisation – of citizenship rights', following the European Observatory on Policies to Combat Social Exclusion (Berghman, 1995: 19). Such a conceptualisation also calls attention to another aspect of social exclusion's multidimensional nature, not addressed by Berghman. This is the ways in which prejudice and discriminatory and oppressive behaviour can, within these four systems, serve to exclude particular groups such as women, racialised groups, disabled people and gays and lesbians.

The dynamic nature of social exclusion encourages a focus on processes and not just outcomes (Wilson, 1995; Byrne, 1999). In doing so, it provides due regard to agency, as well as structure, one or other of which can be lost sight of when attention is fixed, either benevolently or critically, on individual experience and behaviour. Thus, by encouraging the question 'who is excluding whom and how?' the concept draws attention to the role played by social and economic institutions and by political decisions in creating and reinforcing poverty and exclusion. A more dynamic approach also opens up space for the agency of those excluded as political and social actors, rather than treating them as simply passive victims. It places greater emphasis on the political dimension of exclusion, which in turn raises questions about the political status and role of excluded groups (Lister, 2000).

Such a conceptualisation of social exclusion is representative of what Ruth Levitas has dubbed RED, a redistributive, egalitarian discourse. As she notes, 'from the perspective of RED, political inclusion is an aspect of social inclusion' (Levitas, 1998: 173). However, such a discourse is less prominent in contemporary British and EU politics than those of SID (social integrationist discourse), which focuses mainly on the labour market, and, to a lesser extent, MUD (moral 'underclass' discourse). The growing demands to involve people in poverty in decision-making that affects their lives represents a challenge to a narrow conceptualisation of social exclusion, limited to labour market participation, and to a derogatory conceptualisation, which labels people in poverty as passive welfare 'dependants'.

## Citizenship

In contrast, such demands draw implicitly on RED, which, alongside its egalitarian stance, simultaneously represents an expansive discourse of *citizenship*, embracing civil, political, cultural and social rights. Citizenship is, in part, about equality of status and respect (relevant also to recognition politics, see below). As Beresford et al. argue, in a study in which 'poor people speak for themselves', their inclusion in poverty discussions

> is part of the broader issue of addressing the restricted citizenship of people who are poor. It also signifies respect for poor people; an acknowledgement that they have something to offer, that their contribution is important, worthwhile and valued, and recognition of their expertise in their own experience. Much of the social democratic/social administration debate about poverty has focused

on equality. Supporting people to speak for themselves is a basic requirement for such equality.                    (Beresford et al., 1999: 27)

In some strands of contemporary citizenship theory, participation in decision-making is put forward as a citizenship right. Thomas Janoski, for instance, makes the case for 'a right of participation', suggesting that its addition to the panoply of rights 'pushes citizenship rights into the center of more recent welfare state controversies and democratic struggles' (1998: 50). The right to participation can be understood as a bridge between the two main traditions of citizenship: the (social) liberal rights and civic republican traditions, which respectively cast citizenship as a status and a practice. In the latter, the essence of citizenship is active participation in governance and politics for the good of the wider community.

The right to participation has also been promoted as a human and not just a citizenship right. Carol Gould (1988), for instance, has argued for an extension of the human right of democratic participation to include the right of participation in social and economic decision-making. Her argument is grounded in the agency of human beings and in the principle of freedom as self-development. It resonates in the distinction made by Doyal and Gough, in their theory of human need, between simple autonomy as expressed through agency and 'the higher degrees of critical autonomy which are entailed by democratic participation in the political process at whatever level' (Doyal and Gough, 1991: 68).

In some cases, citizenship and human rights discourses are combined to make the case for the involvement of people in poverty in decisions which affect their lives. In a recent consultation document the British Department for International Development argues that human rights 'provide a means of empowering all people to make decisions about their own lives rather than being the passive objects of choices made on their behalf'. The document 'sets out the practical ways in which the human rights framework contributes to the achievement of the objective of enabling all people to be active citizens with rights, expectations and responsibilities' (DfID, 2000: 1).

A concrete example is provided by ATD Fourth World, in its description of a project in which severely disadvantaged families were able to meet with each other and with professionals in a spirit of partnership. The underlying philosophy of the project was that the creation of a democracy, in which 'all citizens have the means to enjoy their rights, assume their responsibilities, and make their contribution', requires us all to 'be ready to change and to consider the poor as partners with whom we will learn how to respect the human rights of each and every one of us' (1996: 61).

ATD claims that 'the project showed us that as people gained self-esteem, self-confidence, and sometimes practical skills as well, they started to see that their views and opinions could be taken seriously' (1996: 58). As a result, they were able to participate more effectively in partnership relationships with professionals. The importance of such a process to citizenship is underlined in some feminist writings on citizenship. Susan James, for instance, has argued that to speak in one's own voice and put forward one's views in the polity, as required of citizens, requires 'self-esteem – a stable sense of one's own separate identity and a confidence that one is worthy to participate in political life' (1992: 60).

The ATD project is an example of how the very process of participation helps to build self-esteem and thus strengthen the agency of people in poverty, thereby enabling them to act more effectively as citizens. As Maud Eduards (1994: 18) has observed, agency embodies 'a transformative' capacity, which has been vital in the development of women's citizenship. It is particularly vital in the development of the citizenship of women in poverty, but also men in poverty. As I have argued elsewhere, 'to act as a citizen requires first a sense of agency, the belief that one *can* act; acting as a citizen, especially collectively, in turn fosters that sense of agency' (Lister, 2003: 39). Indeed, agency has been described as 'the defining quality of citizenship' as a practice (Barnes, 1999b: 82).

Another example comes from a unique parliamentary initiative in which an All-Party Parliamentary Group (APPG) of Members of Parliament has involved, on a regular basis, people with experience of poverty in its meetings. In the first report of the APPG on Poverty, participants were quoted as saying:

'It is good for me to be able to speak out.'

'Taking part in the APPG has helped me to learn what I can do to make differences, to know what I can contribute.'

'We don't make the effort if we don't think that we'll be listened to. Participating in an APPG on Poverty has given me encouragement and it is something that I will take back to my community to encourage them too.'                     (APPG on Poverty, 1999: 4)

The report observes that for most of the participants 'the experience of being listened to and taken seriously is unusual. . . . The APPG on Poverty extends democracy beyond the reach of the already powerful and allows the experts to speak for themselves, and often to significant effect.' It also suggests that 'the humanisation of the democratic process is important for real participation and respectful exchanges to take place' (APPG on Poverty, 1999). Dialogues such as these represent the promotion of citizenship through greater democratic accountability (Cornwall and Gaventa, 2000).

## Democracy

The invocation of principles of *democracy* addresses two concerns: the growing exclusion and separation of those in poverty from the democratic process, and a dissatisfaction in some quarters with the practice of representative democracy. It also chimes with some of the rhetoric of the 'third way'.

One of the most prominent critics of the political marginalisation of those in poverty has been J.K. Galbraith. In the US context, he has written of how the contented majority 'rule under the rich cloak of democracy, a democracy in which the less fortunate do not participate' (1992: 15), and that in the face of inequality of 'power and influence, democracy has become an imperfect thing' (1996: 138). In his vision of 'the good society voice and influence cannot be confined to one part of the population'. The solution, he suggests, 'is more active political participation by a coalition of the concerned and the poor' (1996: 141).

Galbraith is here concerned with electoral politics. His argument is that the non-participation of people in poverty at the ballot box means that their interests and concerns are increasingly ignored by the political parties. The same phenomenon, albeit to a lesser extent, is increasingly true of Britain. Under the British 'first past the post' electoral system, voters in safe seats, which include many of the poorest areas, can safely be ignored. Electoral politics are increasingly played out in a small number of marginal seats. Electoral turn-out in the deprived inner city areas is generally lower than average.

This is one of the arguments used in favour of electoral reform to achieve proportional representation. But the political exclusion of those in poverty also raises questions about the very nature of modern democracy. Political theorists, such as Carol Gould, have argued for the democratisation of all the institutions of society – social, economic and cultural as well as political. Gould propounds the following principle of democracy: 'every person who engages in a common activity with others has an equal right to participate in making decisions concerning such activity. This right to participate applies not only to the domain of politics but to social and economic activities as well' (Gould, 1988: 84; see also Pateman, 1970).

More recently, in his exposition of the third way, Anthony Giddens has argued for the 'democratisation of democracy'. He contends that 'the crisis of democracy comes from its not being democratic enough' in the face of 'the demand for individual autonomy and the emergence of a more reflexive citizenry' (1998: 71). One policy implication, he suggests, is ' "experiments with democratization" such as the use of electronic referenda, revived forms of direct democracy and citizens' juries' (Giddens, 2000: 62). Echoing Giddens, Tony Blair has written of the third way's 'democratic impulse', which 'needs to be strengthened by finding new ways to enable citizens to share in decision-making that affects them' (1998: 15). Initiatives to 'listen to' women and to older people, a 'race relations forum', a 'people's panel' to elicit views on public services, as well as citizens' juries are among the devices introduced to promote this goal.

A study of two citizens' juries describes them as 'just one example of the new approaches to democratic practice which are being developed throughout the public sector' and 'as a practical expression of the notion of discursive or deliberative democracy' (Barnes, 1999a: 1). The increased emphasis on more participatory democratic mechanisms is, though, raising questions about the relationship between participatory and representative democracy, especially at local government level. Some in local government have resisted more participatory forms of democracy on the grounds that they undermine representative democracy. Others have responded that 'an active conception of representative democracy can be reinforced by participatory democracy' (Clarke and Stewart, 1998: 3).

Principles of deliberative and participatory democracy are one element in the case made for 'radical democracy' (Mouffe, 1992; Trend, 1996). The other key principle is that of radical pluralism. Central to the notion of deliberative democracy is the provision of public space in which the voices of different groups can be heard and can deliberate. Iris Young, for instance, tempers her advocacy of participatory democracy with the warning that 'only if oppressed groups are able to express their interests and experience in the public on an equal basis with other groups can group domination through formally equal processes of participation be avoided' (1990: 95). She thus asserts the principle that 'a democratic public should provide mechanisms for the effective re-cognition and representation of the distinct voices and perspectives of those of its constituent groups that are oppressed or disadvantaged' (1990: 184).

Nancy Fraser likewise defines radical democracy in terms of opposi-tion to 'two very different kinds of impediments to democratic partici-pation', namely social inequality and 'the misrecognition of difference. Radical democracy, on this interpretation is the view that democracy today requires both social equality and multicultural recognition' (1996: 198).

## Recognition

Fraser is here talking about the *recognition* and misrecognition of differ-ence. However, the demand for recognition is becoming more vocal in the politics of poverty also, as that politics is increasingly expressed as a politics of 'voice' (Yeatman, 1994; Williams, 1999). In her original *New Left Review* article on the politics of redistribution and of reco-gnition, Fraser (1995; 1997) roots the former in the struggle against socio-economic injustice and the latter in the struggle against cul-tural or symbolic injustice. Poverty is quintessentially the product of socio-economic injustice and anti-poverty campaigns are central to any politics of redistribution. At the same time, though, these campaigns increasingly deploy a discourse of recognition as well as of redistribu-tion. Among the examples of cultural or symbolic injustice cited by Fraser are 'nonrecognition (being rendered invisible via the authorita-tive representational, communicative, and interpretative practices of one's culture); and disrespect (being routinely maligned or disparaged in stereotypic public cultural representations and/or in everyday life interactions)' (Fraser, 1995: 71; 1997a: 14).

In an earlier essay, Charles Taylor identified recognition as a vital human need and underlined the links between recognition and identity:

> our identity is partly shaped by recognition or its absence, often by the *mis*recognition of others, and so a person or group of people can suffer real damage, real distortion, if the people or society around them mirror back to them a confining or demeaning or contemptible picture of themselves. Nonrecognition or misrecognition can inflict harm, can be a form of oppression.
>
> (Taylor, 1992: 25–6; see also Fraser, 2000)

Nonrecognition, misrecognition and disrespect are the typical experience of those in poverty, especially when labelled pejoratively as an 'underclass' or as inhabiting a 'dependency culture' (for a critique, see Lister, 1996). At a National Poverty Hearing in London, organised by Church Action on Poverty (an ecumenical anti-poverty group), one of the most common refrains among those with experience of poverty was the desire to be treated with greater respect. 'I just wish people would give us a chance and treat us with some respect' and 'I just feel very angry sometimes that people are ignorant to the fact that we are humans as well and we do need to be respected' were typical of the comments made (Russell, 1996: 7, 10). David Donnison has suggested that the demand for respect and 'to be treated as the equal of anyone else' is indicative of an emergent new paradigm in social policy (2000: 25; see also Donnison, 1998). In an international context, the *Human Development Report 2000* identifies 'a life of respect and value' as a key aim of human development (UNDP, 2000: 2). The report also emphasises the interrelationship between civil, political, social, economic and cultural rights.

As Fraser acknowledges, economic and cultural forms of injustice tend 'to reinforce each other dialectically' so that 'economic disadvantage impedes equal participation in the making of culture, in public spheres, and in everyday life' (Fraser, 1995: 72–3; 1997: 15). In her critique of Fraser, Iris Marion Young places greater emphasis on the interrelationship between the two forms of injustice and politics. She maintains that 'we should show how recognition is a means to, or an element in, economic and political equality and that 'so long as the cultural denigration of groups produces or reinforces structural economic oppressions, the two struggles are continuous' (Young, 1997: 156, 159). Drawing on Fraser's own work on a 'politics of needs interpretation', she argues for a 'materialist culturalist approach [which] understands that needs are contextualised in political struggle over who gets to define whose needs for what purpose' (Young, 1997: 155).

In a more recent contribution to *New Left Review*, Fraser herself pays more attention to the interrelationship between the economic and cultural and develops her argument in ways that are potentially more directly applicable to the politics of poverty. She suggests that 'properly conceived, struggles for recognition can aid the redistribution of power and wealth and can promote interaction and cooperation across gulfs of difference' (2000: 109). The theoretical move that she makes is to treat misrecognition as a question of social status subordination and injustice, rather than of identity:

From this perspective, what requires recognition is not group-specific identity but the status of individual group members as full partners in social interaction . . . It means a politics aimed at overcoming subordination by establishing the misrecognized party as a full member of society capable of participating on a par with the rest.

(2000: 113; see also 2001)

The obstacles to 'participatory parity' on this model are not just cultural but lie also in the maldistribution of resources. Although Fraser herself does not make the link, such an approach is highly relevant to the politics of poverty. Here a politics of recognition is not about the assertion of group difference, as in the case of women, racialised groups, lesbians and gays, and disabled people (remembering that we are not, of course, talking about discrete groups). Indeed, a successful politics of redistribution could remove the category altogether, as 'the poor' are a group who are primarily the product of the maldistribution of resources. A politics of recognition in this context is, instead, about the assertion of recognition in the sense of equality of status and respect, which, as stated above, are critical to the recognition of the full citizenship of those in poverty.

As Diana Coole has observed, discourses of difference have tended to marginalise social class. While elaborating the difficulties in applying such discourses to class, including the 'underclass', she asserts that respect for those at the bottom of the economic hierarchy is 'patronising' (Coole, 1996: 22). Coole makes the valid point that 'poverty robs groups of the economic and cultural capital needed for participation' (1996: 20). However, she appears to treat this as a given rather than asking how, alongside the struggle to eliminate poverty itself, the cultural and political capital of those in poverty can be strengthened and fostered so as to enable participation. Indeed, as observed earlier, the evidence suggests that the very process of participation and of being treated with respect can itself nourish agency and the ability to participate.

Bob Holman, editor of a book in which seven people in poverty write their own stories, argues that 'the reluctance to listen to the bottom 30 per cent devalues them. They are treated as specimens to be examined and displayed, not as human beings with the rights *and capacities* to participate in public debate' (Holman, 1998: 16; my emphasis). Similarly, ATD Fourth World rejects the construction of people living in poverty as 'objects of other people's knowledge, not as authors of their own development – as problems' for 'they have something to offer, something to contribute' (1999: 16). What is at issue here is the value accorded to poor people's own interpretation of their needs and demands and recognition of and respect for the expertise born of experience (Beresford and Croft, 1995).[4] Moraene Roberts, another participant in the National Poverty Hearing, argued:

> No one asks our views. We are the real experts of our own hopes and aspirations. Service providers should ask the users before deciding on policies, before setting targets that will affect our lives. We can contribute if you are prepared to give up a little power to allow us to participate as partners in our own future, and in the future of our country.                                      (Russell, 1996: 4)

## Empowerment

Roberts points to a crucial element in the equation: that of *power*. As Levitas observes, theories of dialogic and deliberative democracy tend to underplay the importance of 'the structures of power' within which dialogue and deliberation take place' (Levitas, 1998: 176). Beresford and Croft suggest that 'in one sense, it is poor people's powerlessness which lies at the heart of their exclusion from the poverty debate and helps to explain it' (1995: 79). If this powerlessness is not addressed, general strategies to promote participatory democracy could exacerbate rather than redress imbalances of power (Bur, Stevens and Young, 1999: 14).

The 1997 United Nations Human Development Report identifies 'the political empowerment of poor people' as an essential element in 'a political strategy for poverty': 'Poor people should be politically empowered to organize for themselves for collective action and to influence the circumstances and decisions affecting their lives. For their interests to be advanced, they must be visible on the political map' (UNDP, 1997: 94, 10).

Similarly, drawing on the work of Paulo Freire, David Byrne looks to the collective 'empowerment of the dispossessed' as part of 'a popular democratic politics of solidarity' necessary to combat social exclusion (1999: 133). The process of empowerment concerns two aspects of power. One is what Giddens (1991) calls 'generative' power, which is about 'self-actualisation' and which is 'related to energy, capacity and potential' (Hartsock, 1985: 210). It is this kind of power which is developed through the community development process of 'capacity-building' and which can be witnessed in the very process of participation, as confidence and self-esteem grow. However, feminists have also warned against reducing empowerment to an individual social-psychological process, thereby losing sight of the importance of collective empowerment to achieve social change and to alter the distribution of power. Virginia Rinaldo Seitz thus defines empowerment as 'both a process and an outcome of collective identity and political praxis, resulting in a capacity in thought and action to address the condition and position of marginalization' (1998: 234). Integrating the two, individual empowerment enables people to come together to work for change (Mayo, 1994).

This brings us to the other aspect of power identified by Giddens as 'hierarchical', which describes the ability of a group or individual to exert their will over others. Writing in the *Human Development Report 1997*, Else Øyen warns that poverty can serve the interests of the economically powerful, so that the redistribution of resources (political as well as economic and social) involved in poverty reduction 'will sometimes be vigorously opposed' (UNDP, 1997: 95). Thus, ultimately, individual empowerment of a generative kind will need to lead to some redistribution of hierarchical power, if people in poverty are to achieve genuine empowerment through participation. Moreover, individual empowerment may create or exacerbate divisions among groups in poverty, if some are 'empowered' at the expense of others (Taylor and West, 2000).

## Participatory initiatives

The first section of this chapter has argued the case for the involvement of people in poverty in decision-making that affects their lives, with reference to the theoretical concepts of social exclusion, citizenship, democracy, recognition and empowerment. The normative ideal for which it has argued stands in contrast to the reality. As a participatory study with people in poverty in Britain observed, 'one key group has been conspicuous by its absence so far in poverty discussion and policy development – people with experience of poverty themselves' (Beresford et al., 1999). Britain has a strong 'poverty lobby', comprised mainly of middle-class professionals, which speaks out effectively on behalf of those in poverty. It emerged in the 1960s and 1970s, in part because of the collective weakness of people in poverty as a political constituency able to influence governments.

However, increasingly, following the example of the disabled people's movement, demands are emerging for the voices of those in poverty to be heard directly rather than filtered through the professional 'poverty lobby'. A number of initiatives and projects have acted as prefigurative models of what is possible.[5] The paper describes three of them, focusing in particular on the *Voices for Change* project initiated by the UK Coalition on Poverty.

## ATD Fourth World

The longest standing is ATD Fourth World (All Together in Dignity), which operates in a number of countries. It works in partnership with 'the Fourth World' (that is people who, 'due to their poverty, are unable to make their voices heard or to maximise their potential') 'to develop their potential abilities and to enable them to participate fully in the life of their communities' (ATD, 2000: 56). An important aspect of this work is the facilitation of the involvement of people in poverty in an 'exchange of ideas and views with representatives of community services and policy-makers – at local, national and European level' (ATD, 2000: 57).

A recent report describes ATD's 'Public Debate Project'. This aimed to promote the involvement and voice of people in long-term poverty in public debate and the valuing by others of their contribution. A total of 70 people were involved in the project, including around 20 core participants. The project was 'designed to build up the participants' confidence and to enable them to speak to a wider audience, when they were ready' (ATD 2000: 11). At its core was a series of policy forums. These provided a space for the sharing of ideas and skills and for the exploration of policy issues arising from their experiences. More intensive residential training seminars were also held. These helped participants to 'move forward from just speaking about their own lives to learning from their experiences and relating them to how society is run, both locally and nationally' (ATD, 2000: 13–14). Together, these then provided the basis for participation in a series of policy forums with ministers and civil servants, as well as in the meetings of the All Party Parliamentary Group on Poverty, referred to earlier. The overall conclusion reached was that:

> the project demonstrates that people in poverty have ideas regarding policy improvement and are actively seeking to share this experience. In order for this to be possible, however, the policy-making process must evolve and mechanisms must be created that allow for knowledge and expertise from people at grass-roots level to be taken on board.                                                                 (ATD, 2000: 6)

## Church Action on Poverty

Church Action on Poverty (CAP) is an ecumenical group, which established in 1994 a 'Local People, National Voice' project. Among the aims were: to provide opportunities for people with direct experience of poverty 'to speak out for themselves' and to 'create an effective dialogue between policy makers, church members and people experiencing poverty'.

The project consisted of a series of local events and hearings, which provided a platform from which people with experience of poverty could speak out about their experiences and views. Over 20 local and regional hearings, each attended by 100–200 people, were held. They culminated in a national poverty hearing in March 1996. This provided an opportunity for national policy-makers, church, business and voluntary sector leaders and others to listen to people with experience of poverty not only give witness to their experiences, but also talk about their ideas about what should be done and the initiatives in which they were involved. As part of the project, CAP established a small policy group, comprised mainly of people with experience of poverty. This produced a short report in which the group set out its analysis of poverty and policy ideas (Bennett, 1996).

## UK Coalition against Poverty

Both ATD and CAP were founder members of what was to become the UK Coalition against Poverty, which now has over 160 member organisations. The Coalition was originally established to advance the aims of the UN International Year for the Eradication of Poverty in the UK. From the outset, the Coalition was committed to the involvement of people with the experience of poverty in all its activities and decision-making processes. As well as establishing the APPG on Poverty, it organised, in 1996, a national participation event at which people with experience of poverty were able to exchange experiences, knowledge and ideas. The report of the meeting acknowledged that those involved 'were among the more confident and active of the people who suffer from poverty'. Nevertheless, 'there was a wealth of diverse experiences to share and debate'. The workshop provided 'a model of participation' and, as such, was 'a wonderfully empowering and motivating experience for all who attended' (UKCAP, 1997: 2).

As a result, those attending felt strongly that it should not just be a one-off event but should lead to a more sustained initiative to promote participation in decision-making. The outcome was the birth of the

Voices for Change project, funded by the Joseph Rowntree Charitable Trust. Over a two-year period, the project worked from the local level, building up to area meetings and a UK-wide meeting, through a network of area and national steering groups. Much of the local work involved 'capacity-building' and training, as well as investigation into participation and the barriers to it. It used the technique of 'participatory appraisal' (PA), one of a family of participatory methods developed in the southern hemisphere, which has been borrowed as a community development tool to work with disadvantaged communities in the industrialised world.[6] The technique relies heavily on pictorial, non-linear methods, which allow people to share experiences and develop and express their ideas in a non-threatening environment. It involves marginalised people as active participants from the outset and in some cases they are now training others in the techniques and using them in their local communities. As part of Voices for Change, local groups received training in PA techniques and then used them to conduct their own consultations, which fed into area meetings and into what was initially called the Commission of Inquiry into Poverty and Social Exclusion.

### The Commission on Poverty, Participation and Power

The participatory origins of the Commission were one of its features that made it unusual, if not unique. Furthermore, the intention was that area steering groups should continue to be involved in the work of the Commission through Commissioners' visits and in the final stages when they would have the opportunity to discuss and give views on the drafting of the final report. The difficulties in fulfilling this objective underline the difficulties of sustained participation.

The other unusual feature was the Commission's composition: a mixture of 'people in public life' and 'grassroots' people with experience of poverty. This meant developing ways of working which are not typical of committees and Commissions. Meetings were often difficult, as people from very different backgrounds had to learn to work together. It was often impossible to keep to agendas that did not provide the space for 'grassroots' Commissioners to express themselves in the ways that they wanted or to deal with issues arising in their lives, such as one Commissioner's problems with the local Social Security office threatening her benefit because of her absence at Commission meetings. In the early stages, 'public life' Commissioners were sometimes challenged about what they knew about poverty, a sobering experience for those normally treated as 'experts'. Ensuring the full and equal participation of all members was a problem, which was not simply reflective of differing backgrounds. As in all committees, some members (both 'grassroots' and 'public life' and both women and men) were more forceful and talkative than others, but this became more of an issue given the nature of the exercise and the need to balance and respect different kinds of expertise (del Tufo and Gaster, 2002).

Yet, for all the difficulties, there was always an incredible energy in what were long meetings and much was achieved. The Commission's Report described it as 'an extraordinary journey for Commissioners and for the staff supporting their work' (Commission on Poverty, Participation and Power, 2000: v). The formal Evaluation Report, commissioned by the funding body, observed that

> the experiential nature of this *extraordinary process* (commissioner), the informality, laughter, passion, real honesty and energy were major features that distinguish this from other commissions. This was no ordinary set of meetings but a series of dynamic, unpredictable and often exhausting encounters, with a constant tension between seeking good processes and achieving intended outcomes.
>
> (del Tufo and Gaster, 2002: 6; emphasis in original)

Referring back to ATD's observation, cited above, this kind of process 'requires us all to be ready to change' (ATD, 1996: 61). Even for a feminist such as myself, it involved a different way of 'being' on a committee, a way of being which meant that I had to engage as a 'whole person', emotions and all, and not hide behind a bureaucratic committee persona. Yet, one of the most profound lessons I learned was that, even so, I was not engaging at the level of the 'grassroots' Commissioners who had to commit so much more to the project and for whom so much more was at stake. As one woman Commissioner said, 'We've sold a lot of our souls some of us sitting round this table – it better be worth it.' If it is not 'worth it', the costs for 'public life' Commissioners will be relatively small, whereas they will be massive for 'grassroots' Commissioners, both personally and because of the expectations of people in the communities in which they are based. Thus, the boundaries between 'public' and 'private', between 'political' and 'personal' have been much more porous for 'grassroots' than 'public life' commissioners.

The Commission started work at the end of November 1999. One of its first actions was to change its name to the Commission on Poverty, Participation and Power, so as better to reflect what were seen as the key issues. In addition to reviewing the evidence collected through the Voices for Change project and from other available sources, Commissioners visited local projects in all countries of the UK. It quickly became clear that 'participation' was in danger of becoming a dirty word for people with experience of 'token' or 'window-dressing' participation or of superficial consultation exercises, limited to impenetrable questionnaires and/or from which they had seen no positive outcomes or even feedback. Anger was expressed at politicians who attended meetings, made speeches and then left before hearing what people had to say and at officials who simply did not listen. Many felt exploited rather than empowered by what passed for participation. Nevertheless, the demand for genuine participation was strong among some groups, despite the many barriers they faced.

These barriers, as identified by the Voices for Change project, are multiple and interconnected. Some derive from poverty itself, such as the struggle for day-to-day survival, which can sap people's energy and health; the inability to meet the financial costs that can be involved; lacking suitable clothes; feelings of stigma. These overlap with personal barriers such as lack of self-esteem and self-confidence, which may derive in part from limited educational opportunities. Additional barriers can be faced by some groups such as young people, disabled people, travellers, Asian women or asylum-seekers.

More institutional barriers include lacking 'the tools of the trade' that professionals take for granted, such as faxes, computers and internet access; the operation of Social Security rules that inhibit involvement for fear of affecting benefit entitlement; officials who either resist participation or who engage in it in ways that are exclusionary rather than inclusive. What particularly angers people is the use of jargon, which is experienced as exclusionary.

In addition to barriers to participation, there are problems that can arise for which there is no easy solution. These reflect some of the more theoretical points made in the first section of this chapter. Examples are: how to engage the most marginalised people and ensure that minority views are heard and not drowned out by the loudest voices; and how to deal with arguments that, unless people have been elected, they are not 'representative' of people in poverty or have no right to speak on behalf of others. One Commission member suggested that instead of 'representatives' we should think of 'connectors', that is people who help to connect marginalised groups to decision-makers, and vice versa.

The Commission reported in December 2000 (Commission on Poverty, Participation and Power, 2000). The Evaluation suggests that 'the report was generally seen as offering different insights in a different tone – it speaks from the heart and "touches" people, avoids "policy speak", and tries to overcome the deep mistrust felt by people on the receiving end of policies' (del Tufo and Gaster, 2002: 7). As well as specific recommendations, the report puts forward a set of 'principles of participation'. Among these are:

- a recognition of 'participation in the decision-making process of people with experience of living in poverty . . . as a basic human right';
- a willingness among all those involved 'to change how we think and act to make participation genuine and effective';
- a readiness among people who hold power to 'learn to listen properly to the voices of people living in poverty, to understand, to communicate in ways that everyone can understand, to respect people's contributions, and to act on their voices' (Commission on Poverty, Participation and Power, 2000: 45).

### The government's position

The final stages of the Commission's work involved a number of meetings with ministers and officials in government Departments to gauge their reactions to the Commission's findings and line of argument and further meetings were held following publication of the report. There is no single government position, with some parts of government more open than others to the Commission's message. New Labour has accepted and promotes the message of participation at local neighbourhood level. In a Foreword to a consultation document on a National Strategy for Neighbourhood Renewal, Tony Blair acknowledged that 'unless the community is fully engaged in shaping and delivering regeneration, even the best plans on paper will fail to deliver in practice' (Social Exclusion Unit, 2000: 5). The Social Exclusion Unit, who drew up the strategy, attempted to consult people affected by its proposals, although the speed with which it had to work made it difficult to do so effectively.[7] Members of the Unit were very responsive to the Commission's message, having become increasingly convinced of the case for participation as a result of their experience. Increasingly, a degree of community involvement is required in the plethora of neighbourhood and community initiatives that the government is promoting.

The case for participation has also been accepted in a development context. A consultation document from the Department for International Development states that 'a human rights perspective on participation means moving beyond and above local-level processes of consultation through to ensuring poor people's participation in broader formal and informal systems of decision-making' (DfID, 2000: 19). What is significant about this statement is not simply the strong endorsement of participation, but its explicit acceptance that it should not be confined to the local level.

The government has, though, been slower to accept the case for involvement in decisions taken at national level in the domestic context. Yet, this is the level at which some of the most important decisions affecting people in poverty are taken. Until very recently, ministers appeared to consider it sufficient to engage in general consultation exercises on their anti-poverty and welfare reform strategies, which usually involve the publication of a document (and summary leaflets) and possibly meetings with key professional voluntary sector organisations, without any attempt specifically to engage with people in poverty. Questions about representativeness and fears about creating bureaucratic structures have typically been raised. There was little or no acknowledgement that the particular expertise of those with experience of poverty could inform and thereby improve policy-making. However, in response to pressure, including from the EU, which requires participation in the drafting of National Action Plans on Social Inclusion (NAPSincl), the Department for Work and Pensions is consulting on how to involve people with experience of poverty in drawing up future UK NAPSincl. It also included some workshops with adults and children with experience of poverty in a consultation exercise on the measurement of child poverty. Elsewhere in government a Community Forum, half of whose members are people from local communities, has been established to advise on neighbourhood renewal policies. Thus, we are seeing gradual progress.

The same cannot be said with regard to the related issue of service user involvement. There has not yet been acceptance of this principle in the sphere of benefits even though it is now reasonably well established in welfare services. A Green Paper on welfare (Social Security) reform highlighted 'the rise of the demanding, sceptical, citizen-consumer' (DSS, 1998: 16), but did not discuss how the principles of user involvement, developed elsewhere in the welfare system, might be applied to Social Security. Yet a review conducted for the government had concluded that 'user involvement is a viable option for social security', and although challenging, 'it offers a number of benefits' (Stafford, 1997: iii).

# Conclusion

This chapter has attempted to chart, theoretically and empirically, an approach to anti-poverty action, which is part and parcel of the democratic process and both an expression and a recognition of the citizenship of those experiencing poverty. Although the chapter's focus has been on the process rather than the substance and outcomes of anti-poverty action, the latter, of course, must not be forgotten. Ultimately, at issue are not just the promotion of genuine *participation*, but also the eradication of *poverty* and the redistribution of *power*.

# Notes

1. A shorter version of this chapter was originally published in *Social Policy and Society*, 1, 1, 2002. Elsewhere, Fiona Williams (2000) has used the notion of 'recognition and respect', in her case with regard to a set of principles in welfare.
2. See, for instance, a consultation document from the UK Department for International Development on *Human Rights for Poor People* (DfID, 2000); a report by the European Institute of Social Services, *Include Us In, Participation for Social Inclusion in Europe* (Bur, Stevens and Young, 1999); the *Human Development Report 2000* (UNDP, 2000) and a series of documents from ATD Fourth World, including the most recent, *Participation Works, Involving People in Poverty in Policy-making* (ATD, 2000).
3. In fact, the distinction between the concepts of poverty and social exclusion is not that clear cut, but social exclusion does encourage a more relational perspective on poverty (Lister, 2004).
4. Iris Marion Young's recent work (2000; this volume, chapter 2), in which she argues for the importance of the presence of a range of standpoints, perspectives and experiences, in particular those of excluded groups, to good judgement in policy-making, is also relevant here. See in addition Lister and Beresford (2000) for an exploration of the implications of this approach for research into poverty.
5. For further details, see Beresford et al. (2000) and ATD (2000).
6. This is just one example of how much we can learn about participation from the South. Another was provided by Hilary Wainwright in an article about participatory local government budget decisions in Brazil (*The Guardian*, 21 June 2000).
7. The Social Exclusion Unit was set up by Blair, at the heart of government, soon after the Labour Party came to power in 1997. Its remit is to develop 'joined up' solutions to intractable problems of social exclusion.

# References

APPG on Poverty (1999). *Policy, Poverty & Participation, First Report of the All Parliamentary Group on Poverty*. London: APPG on Poverty.

ATD Fourth World (1996). *Talk with us, not at us*. London: ATD Fourth World.
ATD Fourth World (1999). *Influencing Policy in Partnership with the Poorest*. London: ATD Fourth World.
ATD Fourth World (2000). *Participation Works*. London: ATD Fourth World.
Barnes, M. (1999a). *Building a Deliberative Democracy. An Evaluation of Two Citizens' Juries*. London: Institute for Public Policy Research.
Barnes, M. (1999b). 'Users as Citizens: Collective Action and the Local Governance of Welfare'. *Social Policy & Administration*, 33, 1.
Bennett, F. (1996). *Local People, National Voice: Speaking from Experience*. Manchester: Church Action on Poverty.
Beresford, P. and S. Croft (1995). 'It's Our Problem Too! Challenging the Exclusion of Poor People from Poverty Discourse'. *Critical Social Policy*, 15, 2/3.
Beresford, P., D. Green, R. Lister and K. Woodard (1999). *Poverty First Hand*. London: Child Poverty Action Group.
Berghman, J. (1995). 'Social Exclusion in Europe: Policy Context and Analytical Framework', in G. Room (ed.), *Beyond the Threshold*. Bristol: Policy Press.
Blair, T. (1998). *The Third Way*. London: The Fabian Society.
Bur, A., A. Stevens and L. Young (1999). *Include Us In. Participation for Social Inclusion in Europe*. Canterbury: European Institute for Social Services.
Byrne, D. (1999). *Social Exclusion*. Buckingham: Open University Press.
Clarke, M. and J. Stewart (1998). *Community Governance, Community Leadership and the New Local Government*. York: Joseph Rowntree Foundation.
Coole, D. (1996). 'Is Class a Difference that Makes a Difference?' *Radical Philosophy*, 77.
Commission on Poverty, Participation and Power (2000). *Listen Hear: The Right to be Heard*. Bristol: Policy Press.
Cornwall, A. and J. Gaventa (2000). 'Repositioning Participation in Social Policy'. *IDS Bulletin*, 31, 4.
Department for International Development (2000). *Human Rights for Poor People*. London: DfID.
Department of Social Security (1998). *New Ambitions for Our Country: A New Contract for Welfare*. London: Stationery Office.
Donnison, D. (1998). *Policies for a Just Society*. Basingstoke: Macmillan.
Donnison, D. (2000). 'Equality: The New Paradigm'. *Social Policy Association News*, February/March.
Doyal, L. and I. Gough (1991). *A Theory of Human Need*. Basingstoke: Macmillan.
Eduards, M. (1994). 'Women's Agency and Collective Action'. *Women's Studies International Forum*, 17, 2/3.
Fraser, N. (1995). 'From Redistribution to Recognition? Dilemmas of Justice in a "Post-Socialist" Age'. *New Left Review*, 212.
Fraser, N. (1996). 'Equality, Difference and Radical Democracy: the United States Feminist Debates Revisited', in D. Trend (ed.), *Radical Democracy*. New York: Routledge.
Fraser, N. (1997). *Justice Interruptus*. New York and London: Routledge.
Fraser, N. (2000). 'Rethinking Recognition'. *New Left Review*, 3.
Fraser, N. (2001). 'Recognition without Ethics'. *Theory, Culture and Society*, 18, 2/3.
Galbraith, J.K. (1992). *The Culture of Contentment*. London: Sinclair Stevenson.
Galbraith, J.K. (1996). *The Good Society*. London: Sinclair Stevenson.
Giddens, A. (1991). *Modernity and Self-Identity*. Cambridge: Polity Press.

Giddens, A. (1998). *The Third Way*. Cambridge: Polity Press.

Giddens, A. (2000). *The Third Way and its Critics*. Cambridge: Polity Press.

Gould, C. (1988). *Rethinking Democracy*, Cambridge: Cambridge University Press.

Hartsock, N. (1985). *Women, Sex and Power*. Boston: Northeastern University Press.

Holman, B. (1998). *Faith in the Poor*. Oxford: Lion.

James, S. (1992). 'The Good Enough Citizen: Citizenship and Independence', in C. Bock and S. James (eds.), *Beyond Equality and Difference*. London: Routledge.

Janoski, T. (1998). *Citizenship and Civil Society*. Cambridge: Cambridge University Press.

Levitas, R. (1998). *The Inclusive Society? Social Exclusion and New Labour*. Basingstoke: Macmillan.

Lister, R. (1996). 'Introduction: In search of the "Underclass"', in R. Lister (ed.), *Charles Murray and the Underclass. The Developing Debate*. London: Institute of Economic Affairs.

Lister, R. (2000). 'Strategies for Social Inclusion: Promoting Social Cohesion or Social Justice?', in P. Askonas and A. Stewart (eds.), *Social Inclusion. Possibilities and Tensions*. Basingstoke: Macmillan.

Lister, R. (2003). *Citizenship: Feminist Perspectives* (2nd edn). Basingstoke: Palgrave Macmillan.

Lister, R. (2004). *Poverty*. Cambridge: Polity Press.

Lister, R. and P. Beresford (2000). 'Where are "the Poor" in the Future of Poverty Research?, in J. Bradshaw and R. Sainsbury (eds.), *Researching Poverty*. Aldershot: Ashgate.

Mayo, M. (1994). *Communities and Caring*. Basingstoke: Macmillan.

Mouffe, C. (1992). 'Feminism, Citizenship and Radical Democratic Politics', in J. Butler and J.W. Scott (eds.), *Feminists Theorize the Political*. New York and London: Routledge.

Pateman, C. (1970). *Participation and Democratic Theory*. Cambridge: Cambridge University Press.

Rinaldo Seitz, V. (1998). 'Class, Gender and Resistance in the Appalachian Coalfields', in N. Naples (ed.), *Community Activism and Feminist Politics*. New York and London: Routledge.

Room, G. (1995). 'Poverty and Social Exclusion: the New European Agenda for Policy and Research', in G. Room (ed.), *Beyond the Threshold*. Bristol: Policy Press.

Russell, H. (ed.) (1996). *Speaking from Experience*. Manchester: Church Action on Poverty.

Social Exclusion Unit (2000). *National Strategy for Neighbourhood Renewal: A Framework for Consultation*. London: Social Exclusion Unit.

Stafford, B. (1997). *Partnership in Social Security. Giving Benefit Recipients a Voice*. Loughborough: Social Security Unit/Centre for Research in Social Policy.

Taylor, C. (1992). 'The Politics of Recognition', in C. Taylor and A. Gutmann, *Multi-Culturalism and 'The Politics of Recognition'*. Princeton: Princeton University Press.

Taylor, M. and A. West (2000). *Signposts to Community Development*. London: Community Development Foundation.

Trend, D. (ed.) (1996). *Radical Democracy*. New York: Routledge.

del Tufo, S. and L. Gaster (2002). *Evaluation of the Commission on Poverty, Participation and Power*. York: York Publishing Services/Joseph Rowntree Foundation.

UKCAP (1997). *Poverty and Participation*. London: UK Coalition against Poverty.

UNDP (1997). *Human Development Report 1997*. New York and Oxford: Oxford University Press.

UNDP (2000). *Human Development Report 2000*. New York and Oxford: Oxford University Press.

Williams, F. (1999). 'Good Enough Principles for Welfare'. *Journal of Social Policy*, 28, 4.

Williams, F. (2000). 'Principles of Recognition and Respect in Welfare', in G. Lewis, S. Gewirtz and J. Clarke (eds.), *Rethinking Social Policy*. London: Sage.

Wilson, R. (1995). *Social Exclusion, Social Inclusion*. Belfast: Democratic Dialogue.

Yeatman, A. (1994). *Post-modern Revisionings of the Political*. London: Routledge.

Young, I.M. (1990). *Justice and the Politics of Difference*. Oxford: Princeton University Press.

Young, I.M. (1997). 'Unruly Categories: a Critique of Nancy Fraser's Dual Systems Theory'. *New Left Review*, 222.

Young, I.M. (2000). *Inclusion and Democracy*. Oxford: Oxford University Press.

# 9
# Exclusion, Inclusion and Empowerment: Community Empowerment? Reflecting on the Lessons of Strategies to Promote Empowerment

*Majorie Mayo*

## Introduction

In the current policy context, in Britain and elsewhere, there has been increasing emphasis on community involvement and empowerment within the framework of strategies for more inclusive development/ regeneration within the mixed economy of welfare. This chapter explores the contested concept of empowerment in the current policy context, before focusing on illustrations of more (and sometimes less effectively) empowering experiences in practice. Whilst there are encouraging examples of experiences which have been recognised as empowering and inclusive by those involved themselves, counter-tendencies are also identified. As some groups are becoming more empowered others are being left out, and these increasingly margin-alised groups are disproportionately likely to be those already disad-vantaged in terms of 'race', ethnicity, gender, sexuality, age, disability, housing tenure and social class. There are implications for policies and practices at local, national and international levels.

## The contested concept of empowerment in the current policy context

Before reflecting on the lessons of strategies to promote empowerment, the concept of empowerment itself needs to be unpacked. What are the differing definitions and how do these, in their turn, relate to com-peting perspectives on power in society? As Gary Craig and I opined, at the opening of 'Community Empowerment' 'community participation'

and 'empowerment have become more vital and yet more overtly problematic than ever in the current global context' (Mayo and Craig, 1995:
1). Broadly we traced connections between neoliberal economic agendas
and their consequences on the one hand, and agendas for community
participation and empowerment – framed in terms of increasing communities' capacities for self-organisation and self-help, in the face of
increasing social needs but decreasing public welfare provision – on the
other. 'Crucially,' we argued, 'community participation and empowerment have been increasingly widely advocated, both in the North and
in the South, in the context of increasing poverty, polarization and
social exclusion' (Mayo and Craig, 1995: 3).

The results of recession and restructuring in the South were especially
lethal, with famine as an extreme form of a far wider phenomenon of
widespread hunger. Free market, neoliberal strategies which became pre-
dominant globally from the late 1970s through the 1980s and 1990s
were supposed to 'trickle down' the benefits of economic development
to the poor and the poorest. The reality, however, was that structural
adjustment programmes, as these were being advocated by the World
Bank and IMF, were failing most particularly to benefit the poorest and
most excluded, an aspect which came to be recognised by the World
Bank itself. Policies for adjustment with a 'human face' resulted from
this growing recognition that the burdens of restructuring, particularly
the burdens arising from reductions in education, health and welfare
programmes, were being borne disproportionately by the most vulnerable, including women and children (UNICEF, 1989). Strategies for
community participation and empowerment, in this global context,
related to these wider strategies for adjustment with a 'human face',
minimising the consequences of neoliberal economic and social
policies by increasing the contributions of the Non-Governmental
Organisation (NGO) sector, via voluntary sector programmes to stimulate community-based self-help. By the end of the 1990s, even the IMF
had accepted that poverty reduction had to be a core policy objective,
and there was recognition of the need for participation of the poor
themselves in poverty reduction strategies (World Bank, 1999).

Whilst welcoming the increasing acceptance and legitimacy of NGOs,
however, there are many who have also pointed to the limitations of
the NGO sector (Edwards, 2001) As. women in the South have also
argued, NGOs are no substitute for the political process, 'nor can they
bring about structural and systemic change' (Taylor, 2000: 27) on their
own. Effectively, then, despite the efforts of the NGO sector to the
contrary, the poorest and most excluded were to be 'empowered' to

cope more effectively, in face of increasing socio-economic needs and decreasing public provision.

Whilst recognising the significance of neoliberal agendas, globally, however, we emphasised the potential for more transformatory approaches. Faced with pressures towards increasing social polarisation (both locally and globally) relatively powerless individuals, groups and communities were nevertheless managing to do more than simply learning how cope, or even learning how to respond to official programmes – learning the rules of the regeneration/development game. There were also examples where they were developing strategies to empower themselves, to form their own agendas for development and regeneration in both the countries of the North and the South. And global networks such as DAWN (Development Alternatives with Women for a New Era) have been developing their capacity to challenge the ways in which processes of economic and political restructuring have been impeding the translation of international guarantees of social development (such as those agreed at the World Summit on Social Development in Copenhagen, in 1995) into real change in the lives of the women who make up 70 per cent of the poor in the South (Taylor, 2000). These examples illustrate the potential for women (and for men) to develop their own agendas, empowering themselves in ways which would be consistent with feminist approaches to citizenship as processes of active involvement (Lister, 1997).

Before exploring these more transformatory approaches to empowerment, however, the differing and competing meanings of the concept need to be unpacked, and definitions of empowerment need to be related to differing definitions of power, in their turn. Power, like icebergs, it has been suggested, is not only to be delineated in terms of what you can see, unequal relationships where one individual or group demonstrates its ability to impose its will upon another. Lukes' seminal study explored power's less visible dimensions, the second dimension of power as 'non-decision making' or the ability to draw up agendas and limit the range of alternatives to be considered and the third dimension of power as the ability to shape people's desires, to define the terms within which public debates take place – the common-sense assumptions which tend to go unchallenged (Lukes, 1974). This third dimension can be located within wider debates about ideology and hegemony, the power of dominant interests to shape the framework of debates, the generally accepted 'common-sense-view of what is and what is not thinkable (Habermas, 1976; Gramsci, 1988).

Although Lukes' study was published over a quarter of a century ago, this chapter will argue that his work continues to have particular relevance in the context of strategies to promote empowerment through participation in regeneration and development. The zero-sum notion of power which has been associated with his work has been subjected to challenges, including challenges from feminists drawing upon the work of Foucault, suggesting that power is a far more complex and pervasive phenomenon than the zero-sum approach would allow. Feminists have emphasised the importance of the 'power to' act, whether individually or collectively, rather than focusing on power in terms of hierarchy and dominance (Nelson and Wright, 1995). Lukes' analysis, this chapter will suggest, however, does have continuing relevance in relation to both types of concern. Nor does his analysis necessarily imply that socially excluded groups are totally without power themselves, the passive dupes of those with the greatest power in society, those who set agendas and frame the boundaries of 'common sense'. But Lukes' work does raise questions of continuing relevance about the nature of power and the structural and ideological barriers to empowerment which need to be challenged, if the relatively powerless are to find spaces of control. The approach being advocated here, then, would be consistent more generally with sociological perspectives which focus on the nature and processes of the interactions between individuals as social actors and the structures of the social environments and the ideological assumptions which shape, facilitate and/or constrain their actions (Giddens, 1979; Bourdieu, 1984).

Empowerment can be, and too often has been, simply taken to imply gaining power as defined in terms of Lukes' first dimension. Translated into everyday terminology, as expressed by community activists and local professionals working with them this is about learning the rules of the regeneration/development game, within the wider framework of neoliberal economic and social agendas. As respondents in a study of differing concepts of empowerment in south-east London (to be discussed in more detail subsequently) summarised this view, empowerment was about effective communication from the top down, so that individuals and groups in communities could participate effectively in consultations, feeding their views back to decision-makers (Mayo and Anastacio, 1999). The focus here was on the importance of information, knowledge and particular participation skills – learning the rules so that all could play the regeneration game together.

Empowerment, as defined in terms of Lukes' second dimension of power, takes this process further, to include gaining the power to challenge 'non-decision-making', learning how to be effective in getting community-based issues onto regeneration/development agendas. This version of empowerment included the promotion of community initiatives – developing individuals' and groups' abilities to ensure that their own priorities were placed proactively on the regeneration agenda, and that community projects were actively developed and sustained, as part of exit strategies. Although this approach to empowerment involved a more proactive role for individuals and communities, finding the space to put forward their own projects, this was typically still within the overall framework of existing (re)development agendas. Sometimes this might entail little more than determining how to spend the ten per cent or so of the budget which was being allocated for 'community chest'-type initiatives, although individuals and communities' goals and horizons could and often did broaden, and their aspirations increased, as they became more involved, over time.

The most challenging definition of empowerment takes on the implications of Lukes' third dimension of power, questioning the common-sense assumptions about the thinkable and the unthinkable, in the context of neoliberal economic and social agendas for (re)development. This definition included both of the above definitions, together with wider concepts of power, politics and active citizenship, developing the critical understanding to challenge vested interests and to promote strategies to tackle the sources of disempowerment and social exclusion (Mayo and Anastacio, 1999). Whilst this concept of empowerment was less common amongst participants in the south-east London study than the first and second types of definition, there was a significant minority – both amongst community activists and the professionals who were working with them, who did express views of this third type. And here, too, there was some evidence to suggest that participants' views had expanded, as they reflected on their experiences over time. As the following section argues, on the basis of British case studies, official agendas have in any case come to recognise the legitimacy of arguments for allowing more space for the second as well as for the first approach to empowerment – if less clearly for the third.

In summary, then, strategies for participation and empowerment have been developed within the context of developing challenging and indeed transformatory agendas. Relatively powerless individuals and groups have found spaces of control, and reflected on the lessons of their experiences for developing more extensive strategies for participation and empowerment, sometimes with – and at other times without – the support of the professionals working with them, in their communities. But these challenges have been developed within the framework of strategies as these have been developed and promoted at local, national and international levels over the past decade, strategies which have to be located within the context of increasing polarisation as a result of the predominance of neoliberal economic strategies, globally.

Far from representing an alternative to the state on the one hand and the market, on the other hand (as some protagonists of 'Communitarian' and 'Third Way' approaches have suggested) civil society has been deeply affected by these restructuring processes – with emerging evidence of processes of restructuring and polarisation within the voluntary and community sectors themselves (Fowler, 2000). As Edwards has argued, 'civil society is an arena, not a thing, and although it is often seen as the key to future progressive politics, this arena contains different and conflicting interests and agendas' (Edwards, 2001: 1). As such, civil society, then, is an arena for challenge and change. And just as these wider restructuring processes can be and have been increasingly subjected to challenges by social actors, whether individual or collective actors, so too these social actors have been and continue to be affected in their turn (Giddens, 1979; Bourdieu, 1984). These processes of restructuring raise key questions about their impact then, within the voluntary and community sectors. Who might be being most effectively empowered and included and who might be becoming even more marginalised and excluded and how are these processes of differentiation related to existing social divisions in terms of gender, ethnicity, age, disability and social class?

## The British context

Over the past decade, in Britain as elsewhere, neoliberal economic policies have been accompanied by increasing concerns with how to manage their social consequences. Across a range of social policy initiatives, the promotion of the mixed economy of welfare has been accompanied by moves towards enhanced user and community participation (from the rights of families and children in child protection work through user participation in community-based health and welfare (Beresford and Turner, 1997; Lister, 1997), to increasing emphasis on community participation and empowerment in area regeneration programmes (Brownhill and Darke, 1998). There is insufficient space here to trace the history of public policies for user participation and empowerment over these past decades. In summary, for the purposes of this chapter, the key points to note are simply these that, as a number of commentators have pointed out, these policies have contained varying implications. In the case of area regeneration programmes, tightly restrained public resources have been targeted more precisely with increasing emphasis on the promotion of private sector involvement and the marketisation of services, whilst simultaneously enhancing the active involvement of the voluntary and community sectors, particularly programme beneficiaries.

These developments have been taken forward, in a number of ways, since the election of the New Labour government in 1997. For example, in the light of criticisms of regeneration programmes, for failing to take account of the needs and aspirations of relatively disempowered groups such as black and ethnic minority communities, programmes now emphasise the need for more inclusive approaches, with considerably greater emphasis upon the importance of actively involving and empowering all sections of the local community. (The guidance for Round 6 of the Single Regeneration Budget (SRB) bids, for example, clearly indicated the central importance attached to the active involvement of all sections of local communities, including black and ethnic minority groups) (Brownhill and Darke, 1998). As the Guidance from the Government Office for London explained, 'It is crucial to ensure the active participation of local communities in the regeneration of their areas. Involving people who live and work in the area targeted by regeneration schemes right from the outset ensures that schemes are better focused on their needs and priorities. It also helps to ensure that the benefits last over the long term by encouraging ownership of the scheme and identity with the area.' As the Guidance continued, 'Bids should engage the talents and resources of the whole community including black and ethnic minority groups, young people and all sectors of the voluntary sector including faith-based voluntary organisations, the wider voluntary sector and local volunteers' (Government Office for London, 1999: 7). The more recent policy papers on Neighbourhood Renewal similarly emphasise the importance of developing support and learning strategies which facilitate the participation of all sections, with specific recognition of the importance of providing for the needs of minority groups (Neighbourhhood Renewal Unit, 2001). Although, unsurprisingly, this has not ensured that regeneration programmes have actually benefited black and ethnic minority groups in proportion to their needs, let alone ensured that the policy implications have been mainstreamed it has at least provided some benchmarks for further developments.

Whilst ethnic monitoring is required, however, there are still no

requirements for gender monitoring to ensure that regeneration programmes address the needs and aspirations of women – despite the fact
that the British government does require this of development programmes in the South (May, 1997). As May has argued, on the basis
of experience in development contexts in the South, 'it has become
increasingly clear that poverty and social exclusion affect men and
women differently, and interventions that do not reflect this difference
have in many cases reinforced structural inequalities for women. Development (and therefore also regeneration) processes must therefore
understand and take account of the needs and interests of women and
men as a matter of justice and human rights as well as efficiency' (May,
1997: 1). Without systematic monitoring, however, it is not possible to
conclude as to whether or not progress is being made in this respect,
let alone in relation to mainstreaming the policy implications. As it is,
there is evidence to suggest that women's needs are not being sufficiently systematically addressed. For example, an analysis of 121 SRB
Round 4 projects revealed that only 27 projects included childcare,
whilst the SRB Round 5 total of 143 projects included only 14 with
childcare (Bruegel, 2000). Having women representatives on the board
was not of itself, any guarantee that women's needs were being
addressed either (raising questions of representation and accountability
which are explored further in the following section).

Since the change of government in 1997, then, there has been
progress towards more inclusive and more empowering agendas.
Overall, however, programmes are still being criticised, as they have
been in the past, for being top down, rather than bottom-up, with too
much tokenism about the empowerment of the least powerful, and too
little – if any – impact being made on mainstream socio-economic policies and mainspending programmes (Taylor, 1995; Hastings et al., 1996;
Anastacio et al., 2000). There have been few examples of projects, let
alone programmes designed with and by women and ethnic minority
groups, to meet their own strategic needs as they themselves define
these (taking account of the distinctions between women's issues as
others define these for them – for example, issues relating to motherhood and child care – and issues defined by women themselves in relation to their long-term strategic interests for empowerment and social
justice). But there have been some positive examples, as the following
section suggests with encouraging examples of previously excluded
groups empowering themselves through developing effective challenges
to their exclusion.

## Evidence from case studies of the perspectives of community participants themselves and the professionals working with them in the British context

This section draws on evidence from three studies which I have worked on with colleagues, two based in the south-east and one which includes case studies from elsewhere in London, from inner city Birmingham and from Barnsley in the former mining area of the South Yorkshire coalfield. Interviews from the first of these studies (with community representatives, the professionals working with them and decision-makers in south-east London, in an area which has experienced regeneration programmes over a decade or more) have confirmed that participants understand empowerment in varying ways. Broadly, as it has already been suggested, most participants (both community activists and professionals) understand empowerment in terms of learning the rules of the regeneration game, learning the terminology/jargon, the time frames and the mechanisms for intervening to gain (limited) resources for community-based projects.

The following comments illustrate these types of views. There was evidence of considerable acceptance of the overall constraints under which local authorities were operating, and of the expectation that if the reasons for cuts in services were communicated, local people would 'accept it realistically, if they have the case put to them openly and honestly' (Mayo and Anastacio, 1999: 12). Others referred to empowerment more proactively, however, not simply in terms of improved communication from the top down, but also in terms of 'learning how to use the system' and then 'learning' how to 'play them (that is decision makers) at their own game' (Mayo and Anastacio, 1999: 13). There were references to the importance of recognising that 'local people have lots of ideas and are already doing lots of things'. In this context, empowerment was taken to mean, then, enabling local individuals and groups to obtain resources for community priorities, such as the need for more affordable childcare or particular housing improvements on housing estates. 'Empowerment is about local communities having more power and control at the local level' (Mayo and Anastacio, 1999: 13). This also involved learning the decision-makers' jargon, using the key 'buzz words' and learning how to 'go through the hoops' to access to resources.

There was considerable scepticism though about the likelihood of impacting on wider regeneration agendas, let alone affecting the course of mainstream policies and resource allocation decisions. A minority (which also included professionals as well as community activists) expressed wider notions of empowerment however, referring to their developing capacity to challenge official agendas more effectively and to develop alternative agendas, rooted in their own definitions of needs and priorities. As one community activist expressed this, she had 'gained a better understanding of the real world and the political game' – that is, the structural constraints – and how to find the space to develop alternative agendas effectively (Mayo and Anastacio, 1999: 14). As one of the professionals expressed this, it was about education for active citizenship, learning about 'who has power and about how power can be taken, who is excluded and why and how this can be challenged' (Mayo and Anastacio, 1999, pp. 14–15).

Evidence from the second study (the case studies in four areas – two in London, one in Birmingham and one in the south Yorkshire former coalfields area) confirms that despite major criticisms and very considerable scepticism about official programmes to promote participation, empowerment and social inclusion, there have nevertheless been encouraging examples of positive outcomes. Over time, individuals and groups have become knowledgeable and skilled in learning the rules of the regeneration game, and some have gone on to frame their own agendas and to develop their own projects and programmes, challenging their initial exclusion and building solidarity with other previously excluded groups and organisations.

## Examples which have been particularly striking

### Issues of gender and ethnicity: The Bangladeshi Youth Forum, Aston/Newtown, Birmingham

Aston/Newtown is a small inner city area just north of the centre of Birmingham, Britain's second city. The area was selected for regeneration (via a 'City Challenge programme' of £37.5 million) in 1993, and this was followed by a smaller (Single Regeneration Bid) programme, focusing particularly on capacity-building and training with a strong emphasis upon tackling racism. The fact that issues of race and racism were so firmly on the current regeneration agenda can be explained, at least in part, as resulting from successful challenges to previous agendas. Young Bangladeshis, young women as well as young men, have played key roles in these processes of challenge.

The first regeneration programme, the City Challenge, focused on the need for improvements in public housing, as well as the need to tackle other economic and social issues. The focus on public sector housing was a key factor in defining the boundaries of City Challenge. Only these boundaries effectively excluded those who had been outside public housing in the first place, including the Bangladeshi community which tended to be located within the private housing sector, just outside the City Challenge area.

The Bangladeshi community organised to challenge their initial effective exclusion. In particular, the Bangladeshi Youth Forum (BYF) which had already been established by young Bangladeshi people in the area to provide services to young Bangladeshi people, took up the challenge. The BYF needed resources to enable them to develop the services which they were already providing – services such as youth clubs, social activities and training, including information technology training. With support from key activists within the Bangladeshi community, as well as from particular local community workers, the BYF challenged their effective exclusion from City Challenge, and by dint of their sheer determination they made their case convincingly. As a BYF activist commented, 'their activities spoke for themselves' (Anastacio et al., 2000: 9). Eventually, BYF obtained space within the City Challenge offices and gained access to City Challenge resources, running a series of programmes to meet the needs of young Bangladeshis as they themselves defined these. Since then BYF has become a partner in the voluntary sector-led SRB programme which has succeeded City Challenge. They have a thriving centre which includes young women as well as young men at every level from the management committee through to the volunteers and centre users.

BYF's success has been attributed to their determination, coupled with strong leadership. In developing this proficiency, they have acknowledged their debts, both to community activists within their own community and to professionals outside it. The issue of gender has been a continuing theme here. Young Bangladeshi women have determinedly rejected stereotypes of themselves as passive victims, strongly asserting their own views and interests and refusing to accept that older men in their community should have the right to represent their interests or speak on their behalf. As the following section will suggest, however, they have had to contend with powerful pressures, both within their community and outside it, including pressures from decision-makers and professionals who espouse the causes of equal opportunities and empowerment in principle – but do not necessarily recognise the significance of differences of interest and perspective within as well as between different ethnic groups within communities of locality. Differences of gender were key in this case, as well as differences of ethnicity and young Bangladeshi women were not prepared to have these differences submerged, or to allow their interests to be (mis)represented by older Bangladeshi men (the 'beards', as they described them).

## Issues of gender, ethnicity and class in north London

The north London case study provided further illustrations of the interrelationships between gender, ethnicity and social class. Kings Cross is a strategic development site for redevelopment on a major scale, with potentially international dimensions (linked to a long-stalled proposal for a Channel Tunnel rail link). Given its central and strategic location, Kings Cross has attracted interest from property developers and there have been significantly different views on how the area should be developed, in whose interests, and taking account of whose needs, the interests of private developers, local residents and/or the homeless who tend to congregate around major transport interchanges in the capital city?

The chief executive of the first regeneration partnership (which was subjected to a number of criticisms for failing to involve local people effectively) was a woman and so was her successor, who was welcomed for being more committed to working in partnership with the local community. There were women representatives too, on the partnership board, as well as women involved as community activists and local professionals. Differences according to gender alone do not seem to provide adequate explanations in this context. The issues in Kings Cross are more readily understandable when linked to differences of interest in relation to class, as well as to ethnicity and housing tenure. There were strong and determined women, fighting to have their areas included, with programmes to meet their needs as local tenants and residents defined these themselves. And there were examples of professionals who were committed to working to support them, just as there were examples of decision-makers and professionals whose perspective on the area's needs were closer to the perspectives of private property developers.

In addition to the determination which was demonstrated by working-class women (and men) to develop their own regeneration agendas, there were also examples of positive and empowering professional practice, in the neighbouring area of west Euston. Here the Women's Design Service developed the 'Women and Regeneration Project', working with Somali, Bangladeshi and white British communities to enable them to develop their own priorities for regeneration. The Women's Design Service took particular care to ensure that all women's voices were heard and that all their concerns including concerns about safety for themselves and their children were fully represented (particularly important in an area which had been affected by racial harassment and abuse) (Women's Design Service, 1999).

More generally, however, there were questions about how far either women or men had been able to impact upon the strategic issues, or whether as one officer reflected 'People had most say on the smaller projects' – 'but nothing on the big issues' as a community representative from the same area commented (Anastacio et al., 2000: 31). On the issue of social housing, for example, one of the women community activists reflected that whilst improvements to the existing stock were still on the agenda, housing more generally 'is off the agenda' (Anastacio et al., 2000: 32)

### Other examples of empowering practice

There is not the space here to develop the discussion of other examples of empowering practice, examples where groups and individuals have found the space to develop their own agendas for social inclusion and social justice. One of the most striking was the case of Lewisham Young People's Participation Project, for instance, a project to promote the involvement of young people in Lewisham, south-east London. These young people had been labelled as 'disaffected, hard to reach'. Prejudices and negative stereotypes about these young people – including young black women as well as young black men – were rife, not only amongst decision-makers, but also amongst adults in their own communities.

Over a five-year period, youth workers supported groups of young people to develop their own approaches to participation, resulting amongst other outcomes in a major event which the young people themselves ran in February 2000. As one of the youth workers commented, 'without doubt, this is one of the most exciting pieces of youth work I've seen in a decade' (Back et al., 2000: 8). (The contribution of the youth workers was centrally important, supporting, encouraging and enabling the young people to organise in ways of which many would not, initially, have believed themselves capable.) The young people themselves were for the most part extremely enthusiastic, reflecting upon how they had gained in knowledge, skills and confidence as they had been involved in 'making things happen' . . . speaking up about 'the things we want to see changed' (Back et al., 2000: 14). The young people's reservations were mostly around the question of how far adult decision-makers were genuinely prepared to listen. As one young black woman put this, 'Councillors would say they are going to do something and [subsequently] push it to the back of their heads' (Back et al., 2000: 16).

There are key issues to be addressed here, in the programmes for education for citizenship which are currently being developed in schools in this area and beyond. The south-east London experiences are far from being untypical and there is a developing literature on strategies and successful practices to promote the empowerment of young people as active citizens, both in Britain and beyond, internationally (for a review of this literature, see Mayo, 2001).

In addition to such encouraging examples of participation and empowerment within groups and communities coalitions and networks of solidarity between different groups and organisations have also been developing. For instance, in Birmingham the Residents Association Information Link (RAIL) developed as a forum as a way of 'informing each other and developing solidarity' (Anastacio et al., 2000: 29). RAIL enabled its members to run their own projects as well as working together, advocating and campaigning on key policy issues. Here, too, RAIL enjoyed excellent professional support, with its own community worker, working to RAIL's own agenda. In New Cross, south-east London, there are comparable examples of the development of forums, arising out of the experiences of participation in regeneration programmes. Here too, there are now examples of community-led regeneration programmes, including a programme to develop active citizenship and a programme to build a community development trust.

Whilst previous experiences of cooperation have clearly been significant, the development of solidarity was not to be assumed, though. Barnsley, for example, had a strong tradition of collective working, during the 1984–85 miners' strike. These experiences clearly had continuing resonance. Despite the mobilisation of women during this period (and the key role played by miners' wives groups) some women (and some men) reflected that this impetus had not necessarily been taken forward. As one woman commented: 'It's very male-dominated . . . it's got a long way to go' despite the 'huge impact of the miners' strike' (unpublished interview). 'There's a background of voluntary and community work being done by women' commented another interviewee but 'there no longer seems to be a women's agenda' (unpublished interview). Despite their community activism women were still being considered as disproportionately likely to be amongst the excluded, along with young people. (There were very few black and ethnic minority groups in the area so these groups were less likely to be identified as excluded in this context, although they certainly were identified as such in London and Birmingham.)

Despite these caveats, there have been some very positive examples though, illustrations of the potential for empowerment, as defined in its fullest and most transformatory terms. Whilst celebrating these achievements, it is also relevant to recognise, too, that in addition to the energy and determination of the local participants there were other factors which contributed to these favourable outcomes. These factors included a more favourable policy climate, generally (local authorities being required to demonstrate that local people, including black and ethnic minority groups, have been involved in regeneration bids). Although there were no formal requirements for gender impact assessment, in terms of national policy, in some areas there were also pressures on groups to demonstrate that women were involved before receiving funding – a factor that seemed to have some relevance in the case of one of the more established/traditional Asian organisations in Birmingham, for example. In addition, there was also evidence that some of these more successful challenges had been supported by local professionals (including community and youth workers and community education workers). The contribution of these professionals had been valued, in particular, because these professionals had been working in empowering ways, acting as facilitators to enable the groups and organisations to develop their own agendas effectively and to build solidarity with groups and organisations with common interests and concerns.

## More problematic outcomes

More negatively, however, there was evidence that programmes to promote participation and empowerment were in some cases reinforcing existing divisions, leading to further polarisation. Communities are diverse rather than heterogeneous. Despite this well-recognised fact, public interventions still too often fail to take account of diversity and difference, in terms of factors such as class/occupation/lack of paid occupation, ethnicity/race, gender, age and disability. This applies in both Northern regeneration and Southern development contexts (Gujit and Shah, 1998). Officials may perhaps tend to imagine a simpler reality, in which a few voices can be taken to represent the range of diverse interests within localities. But such failures to address diversity may effectively reinforce differential outcomes.

The case studies provided a range of illustrations of these negative processes. Individuals were being taken up by officialdom and turned into 'community stars' – and then subjected to pressures – sometimes literally unbearable pressures – from all sides. Some 'community stars' (or community 'godfathers' and 'godmothers' as they have also been called) became increasingly detached from those they were supposed to be representing. Others became increasingly marginalised. (There were cases of individuals experiencing breakdowns, personally, as a result of these pressures.)

'Community stars' can also be unmade, especially if they turn out to raise challenging issues. (At this point officials may seek to undermine them by simply labelling them as 'unrepresentative'.) As one community activist commented, in his/her view the local authority and the private developers they were working with wanted community representatives who were 'solid establishment figures, people who will not under any circumstances rock the boat' (Anastacio et al., 2000: 24). Those who were defined as not being 'yes people' were being effectively excluded from key discussions, it was widely believed, in this area, at that point in the regeneration process.

Overall, these processes can lead to further polarisation in the community sector, as some individuals and some groups become increasingly empowered and others become even further marginalised and excluded. To some considerable extent the community sector is being restructured and professionalised. The emergence of community-led regeneration programmes, whilst evidence of empowerment in some respects, raises continuing issues, including issues about the boundaries between the voluntary and community sectors themselves, and the boundaries between paid and unpaid efforts in the community. Local community activists and professionals were well aware of these tensions and of the dilemmas inherent in community representation and accountability more generally. Both expressed particular concerns about the further marginalisation of black and ethnic minority groups, refugees and asylum seekers, homeless people, young people more generally and people with disabilities.

The evidence is not as straightforward in terms of how this relates to gender, however. As feminists, including socialist feminists, have been arguing, gender oppression needs to be understood in the context of other forms of oppression and discrimination, particularly those relating to class and ethnicity (Skeggs, 1997). On the basis of the evidence from the case studies, there were examples of women who were effectively taking up their concerns at decision-making and professional levels as well as at the level of community representatives. To understand these issues around polarisation within the community sector, as they affect women, gender has to be related to both ethnicity and class. The previous examples illustrate these processes of marginalisation and exclusion together with some of the challenges which were being effectively posed to them – for example, the Bangladeshi young women in Birmingham, the tenants in London and the young black women and men in Lewisham. Other examples illustrate some of the complexities of these interrelationships, suggesting that there is no automatic connection between experiences of mobilisation in one sphere and the propensity to continue to mobilise in another, (as in the case of Barnsley former miners' wives, some but by no means all of whom were continuing to be active in their communities).

Learning also emerges as a key outcome of participation in the informal sector. This finding is consistent with the findings of other studies (McGivney, 1999) with particular implications for those women who are more likely to become involved in informal than formal activities, at least in the first instance. This learning can be reinforced and valued in ways that promote further learning (including progression to more formal learning situations) and to empowerment. This positive potential has already emerged powerfully from another study (the third case study referred to in this chapter) evaluating a project to promote access to higher education for previously excluded groups via action learning in the community. Action Learning in the Community (the ALIC project) in south-east London has already demonstrated the importance of building on informal learning in the community sector as a mechanism for facilitating the progression of adults who have experienced long-term unemployment – into higher education and enhanced employability. Whilst celebrating the achievements of the participants (the majority of whom have so far been women, including black and ethnic minority women) however, ALIC also raises a number of questions.

There are often implicit assumptions, for example about pathways for women, assumptions that can reinforce existing gender stereotypes. Women can be encouraged to take up training opportunities in the caring services and childcare in particular. Whilst this may indeed be what many women are seeking (building on existing knowledge, skills and confidence) ALIC has ensured that women are also offered other choices. In the first year, for example, as a result of being encouraged to test out wider possibilities, there were examples of participants then opting for design and photography. In addition, ALIC has also been raising key issues about the need for wider policy changes. In particular, the welfare benefits system, together with student fees and the abolition of student grants, represents a major and continuing barrier for widening access, as the government is increasingly coming to recognise (Collymore and Mayo, 2000). There is not the space here to develop the discussion of the implications, although they have key significance for the development of more inclusive strategies for lifelong learning and active citizenship.

## Finding ways forward

The need for wider policy changes emerges as central, if participation for empowerment is to be more than tokenistic for socially excluded groups. Whether these are strategies for lifelong learning and active citizenship, or whether these are strategies for regeneration and development, there are implications for the surrounding framework of social policies, from the welfare benefits system, through education and training policies, health, housing, planning and economic development. If Luke's third dimension of power is indeed to be addressed via transformative strategies for empowerment, there are implications at local, regional and national levels and beyond, taking account of the global policy issues which were raised at the beginning of this chapter.

The wider the policy arena, however, the more problematic the issues around representation and accountability. As the discussion of the British case studies has suggested, the achievement of democratic representation and accountability has proved challenging enough, at the local level. Addressing the democratic deficit effectively at national level continues to represent further challenges. Despite these limitations, though, there are examples of transformative practice in the British context, including examples where professional support has been both effectively supportive and empowering.

Whilst potentially more problematic still, at the global level, the case of DAWN illustrates a possible way forward for feminists concerned to challenge the global as well as the local causes of their oppression. As DAWN's publication on the Marketisation of Governance argues, on the basis of critical analysis, rooted in the experience of women, 'DAWN seeks to articulate a vision of genuine political restructuring to achieve the social transformation necessary for the realisation of equitable, environmentally-sustainable, and gender-just development' (DAWN, 2000).

## References

Anastacio, J. et al. (2000). *Reflecting Realities: Participants' Perspectives on Integrated Communities and Sustainable Regeneration*. Bristol: Policy Press.
Back, L. et al. (2000). *A Voice for Young People: An Evaluation of the Lewisham Youth*

*Participation Project.* Occasional Paper, Centre for Urban and Community Research, Goldsmiths College, University of London.

Beresford, P. and M. Turner (1997). *It's Our Welfare.* London: National Institute of Social Work.

Bourdieu, P. (1984). *Distinction.* London: Routledge and Kegan Paul.

Brownhill, S. and J. Darke (1998). *Rich Mix: Inclusive Strategies for Urban Regeneration.* Bristol: Policy Press.

Bruegel, I. (2000). 'Gender Issues in Regeneration Partnerships'. Unpublished paper delivered to LEPU Seminar on Partnerships, 23 May 2000, South Bank University, London.

Collymore, X. and M. Mayo (2000). 'Widening Participation through Action Learning in the Community', in J. Thompson (ed.), *Widening Participation and Lifelong Learning in Higher Education.* Leicester: National Institute of Adult Continuing Education.

Edwards, M. (2001). 'Introduction', in M. Edwards and J. Gaventa (eds.), *Global Citizen Action.* London: Earthscan.

Elsdon, K. et al. (1995). *Voluntary Organisations: Citizenship, Learning and Change.* Leicester: NIACE.

Fowler, A. (2000). *Civil Society, NGDOs and Social Development: Changing the Rules of the Game.* Geneva: UNRISD.

Giddens, A. (1979). *Central Problems in Social Theory.* London: Macmillan.

Government Office for London (1999). *Single Regeneration Budget Round 6 Bidding Guidance; A Guide for Partnerships in London.* London: Government Office for London.

Gramsci, A. (1988). *A Gramsci Reader* (edited by D. Forgacs). London: Lawrence and Wishart.

Gujit, I. and M. Shah (eds.) (1998). *The Myth of Community: Gender Issues in Participatory Development.* London: Intermediate Technology.

Habermas, J. (1976). *Legitimation Crisis.* London: Heinemann.

Hastings, A. et al. (1996). *Less than Equal? Community Organisations and Estate Regeneration.* Bristol: Policy Press.

Lister, R. (1997). *Citizenship: Feminist Perspectives.* London: Macmillan.

Lukes, S. (1974). *Power.* London: Macmillan.

May, N. (1997). *Challenging Assumptions: Gender Issues in Urban Regeneration.* York: Joseph Rowntree Foundation.

Mayo, M. (2001). 'Children and Young People's Participation in Development in the South and in Urban Regeneration in the North'. *Progress in Development Studies*, 1, 4.

Mayo, M. and J. Anastacio (1999). 'Welfare Models and Approaches to Empowerment'. *Policy Studies*, 1.

Mayo, M. and G. Craig (1995). 'Community Participation and Empowerment: the Human Face of Structural Adjustment or Tools for Democratic Transformation', in G. Craig and M. Mayo (eds.), *Community Empowerment.* London: Zed Books.

McGivney, V. (1999). *Informal Learning in the Community.* Leicester: NIACE.

Neighbourhood Renewal Unit (2001). *A Learning and Development Strategy for Neighbourhood Renewal; A Discussion Paper.* London: Neighbourhood Renewal Unit.

Nelson, N. and S. Wright (1995). 'Participation and Power', in N. Nelson and

S. Wright (eds.), *Power and Participatory Development*. London: Intermediate Technology Publications.

Skeggs, B. (1997). *Formations of Class and Gender*. London: Sage.

Taylor, M. (1995). *Unleashing the Potential*. York: Joseph Rowntree Foundation.

Taylor, V. (2000). *Marketisation or Governance*. Cape Town: SADEP, University of Cape Town.

UNDP (1999). *Human Development Report 1999*. Oxford: Oxford University Press.

UNICEF (1989). *The State of the World's Children*. Oxford: Oxford University Press.

Women's Design Service (1999). *West Euston Neighbourhood Health and Safety Audit*. London: Women's Design Service.

World Bank (1999). *Entering the 21st Century*. Washington, DC: World Bank.

# 10
# Redefining Citizenship: Community, Civil Society and Adult Learning

*Pauline McClenaghan*

## Introduction

The last two decades have seen an extraordinary revival of interest in a number of core concepts in economic, social and political thought. Pivotal among these is the concept 'community'. In economics, as part of the attempts to incorporate socio-cultural variables into economic theory, 'community', as an expression of norms and values associated with social ties and networks, has been redefined as *social capital* and accorded important relevance in explanations of variations in economic development and has been identified in 'public choice' economics and new public sector management theories as the appropriate site for socially oriented 'not-for-profit' economic activity, now conceptualised as the *social economy*. In sociological theory 'community', linked to processes of social integration, fragmentation and social closure (expressed as *social inclusion/exclusion*), is increasingly replacing class as a conceptual tool for the analysis of inequality, solidarity and social and political identity. In political science 'community', associated with new conceptualisations of *citizenship*, is displacing 'the social' as the focus of public sector and administrative reform and as the 'key zone, target and objective of strategies of government' (Rose, 1996). In philosophical thought 'community', as an important facet of reconstituted notions of *civil society* (with a special relationship to or located within the 'life-world'), is increasingly deemed to have a key role in the 'reflexive continuation of the democratic revolution' (Cohen and Arato, 1992); and in learning and education theory 'community' as a collection of cultural practices or networks, expressed in the concept *lifelong learning*, has become an important conceptual tool for analytical research into learning identities and processes and, in particular *social learning processes*, deemed necessary to economic and social inclusion and democratic participation.

The re-emergence of the concept of 'community' in these different academic fields reflects the evolution over the last two decades or more of what has become an increasingly unified interdisciplinary discourse encompassing a broad range of ideological and theoretical perspectives yet generating similar sets of prescriptions for a wide range of social ills. Cohen and Arato go so far as to suggest that we are 'on the threshold of another great transformation of the self-understanding of modern societies', a threshold to which we have been pushed, they suggest, by the disintegration of the old hegemonic paradigms of pluralistic industrialism and Marxism and 'the certainties and guarantees that went with them' (1992: 1); and by implication the philosophical and scientific traditions and practices which have informed these opposing perspectives. However accurate these broad assertions may be, we are undoubtedly living in an era of considerable socio-economic transformation and politico-institutional change. In virtually every society in the industrial world, economic globalisation, informationalism and the growing influence of both supranational institutions and regional economic and political bodies (effectively new forms of international and local corporatism) have been articulated with neo-liberal policies of privatisation, deregulation and structural change in modes of welfare and social service provision; processes which are in many societies restructuring the relationship between the market, civil society and the state, changing the balance between the public and private spheres, transforming the nature and form of 'political community' and creating, some would argue, 'new forms of governance and politics both within states and beyond their boundaries' (Held, 2000: 394).

But the ideas that underpin this new discourse are far from new. They address questions that have long been central to social theory, regarding the reconciliation of the interests of the collectivity (the common good) with individual freedoms and the squaring of justice and solidarity, of the public and private spheres, of particularlism and universalism and of individual and group autonomy with social integration and social cohesion. By linking individual identity, self-consciousness, social competence, self-esteem and social integration, through localised and particularistic solidarity mechanisms, to higher level tiers of social action, the discourse seeks to link, in apparently new ways, the private world of the individual, family and voluntary association to the more public spheres of social and economic organisation, citizenship and governance. As such it finds advocates and proponents in a broad spectrum of opinion. For some it represents a renewed awareness of the salience of traditional social and family values, responsibilities and ties, a moral justification of the 'free market' economy balanced by civic virtue, and a rationale for privatised and voluntarist forms of social care and for limiting or dismantling state intervention and bureaucracy in the name of democratic politics and good government. While, at the other end of the spectrum, it is a discourse about social transformation, emancipation, 'developmental citizenship', empowerment, equality, social justice and democratisation, the building of alternative and more effective ways of meeting economic and social need or of socially re-embedding the marketised economy or opening it up to social influences.

The discourse also has its critics, of course, both as a general paradigm and in terms of its constituent parts. Some see it as a crude attempt to manufacture a new social consensus (Hoggett, 1997) inflated into a social theory built around methodological approaches that have long infused, with only limited success, developmental strategies in the Third World and voluntarist and professional practice in social problem management in the United States and elsewhere. Others see it as the colonisation of social theory by neoclassical economics, the triumph of methodical individualism over collectivism (Fine, 2001), expressed in a discourse in which the intangible 'assets' of values, networks and relationships have been economised (social capital), where socialised public goods are being recommodified (the social economy), in which the structural processes generating class inequalities and unemployment have been individualised and personalised (social exclusion), in which solidarity is localised and particularised (civil society), where citizenship has become conditional and in which adult education and collective learning are being de-radicalised, de-theorised and instrumentalised in the interests of a flexible, segmented and gendered labour market and to legitimise and serve new public management technologies and neo-state governance strategies. For critics and proponents alike adult learning and education are central to the discourse, either as important vehicles for the generation of subjectivities necessary to the maintenance and reproduction of the new consensus it seeks to define, or as vital elements of integrationist and/or empowering and democratising processes arising from civic action and the social capital it is assumed to generate.

Drawing on insights gained from 15 years of research, teaching and consultancy experience related to the provision of community development adult education at the University of Ulster, this analysis critically assesses the democratising potential of civil society engagement in the context of the new social field currently being constituted through the discourse of active citizenship and community participation and evaluates the role of community development education in the formation of a habitus for what is an expanding but highly structured social field wherein the concept 'community' has central place.

## Reimagining the public sphere

Just as in the nineteenth century, another period of immense economic and social transformation when the concept of community held pivotal importance in social thought, so too at the beginning of the twenty-first century has community emerged as a unit idea in social and political analysis. In its archetypal form it expresses relationships based on personal intimacy, solidarity, social cohesion and moral commitment in contrast to those governed by competition, utility or contractual assent – that is, the relationships of the market (Nisbet, 1976). In its twenty-first-century guise the concept still incorporates the essential characteristics of mutuality, reciprocity and solidarity, but unlike its nineteenth-century counterpart the 'sense of community' in the contemporary moment has been detached from a 'sense of place' (Hoggett, 1997). The separation of community from market processes is also now more ambivalent, and relations between community, the state and the political sphere, in contradictory fashion, have become at once closer and more distanced.

Unlike traditional nineteenth-century communities, in late modernity human individuals are members of a multiplicity of overlapping communities and to a certain extent political jurisdictions, some of which are ascriptive but many of which are elective and intentional, organisational or action- or practice-based or reflective of some kind of aesthetic attachment or appreciation. Hence in a highly individualised, fragmented and de-traditionalised social world, characterised by plurality, ephermerality, indeterminacy, uncertainty and risk, 'community' is now understood to express a complex multiplicity of social spaces in which processes of human bonding and identity formation are persistently re-enacted, reconstructed and renewed; bonding and deeply complex bridging and integration processes which, in a highly fragmented social order, provide biographical coherence and new forms of social solidarity which have the potential, some theorists suggest, to 'generate and ground moral judgement and to provide a source of inspiration for forms of normative and moral commitment' (Frazer and

Lacey, 1993); commitments which might serve as a basis for more fully rationale, participative and associative forms of democratic governance.

Yet ironically, as new forms of community emerge and are accorded a privileged role in the 'deeper democratisation of late modern societies' (Hall, 1995), the de-socialisation of the economy has bundled risk and uncertainty downwards onto the most vulnerable – the poor, the socially disadvantaged, the underprivileged, the undereducated, the lower or inappropriately skilled, the less socially or culturally adaptive, the victims of discrimination and negative societal ascription – who, as a result of the distributional and relational dimensions of social inequality, find themselves locked into place more and more; a place of restricted opportunities and limited capacities for engagement in both the social and market economy, where identity and belonging are *given* rather than matters of *choice* and where propensities 'to be engaged in activities which diminish rather than amplify local *social capital formation*' (my emphasis) (deemed essential to economic survival in a globally competitive world) are understood to be inter-generationally reproduced (Bahalla and Lapeyre, 1999).

In this context the rediscovery of community in the contemporary moment reflects concerns over the possible anomic tendencies of a social order based entirely on 'the entrepreneurship of self' implied in marketised individualism and neo-liberalism, and the inherent empirical assumption in both that it is possible and appropriate to base virtually all social relations on the autonomous consumer's right of choice in the market place; and more especially so in societies still plagued by the vestiges of old social inequalities and increasingly faced with the social consequences of new, and now less socially and politically manageable, forms of social polarisation and social closure. The function of 'community' in current Western discourse, therefore, represents a 'quest for moral integration' (Kildal, 1999); for the reconstruction of 'a new long-term social consensus' (European Commission, 1994: 19) based on values and virtues underpinning new conceptualisations of citizenship embodying a tacit social contract based on responsibility and reciprocity rather than as 'a passive legal status' defined by entitlements and rights.

Within this emerging discourse 'the responsibility frame occupies the central place vacated by rights and justice' (Strydom, 1999) in a global context in which the ever-widening circulation of the symbolic media of exchange is gradually undermining collectivist and quasi-collectivist societal responses to human need. But market efficiency also requires a semblance of social and political integration and stability that, in current political discourse, is deemed to be achievable *without* socially embedded forms of regulation and intervention, understood to inhibit productivity and international competitiveness. Social cohesion, therefore, necessitates the generation of new *less passive and more active* 'collective solidarity mechanisms' (EU Commission, 1994: 15) capable of generating a broad social consensus and of integrating detached individuals and groups, including those outside the paid labour force, by encouraging all 'societal stakeholders' to recognise their communal responsibilities. Every citizen is exhorted to practise 'neighbourhood solidarity' (1994: 16) which will empower individuals and involve them as citizens, providing the basis for the evolution of more participatory and democratic forms of governance, preferable to both bureaucratic modes of welfarism and to the more recent, consumer-driven framework of new right marketisation. Community, in this context,

> implies a recognition of interdependence but not overweening government power. It accepts that we are better equipped to meet the forces of change and insecurity through working together. It provides a basis for the elements of our character that are co-operative as well as competitive, as part of a more enlightened view of self-interest.
>
> (Blair, 1995)

– a utilitarian and individualised notion of the social where altruism and solidarity have been reduced to strategies for self-advantage and 'sociality to the borderline of imagined communities' (Jansen et al., 1998: 90); a perspective that ignores class-based and other collective forms of interest, inequality, social organisation and conflict in favour of a form of 'voluntarist moralism' assumed to have the capacity simultaneously to enhance economic efficiency and open market forces to social influences through the promotion of community values, the generation of social capital and the engendering of active citizenship in a mixed economy of care.

> The only effective answer . . . is a mixture of social crusading by those 'haves' who care and the empowerment of the 'have nots'. That can best be achieved by adequately funded and committed voluntary associations working in partnership with the poor and excluded.
>
> (Hirst, 1994: 10)

Community action, as an expression of active citizenship, becomes, therefore, a desirable social asset and the quality of a democracy is no longer to be determined by the 'justice of its basic structures', but by the 'qualities of its citizens' (Kildal, 1999). Citizenship thus acquires a conditional status; conditional on the individual's capacity to fulfil the obligations associated with it and on his/her willingness to do so. Learning and socialisation, therefore, acquire even greater significance since the economic and political potential of civic and community action rests on the dispositions and capacities – the habitus – of an active, participative and socially and morally committed citizenry, with communicative and other forms of competence.

## Imagined communities: from civil society to community development

It is no coincidence that the emergence of community in political discourse, and as the focus of new governance strategies, has been paralleled by the (re)emergence of the concept 'civil society' in social and political thought. Civil society, defined as a distinct social sphere of self-organising, self-governing autonomous groups, separated from the state and in most analyses now also the formal mainstream economy, has become another key concept in the analysis of contemporary society and its possible futures. Its revival has been associated particularly but not exclusively with critical theory, post-Marxist, post-feminist, civic republican and communitarian perspectives. Originally focused on new social movements, the concept has more recently come to include virtually all forms of autonomous groupings outside the spheres of the state and the economy, with increasing emphasis being placed on community and voluntary sector organisations (the 'third' or 'non-profit' sector), as social and welfare policies in many Western societies shift away (or further away) from universalistic and redistributive forms in the direction of moral authoritarian welfare regimes involving mixed, targeted and conditional forms of provision wherein interventions aimed at 'communities of fate', the unemployed, the poor and the socially and geographically disadvantaged or marginalised are increasingly being resourced and administered through civil society entities.

These attempts to redraft and re-envisage the universalist welfare state, which had previously subordinated the capitalist market to social democracy's tenets of social justice, reflect in part the interrogation of the politics of redistribution by the particularisms associated with the sub-politics of recognition and identity and new social movements' concerns regarding the marginalisation from social citizenship of particular groups on the basis of gender, ethnicity, social disadvantage or individual impairment; interrogations expressed through a groundswell of grassroots activism and organisation based on efforts to extend the liberal philosophy of rights and justice to include notions of identity, personal and group development, autonomy and empowerment; efforts that have their roots in the collectivist ethos of the postwar welfare state itself. But other more influential and powerful challenges to universalist welfarism have since entered into civil society discourse, neo-conservative elements, reasserting the primacy of the market, the communitarian aspects of social obligation and the alleged ineffectiveness and inefficiency of the welfare state associated with its propensity to constrain and distort the 'economically sound' functioning of market and wage systems, its alleged tendency to over-supply public goods, to foster passivity and dependency in client groups and to encourage long-term distributive coalitions between clients and 'rent-seeking' politicians and state-employed professionals and bureaucrats motivated to expand their resources and patronage and to respond to the demands of lobbying organisations and groups.

These challenges and other problems facing welfare states, including longevity, falling birth rates, advances in medical care, unemployment, falling taxes, the greater interdependence of national economies, problems arising as a result of market integration, regime competition and engagement in increasingly complex multi-centred forms of policy-making (in the EU countries especially) and tensions arising from state efforts to deal with and take advantage of globalised and networked forms of accumulation, have resulted in a remarkable degree of policy convergence on the desirability of encouraging civil society and 'bottom-up' community participation in welfarism, social problem management, labour market restructuring, urban and rural regeneration and regional economic development, through a mixture of consultation, subcontracting, synergetic partnerships, localised and neighbourhood initiatives, community education, capacity-building and empowerment programmes and, in the case of certain social groups, enforced inclusion through financial and/or moral compulsion. The restructuring of welfare states along these lines and the greater emphasis now being placed on community and grassroots participation in social policy implementation and economic regeneration has brought community development into the policy framework in many European societies, in some cases for the first time, in others as the resurrection or extension of earlier interventionist methodologies and practices reconstituted in the context of new policy and governance paradigms; variations reflecting the different 'states of welfare' generated by the vernacular articulation of modernisation processes and political traditions and cultures in different societies, processes which have structured the social space in which civic activity has evolved and the manner in which it is socially and culturally understood.

As a specific cluster of related concepts, processes, principles, values and practices, community development also has a long but relatively conceptually consistent history; a history embedded in and related to the processes and consequences of modernity. Its origins can also be traced back to the nineteenth century, to the reform and settlement movements in Britain and the United States, particularly the Educational Settlements Association and the Federation of Residential Settlements, both of which represented endeavours in adult education aimed at the socio-economic integration of emerging industrial working classes, immigrant populations and, in the United States, 'pre-modern' indigenous socio-cultural groups. In postwar conditions it gradually formed into a distinct discourse within the context of emerging contradictions in the social regulation of mature capitalism and in Western interventions in post-colonial societies (Batten, 1957), where it was articulated as *a social learning and educative process* which would establish values and relationships, forms of interaction and solidarity underpinning a transition from kinship to community to associational forms of integration and identity, deemed necessary preconditions for economic growth and development; a form of intervention which expanded rapidly in developing countries in the 1950s only to decline as quickly in the early 1960s in the face of widespread disillusionment as projects failed to produce expected economic outcomes (Holdcroft, 1982).

While Western financial support for community development in Third World countries declined in the 1960s, it continued domestically as a facet of social service provision in the United States, Britain, Ireland and the Netherlands. Within the context of the liberal and minimalist welfare system in the United States, it came to be closely associated with the evolution of the public service professions of social work, adult education and public health, re-theorised with the 'rediscovery of poverty' in the 1970s, and representing a specific methodological approach and set of practices, based on 'community organising and community building' (Brager and Specht, 1973; Minkler, 1998) which were, and continue to be, adopted in public, professional and voluntarist and charitable interventions aimed at communities of the poor and the socially disadvantaged.

In the Republic of Ireland, the social role of the Catholic Church ensured the hegemony of a political discourse which emphasised 'traditional community and family values' and minimal state intervention in the private sphere, allowing for the evolution of a significant community and voluntary sector, theorised and legitimated by subsidiarity principles derived from Catholic social ethics, which later came to be secularised and more broadly popularised by the European Union, which formally endorsed community development at the Council of Europe in 1989. While the impact of European Union Poverty and other programmes on the size and structure of the community and voluntary sector in Ireland has been considerable, the sector has no statutory basis and government support for it has traditionally been ad hoc and piecemeal until the more recent period of rapid economic growth, when community participation through community development activity has become an important and relatively more integrated and contractually-based feature of the 'social partnership' model of governance adopted by Irish governments (Department of Social, Community and Family Affairs, 1999); defined now as 'assisted self-reliance', but which in some facets of Irish political discourse is increasingly expressed as the foundation of a post-liberal/post-welfare social consensus.

The more quasi-collectivist approach to welfarism adopted in Britain for a time residualised community development, submerging it into the professional realms of social work and public health as a third and minor partner in an interventionist approach based mainly on family casework and group work, until its re-emergence in the 1970s in specialised poverty and local authority programmes funded under the Urban Programme. Initially influenced by American theoretical frameworks, aimed at encouraging social integration and cultural adaptation by changing community behaviours and practices, in 1970s Britain it began to take on more radical and transformative dimensions. While generally its focus remained local, specific and partial, based on immersed and located subjectivities and particularistic responses to human need, in many incidences community development practice came to reflect a more critical stance involving new forms of cultural politics linked to social learning and community action aimed at wider, systems-level and societal change, involving demands related to the acquisition of social rights and the affirmation of citizenship on behalf of 'communities of special need' that is the urban poor, the disabled, the homeless, the mentally ill, women, immigrants and ethnic minorities. With the ascendance of the New Right and economic recession and austerity, state support for the Community Development Projects was ended, residualising Community Development once again until its reconstitution within the context of New Labour's communitarian politics of the 'third way' where it has become an important facet of social and health policy and practice and new corporatist forms of urban regeneration, but now increasingly *replacing* rather than paralleling and extending state provision.

The 'democratic deficit' in Northern Ireland generated by decades of political exclusion, instability and communal conflict also created a social space in Northern Irish society which came to be occupied by a significant community and voluntary sector some elements of which took, until relatively recently, a strong anti-state and generally oppositional stance, creating circumstances whereby social, political, economic and socio-cultural issues where contested at the level of the 'sub-politics' of community. The considerable expansion in the sector over the last ten years and its now more accommodating stance vis-à-vis the state apparatus is largely the result of state funding initiatives and European Union and other support programmes aimed at regulating and managing the political conflict by addressing local problems associated with economic underdevelopment, unemployment, poverty and sectarian division. In a society now struggling to re-establish democratic forms, the role and significance of the community and voluntary sector is changing. As representative politics are re-established, the sector's direct influence in the political sphere is weakening, while its role in the implementation of social and health care strategies and in rural and urban development is expanding as the British government acts to extend, strengthen and promote further community development in the region and to mainstream it in all health and social services agendas (Department of Health and Social Security, 1997; 1998; 1999).

On mainland Europe, in countries such as Germany and the Netherlands, social participation via associational membership and volunteering has long been identified as a major ingredient of social integration, reflected in the social pedagogical approach to social work in these societies. The decommodified distributive model of social democracy in Denmark and Sweden, on the other hand, left little space for a vigorous community and voluntary sector. Associational forms in these societies have tended to reflect an expressive rather than a service role associated with activities organised around aesthetic attachment or appreciation – leisure, hobbies, the arts, and so on, or different socio-cultural or socio-political interests or tendencies, for example the trade unions, ethnic cultural organisations and the environmental, peace and women's movements. But even here efforts to reduced unemployment, to combat alienation, to increase efficiency, to make services more responsive to the growing heterogeneity of the population structure (Esping-Andersen, 1996), coupled with the drift towards decentralisation, active labour market policies and, in Sweden at least, privatisation, have challenged the traditional universalism of the welfare state edging in new forms of social regulation and corporatism involving active citizenship and community participation (Ronnby, 1995). In fact, in virtually every society in the developed world, a discrete social field is either emerging or being extended and redefined as a social space, occupied by an active citizenry, between private households and informal communities and the public domain, represented by the market and the state. A social field increasingly mediated by community and voluntary organisations and other civil society entities many of which are communities without propinquity, in reality simulacra of communities, that is the associations and networks, 'communities' of civil society – organisations and groups functioning as 'staged' (Alheit, 1996: 43) or constructed communities – 'not the renaissance of the people but the renaissance of the staging of the people or the staging of the renaissance of the people!' (Beck, 1994: 43).

These entities are deemed as 'schools of democracy', generating 'internal learning' effects fostering sentiments of attachment, belonging, trust, social obligation and moral commitment and through strategic relations with the state and private sector providing 'thick welfarism through thin collectivism' (Hirst, 1994) thereby simultaneously contributing to social solidarity and economic growth and efficiency. Yet it is a field where these entities and others, both public and private, compete for access to resources, to processes and channels of decision-making and for social and political influence, a field structured by power relations rooted in varying levels of capital endowment. So what are the democratising possibilities of this new form of social regulation, and how can these be linked through learning to higher tiers of social and economic organisation and action?

## Democratising the social field?

Central to many theorisations of civil society and its links to learning is the Habermasian distinction between system and life-world, his understanding of rationality and of the structure of power relations related to the reification of knowledge and expert systems and the implications of these arguments in relation to the potential for increased democratisation through shifting patterns of relationships between the state, community and the private sector expressed in new governance practices and in synergetic partnerships. The systems world of the state and the economy function, in the Habermasian view, on the basis of purposive rationality; the former governed by legally codified rules and procedures and the latter characterised by the instrumental rationality of the marketplace, generating respectively the steering mechanisms of modern society – power and money. The life-world, on the other hand, is characterised by a different form of reasoning – communicative rationality – which draws on the moral-practical world of norms and values; it is a process-oriented sphere of communicative action where ends are achieved through dialogue, mutual understanding and agreement. The expansion of the systems world, associated with modernisation, has brought with it the invasion and colonisation of the life-world through the increasing monetarisation and bureaucratisation of social life; processes by which human subjects have been constructed as the passive consumers of the products of an economy over which they have little control or as the objects of professional discourses and services without which they are deemed to be 'impoverished and pre-modern creatures, lacking subjectivity and individuality' (McKevitt and Lawton, 1995). Only the 're-birth of civil society' as a third sphere of social action, it is argued, is capable of offsetting the standardisation, commodification, formalism and proceduralism of the systems world and of revitalising human inter-subjectivity, identity, solidarity, democracy and community to an extent compatible with the wide degree of pluralism characterising late modern societies.

Community in this variant of the discourse becomes an inter-subjective space generated and expressed through civil society engagement with the potential to preserve the communicative infrastructure of the life-world and to extend communicative action into the systems world of state and economy, and adult education and learning linked to community action the vehicle by which a communicative attitude is encouraged and diffused at societal level (Collins, 1991; Mezirow, 1991; Welton, 1995; Connelly, 1998).

> Part of the task then of a transformative adult education practice within community-based settings is to disclose the rational basis of vital life-world interests threatened by seemingly commonsensical, though fundamental irrational, initiatives from a system-world whose imperatives . . . nullify a need for genuine democratic discourse. (Collins, 1991: 112)

But the extent to which community-based and other associational forms might contribute to the generation of a genuine democratic discourse depends to a considerable extent on the *inclination* as well as the capacity of these new civil society communities to shift, in the interests of social justice and equity, the structural imperatives and power matrices in the social field formed by the new nexus of relations between the state, civil society and the economy and to reconcile their particularisms with a recognition of the bonds of common citizenship previously associated with universalist welfarism.

In Ireland and Britain the political discourse of active and participative citizenship is placing community and voluntary sector groups in stakeholder and multi-agency partnerships with statutory authorities, local, national and supranational state bureaucracies and a whole range of semi-autonomous bodies and private sector agents, as governance structures shift from the traditional, nation state-centred form of government to more multi-centred, multi-layered and networked patterns of governance (Rhodes, 1998). In the context of the purchaser/provider split in state service provision and new forms of local corporatism, community and voluntary organisations are now finding themselves drawn into a highly competitive business world where caring and altruism, in their various forms, are being turned into commodities, where social purpose is redefined as social entrepreneurship and community relationships and networks have come to be viewed as a form of capital. In this complex, yet relatively well-organised social field, groups are required to compete with one another, with larger and longer-established voluntary organisations, commercial enterprises and often state or semi-state agencies for service contracts or inclusion in partnership structures, forcing them to respond to market forces and to adopt features and behaviours characteristic of 'for-profit' firms.

At a time when the volume of alternative forms of economically necessary work is diminishing, especially for the lower skilled, the community and voluntary sector has become a significant employer. As groups respond to the siren call of the contract culture, many have evolved into major suppliers of services and are being forced to 'professionalise' (Powell and Guerin, 1997; Drake, 1998; Cowen, 1999; McClenaghan, 2000), that is to adopt the imperatives of the systems world. Like the more traditional charitable organisations that pre-dated them, they too are becoming virtually indistinguishable from the state bureaucracies with which they interact and, in the new climate of quasi-markets, the private firms with which they compete. Market effects and state contractual procedures are reconstituting community activist and group roles and responsibilities, transforming volunteers into employees and community members into consumers. In the new environment generated by 'community governance' economic and bureaucratic forms of rationality, related to managerialism and quality assurance, budgeting imperatives, monitoring and evaluation systems, employment rules, health and safety regulations and the necessity of accredited educational and training qualifications, at the very least as a defence against litigation, are being further extended into the civic sphere. Civil society, rather than defending and extending the lifeworld, is in many respects being collapsed into the market (Levitas, 1996: 16) and/or absorbing the bureaucratic forms of rationality characteristic of the state; a form of state administration at a distance. Even where community groups emerged within the context of local articulations of new social movements, which rejected the subjectivites constructed by the systems world (the women's movement is an important case in point), activists are finding themselves functioning more as the administrators and managers of state-funded programmes than agents of social change. In many instances these processes are undermining the community sector's representative function, stifling protest and leading to fragmentation and compartmentalisation (Drake, 1996) or amalgamation and rationalisation as governance structures act to mould and shape civil society in the interests of system imperatives. As organisations become more like professional enterprises, rather than membership groups, their capacity to act as generators and carriers of democratic values is increasingly diminished. Evidence already suggests that the composition and governing structure of many civil society communities is neither democratic, representative nor inclusive. Contractual conditions and procedures specify the nature of services to be provided, for whom and at what cost. Self-selected members from the systems world, public and private, disproportionately occupy places on partnership boards and business and professional management interests continue to set board agendas and to structure the language and procedures adopted. Validity claims when made are more often about increasing revenue streams and funding support and reducing regulation than they are about rights and justice. The extent to which the community and voluntary sector in the UK has absorbed the language and values of the market is evidenced by the current application to the Financial Services Authority by the Charities Aid Foundation to transform its £9 million 'Investors in Society' fund into a new charity bank and to allow community and voluntary groups to operate more effectively as enterprises by permitting them to offer investors equity and a return on their investment.

However, unlike their commercial and other competitors, many, locally based community initiatives especially are financially insecure, with limited capital assets and unreliable revenue streams as a result of the complexity and short-term scale of the funding regimes upon which they must rely. Only 3 per cent of social economy projects in the UK, for example, are financially independent. The rest rely on a whole series of support structures administered through a complex web of regional and national infrastructures with different and changing priorities (Amin, notes: 95); new governance infrastructures which have shifted the power to influence local regeneration and service provision away from local authorities to central government and to unelected regional development agencies, advantaging the larger civil society organisations able to employ professional managerial staff, fund-raisers, public relations and legal teams, those with better field connections and networks (social capital) and with closer links and attachment to the mainstream economy and disadvantaging those in the poorest localities and neighbourhoods, with more limited funding and trading opportunities. Community in civil society has now been reduced to a series of marketised networks in a social field increasingly governed by the 'public choice' imperative by which profit is privatised and cost and risk socialised; and those who carry the greater burden of risk are the consumers of services and sector employees.

The idea of a public sphere in which autonomous self-governing groups establish normative principles, social responsibilities and citizenship rights on the basis of rational argument and validity claims, while an attractive notion, fails to address the different levels of social and economic power permeating society at large, civil society itself and the social field in which many civil society organisations are now operating, Granting communities the power to create their own ethical and value frameworks and to participate in decisions about the nature of services to be provided and their distribution, by subcontracting services to organisations community members, in theory at least, own and control, may not only prove to be unsustainable in marginalised communities and poorer localities (Powell, 1999; Ambrose, 2001; Amin, 2001), but may also be inimical to democracy. Evidence from the United States, which has long had a large voluntary sector providing services, many of them essential services which in social democratic countries would have been provided by the state, suggests gaps in accountability and the formation of a different kind of distributive coalition in which solidarity within groups works against wider configurations of solidarity, leaving hard core social problems and less popular causes unaddressed and some social groups less well served than others, that is single homeless people, the mentally ill, alcohol and drug abusers, ethnic minorities, homosexuals and lone parents (Johnson, 1999). Even where individuals *do* have social rights, civil society may have little sense of a reciprocal obligation.

The precarious financial position of many community and voluntary sector groups, especially those working and locked into places and communities of particular disadvantage, has created an expanding secondary labour market, swollen by the extensive use of government employment schemes, where the distinction between the formal and informal economy has become blurred and where employees bear the burden of organisations' financial insecurity. In spite of the drift towards professionalisation and the resultant emergence of a cadre of social entrepreneurs, the majority of paid staff in community organisations, working directly with the poor and the disadvantaged, are themselves poorly paid, low-status, marginal staff, working long hours on temporary contracts; a career structure in some important respects resembling 'a giant workfare programme' for the ghettoes (Graefe, 2001), supplemented by the informal and unpaid participation of users and members, a significant proportion of whom are local women performing functions, which when socialised in Sweden and Denmark made an important contribution to the fuller integration of women in these societies, largely through the expansion in public sector employment generated by this process. The gender-blindness inherent in many civil society theories, even with the inclusion of women's organisations in broad definitions of the concept, is paralleled by the neglect of other structural processes generating inequality. The effects of class location, poverty, de-industrialisation, unemployment, low pay, racism and sexism, and their intersection and articulation, are effectively reduced to the attributes of individuals and neighbourhoods.

> Where you live, who else lives there, and how they live their lives, co-operatively or selfishly, responsibility or destructively, can be as important as personal resources in determining life chances.
>
> (Commission on Social Justice, 1994: 307–8)

The focus has now shifted from systems change to the life-worlds of the poor, the marginalised and the disadvantaged as repositories of meaning, values and identity requiring change through self-help, organisation and social learning.

For Habermas the potential of civic engagement to democratise the systems world refers to the capacity of civil society to extend communicative rationality into both the economy and the state. In many contemporary analyses, however, the question is not so much one of democratising the state but of replacing its redistributive functions, and democratisation stops at the boundaries of the economy. The capitalist market is reified as an invisible and 'natural' set of processes, governed by inevitable social laws and the sociality of capital (that is, the social relations on which capitalism depends) is denied or ignored. Work becomes the anchor of the individual's moral obligation to and con-tract with society but the responsibility to earn is no longer reciprocated by the *right* to earn. The democratisation of work enters into but a very few, more radical, theories of civil society and in many analyses civil society entities that have long articulated validity claims regarding the organisation and quality of working life, the trade unions, are regarded as part of the systems world or as too closely associated with the disin-tegrating 'guarantees and certainties' of pluralistic industrialism to have relevance now; a view that may not always be shared by the growing number of unprotected workers employed in the civil sphere.

Linked to these issues is the Habermasian understanding of the state, also an ideal-typical reified abstraction, and the conceptual separation of the state and the public sphere implied in his analysis. The state and its instrumental and procedural activities, imbued and sustained, by the professionalised and reified validity claims which underpin its various spheres of expertise, is treated by civil society theorists in a mechanical way, as the coloniser and enemy of civil society, inhibiting the processes of democratisation, equalitarianism and individual and community autonomy. But the state is a very complex structure, wherein politically, economically and procedurally determined imperatives (often mere taken-for-granted assumptions about the social world) are enacted by human agents, functioning within communities of practice which incorporate communicative action by agents, who also simultaneously occupy the life-world. It is a complex arena of conflicting discourses and struggles – economic, managerial, bureaucratic, political and pro-fessional. Underpinning much of civil society theorising is an anti-pathy towards and distrust of professionalism, an antipathy which in community development theorising and practice goes back to its nineteenth-century 'practical socialism' origins (Barnett, 1888; 1904). The very valid criticisms of professionalisation, the technologies of power and social closure associated with the reified knowledge systems underpinning professional practice and the arbitrary and normative judgements they contain, which have served to objectify and subjugate human individuals and socio-cultural groups are an important compo-nent in the civil society critique of the state. Yet even while recognising the many-layered links between the state and powerful interests, in the context of the necessarily abstract solidarity associated with universalistic forms of welfarism, professional practice has also been the prime collective action in the administration and legitimation of social rights and social citizenship. A sharp distinction between the state and the public sphere may well lead to an underestimation of the function of the state and the professionals within it as the guarantors of citizenship rights.

In Britain and Northern Ireland the increasing hegemony of a political discourse based on civic responsibility and community participation has already begun to break down professional demarcations and the autonomy of a number of professional groupings, reconstituting professional and other knowledges to accommodate this process. The 'technologies of power' traditionally associated with professionalism are, to a growing extent, being replaced by new technologies of power associated with managerialism, and those professionals who are being most affected are workers with the least powers of social closure, who are less able to insurance themselves, in an increasingly de-socialised economy, against the risk of error or poor judgement or often, for that matter, unemployment as their professional functions are taken on by even less secure, lower-paid, unprofessionalised and unprotected workers; professional staff working with the social consequences of poverty and inequality and social marginalisation, already aware of the multidimensionality of the social problems they have been employed to address.

As the welfare system continues to be restructured and many services further de-socialised, new spaces are daily being created for the formation of strategic alliances between the least privileged and those employed to manage them, both within the public sector and beyond its boundaries, many of whom are themselves neither highly privileged nor economically secure. Recent examples include industrial action taken by social workers in Northern Ireland in support of demands for increased resources for childcare services or that of health visitors leading community campaigns to defend local health clinics. These forms of collective action would no doubt be interpreted by some theorists as efforts by these professionals to maintain or re-establish rent-seeking distributive coalitions in their own interests, but such an interpretation is based on the atomised, economically rational, self-seeking and under-socialised self assumed in much of this kind of theorising; an assumption which ignores the application of values and ethics to professional reasoning by genuine actors struggling through associational action to maintain the welfare state and to democratise its agencies and structures; and perhaps it is in these spaces and others that the democratising potential of learning linked to associative action actually lies.

## A civil labour habitus: learning democratic competence?

Community development adult education, with its emphasis on personal and community autonomy, responsibility and empowerment, on communicative competence and democratic participation, on communal identity, social cohesion and solidarity, on flexible and particularistic responses to need and on forms of pedagogical practice based on contextuality, collective participation and experiential and situated learning, mirrors in many respects the perceived learning needs of the active and morally committed citizenry of reconstituted notions of civil society. The evolution of the community development education in Northern Ireland mirrors the changing context in which community action in the region has been taking place and its gradual integration into policy frameworks and practice in the field of social welfare and in economic regeneration. Just as in the nineteenth century when Samuel Barnett established the first University Settlement Association providing adult education in working-class communities, so too were the first formalised and accredited engagements in community development education established in Northern Ireland by a university. These initiatives emerged from an Extra-Mural Certificate programme in Community Studies begun at the Magee Campus in Derry in the early 1970s. The acquisition of European Union funding in 1987 allowed for the design and implementation of a two-year action research that would establish, through provision, an adult education programme in community development targeted at the unemployed volunteer members of community organisations and the communities and social groups they represented or served (McClenaghan, 1989). Extended EU support allowed for the continuation of the programme for a further six years by which time 230 men and women had completed the course. In 1996 a major study was carried out examining the contribution of the programme to 'social learning', and identifying changing organisational perceptions of educational and learning needs within the community and voluntary sector as the emerging social field in which local community action took place developed and evolved (McClenaghan and Robson, 1996a; 1996b; McClenaghan, 2000). As EU funding strategies shifted from a focus on institutions to the more direct funding of organisations or the implementation of funding regimes through partnership structures, European funding for the programme was ended. Through the efforts of university staff working in collaboration with the Community Development Access Network, a loose network of community organisations and groups interested in maintaining the access opportunities into higher education the programme provided, provision was gradually mainstreamed into the university's internal award structure; initially at Certificate/Diploma level offered partly in a community location and partly in the university itself and later as a pathway in the multidisciplinary modular degree in Combined Studies, attracting traditional undergraduate students as well as employed and volunteer community development workers. Provision will be fully integrated as a discipline area in undergraduate studies with the introduction of an Honours Degree in Community Development in 2003. At postgraduate level mainstreaming has occurred through the Diploma/MSc 'Professional Development in the Community' which provides shared learning environments involving practitioners – health workers, social workers, planners, regional development workers and educationalists – and their community counterparts. Postgraduate provision has, however, been increasingly shifted into the framework of professional social work education, as the regime of active citizenship and community participation has engendered a 'rediscovery and modernisation' of community development within the profession (Bahalla and Lapeyre, 1999).

Outside these developments, with their sources in higher education, the social field is now also permeated with an extensive range of community education and training programmes, emanating from a wide variety of semi-state, voluntary and community organisations and ranging from specific forms of employment training to personal development training, community enterprise skills, community leaderships skills, fund-raising skills, capacity-building, confidence-building and assertiveness training, organisational development and problem-solving skills, proposal writing courses, managerial and budgetary training, community health courses, IT skills, research and evaluation skills, parenting courses, group work skills, community relations courses, civic education and more. These different forms of community learning have engendered the proliferation of accreditation systems and bodies whereby community members are encouraged to build up a portfolio of accredited 'vocational' qualifications (NVQs) which, it is assumed, will enable them to participate as citizens, acquire employment and to take control of their own lives and their immediate environment. In a discourse which understands inequality, unemployment and poverty as social exclusion and conscious of the 'constraints' placed on intervention by globalisation, education, at every level, has been subordinated to the labour market and adaptation to market change has become a lifelong endeavour.

> The objectives of . . . adult education as a lifelong learning process, is to develop the autonomy and the sense of responsibility of people and communities, to reinforce their capacity to deal with the transformations taking place in the economy, in culture and in society as a whole'.
>
>      (*Hamburg Declaration 1997*, quoted by Longworth, 1999: 28)

While many individuals clearly benefit from their participation in community education programmes, in that they are able to use these qualifications to gain some form of employment in the civil sphere or indirectly as an avenue into formal accreditation systems, as many of our own students have done, many others are trapped in a repetitive cycle of short-term training and temporary work and still others fail to complete or reach the minimum level of competency required for accreditation. But even where they do succeed, the emphasis on personal competency and empowerment, reformulated as they have been within the context of the active citizenship discourse, and drawing on facets of humanistic psychology associated with human awareness training and group dynamics (Shaw and Crowther, 1995: 207) designed to assist human individuals to rediscover their 'true self', may well not be empowerment at all since, in the adoption of these approaches, less emphasis is often now placed on the transformation of the social structures which 'shape the very lineaments of self' (McLaren, 1995: 83) and more on adapting to and coping with the 'realities' of social and community life – *learning to live in the world*. The focus on the enhancement of the particularistic identities of community and the specificity of localised communal experience serves to obscure the non-local dimensions of identity, the wider meaning systems that act on the repositories of beliefs, assumptions and values, underpinning identity and the social relations which organise and shape experience; a feature of community education which has a tendency to lock communities into local narratives, thereby limiting the capacity of communities members to form bonds of solidarity beyond the local and immediate sphere – an important limitation in any society, but more so in one divided along communal lines.

The largely untheorised, instrumental and often anti-intellectual tendencies characteristic of many community-based adult education programmes also serves to reduce the social purpose of organisations to the acquisition of technique, 'a critical aspect of achieving positive and tangible change for communities and individuals' (Ministerial Working Group, 1998, n. 101). Training is inevitably practice- and competency-based and aimed at the managerial principles of best value and best practice, the latter generally reflecting the imperatives of the former. Organisational members become skilled in performance and evaluative procedures and techniques based on pre-set outcomes and a series of normative principles and values, which effectively become ends in themselves, for example, participation for participation's sake; a fixation with process which serves to legitimatise the activities of the 'enabling state'. While this emphasis has long infused government-sponsored community training programmes, the failure of many initiatives to bring about expected levels of community change and to learn form one another 'what works' has led to further experiments in community education, the latest involving the establishment of 'community learning chests' which will fund community leaders to gain even more 'training and skills' in community regeneration and professionals to acquire 'knowledge' of deprived communities, they are assumed to be lacking, by joint participation in skills and knowledge programmes (*New Start*, 2001).

University provision in community development adult education was also originally funded on the basis of pre-set outcomes associated with skills acquisition aimed at increasing the self-reliance, creative problem-solving capabilities and employability of participants and through them enhancing the skills base and technical and procedural competency of the organisations of which they were members. The EU-funded Socrates Intensive Programme, a postgraduate module on the Masters' degree in Professional Development in the Community, was also competency-based, as is the entire degree, since it was designed to improve the inter-sectoral practice of professionals and community actors. While a significant proportion of the curricula did involve skill and competency components and the pedagogical approach adopted on both courses began with the embedded, situated, local and concrete knowledge of students, in order 'to validate their historical agency' (McLaren, 1995: 255), like most adult educators in the radical tradition staff sought in dialogue with students to go beyond the local and the particular, to link the specificity of situated experiences to the situations and social relations which order and shape experience, to theorise and problemise

themes in community practice and in everyday life, to identify the economic and power relations and their representations in the practice field
and to explore the constitutive discourses structuring the field and the
subjectivities they create – *learning to read the world*.

These experiences have taught us that the field remains a contested
one. Examining the concept 'community' in the context of the political discourse of active citizenship operating to structure the field in
which civil action takes place, to prompt certain attributes and values
among disadvantaged population groups and to reconstruct the self-
identity of community members and the professional identity of whose
who work with them, can generate a false assumption of widespread
community and professional compliance. Some community agents and
their professional counterparts have already begun to identify common
counter-discourse agendas and to act on these through their different
associational forms. While these may as yet be limited in number, the
language of the discourse, the signifiers of democratisation and participation, codified and contained as they are in the procedures and techniques of inter-sectoral partnership and practice, has opened a dialogical
space containing, perhaps, new sites of cultural production, where subjectivities might be renegotiated and new constellations of solidarity
formed capable of destabilising the power regimes dominating the field.

## Conclusion

Just as Alderidge (1998) identified an emerging social field in personal
finance, arising through a project of cultural reconstruction requiring
those in employment to take active responsibility for their own welfare,
so too are the same forces generating a new social field expressed in the
changing orientation of social policy to civil society. Like its personal
finance counterpart this new field may not currently be in the consciousness of all social actors, but the project is to make it so by forming
a habitus through the political discourse of active citizenship and social
and community responsibility. In many respects community development education both within communities and in educational institutions may well be contributing significantly to the formation of such a
habitus. The challenge for adult educators is to identify in dialogue with
students the underlying economic and political discourses constituting
this new social field and to interrogate the meaning systems and subjectivities constituted by them with the aim of generating new forms
of 'culturally constitutive knowledge' (Salling Olesen, 1996: 33) in the
interests of equality and justice.

There is no more reason now than there has ever been to believe that we are constrained by mysterious and unknown social laws, not simply decisions made within institutions that are subject to human will – human institutions which have to face the test of legitimacy and if they do not meet it, can be replaced by others that are more free and more just, as often in the past.          (Chomsky, 2000)

# References

Alderidge, A. (1998). 'Habitus and Cultural Capital in the field of Personal Finance'. *Sociological Review*, 46.

Alheit, P. (1996). 'Research and Innovation in Contemporary Adult Education', in S. Papaioannou, P. Alheit, J.F. Lauridsen and H.S. Olesen (eds.), *Community Education and Social Change*. Anogia Workbooks Vol. 2. Roskilde: Roskilde University.

Ambrose, P. (2001). 'Bringing Together the Partners in Community Regeneration'. *New Start*, 3, 134.

Amin, A. (2001). 'Bringing together the Partners in Community Regeneration', *New Start*, Vol. 3, No. 139.

Bahalla, A.S. and F. Lapeyre (1999). *Poverty and Exclusion in a Global World*. New York: Macmillan Press.

Barnett, S.A. (1888). *Practical Socialism*. London: Longmans.

Barnett, S.A. (1904). *Towards Social Reform*. London: T. Fisher.

Batten, T.R. (1957). *Communities and Their Development. An Introductory Study with Special Reference to the Tropics*. London: Oxford University Press.

Beck, U. (1994). 'The Re-invention of Politics: Towards a Theory of Reflexive Modernization', in U. Beck, A. Giddens and S. Lash (eds.), *Reflexive Modernization: Politics, Tradition and Aesthetics in the Modern Social Order*. Cambridge: Polity Press.

Beck, W., L. van der Maesen and A. Walker (eds.) (1997). *The Social Quality of Europe*. The Hague: Kluwer Law International.

Blair, T. (1995). 'Allied Dunbar lecture'. *The Spectator*, 25 March, p. 18.

Brager, G. and H. Specht (1973). *Community Organising*. New York: Columbia University Press.

Chomsky, N. (2000). In D. Macedo (ed.), *Chomsky on Miseducation*. Boston, Mass.: Rowan & Littlefield.

Cohen, J.L. and A. Arato (1992). *Civil Society and Political Theory*. Cambridge, Mass.: MIT Press.

Collins, M. (1995). *Adult Education as Vocation; A Critical Role for the Adult Educator*. London: Routledge.

Commission on Social Justice (1994). Dublin: Government of Ireland.

Connelly, B. (1998). 'Lifelong Learning Through the Habermasian Lens: Providing Theoretical Grounding to Adult Education Practice', in J. Holford et al. (eds.), *International Perspectives on Lifelong Learning*. London: Kogan Page.

Cowen, H. (1999). *Community Care, Ideology and Social Policy*. Hemel Hempstead: Prentice Hall Europe.

Department of Health and Social Services (1997). *Well into 2000: A Positive Agenda for Health and Wellbeing*. Belfast: The Stationery Office NI.

Department of Health and Social Services (1998). *Building Real Partnership, Compact between Governament and the Voluntary and Community Sector in Northern Ireland*. Belfast: The Stationery Office NI.

Department of Health and Social Services (August 1999). *Mainstreaming Community Development in the Health and Personal Services*. Belfast: The Stationery Office NI.

Department of Social, Community and Family Affairs (1999). *United against Poverty. The National Community Development Programme Handbook*. Dublin: Government Publications Office.

Drake, R. (1996). 'A Critique of the Role of the Traditional Charities', in L. Barton (ed.), *Disability and Society: Emerging Issues and Insights*. London: Longman.

Drake, R. (1998). 'Professionals and the Voluntary Sector', in A. Symonds and A. Kelly (eds.), *The Social Construction of Community Care*. London: Macmillan Press.

Esping-Andersen, G. (ed.) (1996). *Welfare States in Transition*. London: Sage.

European Commission (1994). *European Social Policy: A Way Forward for the Union*. Luxembourg. European Commission.

Fine, B. (2001). *Social Capital versus Social Theory. Political Economy and Social Science at the Turn of the Millennium*. London and New York: Routledge.

Frazer, E. and N. Lacey (1993). *The Politics of Community: A Feminist Critique of the Liberal-Communitarian Debate*. London and New York: Harvester Wheatsheaf.

Graefe, P. (2001). 'Whose Social Economy? Debating New State Practice in Quebec'. *Critical Social Policy*, 21.

Hall, J.A. (1995). *Civil Society: Theory, History and Comparison*. Cambridge: Polity Press.

Held, D. (2000). 'Regulating Globalization? The Reinvention of Politics'. *International Sociology*, 15, 2.

Hirst, P. (1994). *Associative Democracy: New Forms of Economic and Social Governance*. Cambridge: Polity Press.

Hoggett, P. (1997). *Contested Communities: Experiences, Struggles and Policies*. Bristol: The Policy Press.

Holdcroft, L.E. (1982). 'The Rise and Fall of Community Development in Developing Countries, 1950–1965: A Critical Analysis and Implications', in G.E. Jones and M.J. Rolls (eds.), *Progress in Rural Extension and Community Development, Vol. 1*. New York: John Wiley & Sons.

Jansen, T., M. Finger and W. Wildemeersch (1998). 'Lifelong Learning for Social Responsibility: Exploring the Significance of Aesthetics Reflexivity', in J. Holford (ed.), *International Perspectives in Lifelong Learning*. London: Kogan Page.

Johnson, N. (1999). *The Mixed Economy of Welfare, A Comparative Perspective*. Hemel Hempstead: Prentice Hall Europe.

Kildal, N. (1999). 'Justification of Workfare: the Norwegian Case'. *Critical Social Policy*, 19, 3.

Levitas, R. (1996). 'The Concept of Social Exclusion and the New Durkheimian Hegemony'. *Critical Social Policy*, 16, 1.

Longworth, N. (1999). *Making Lifelong Learning Work: Learning Cities for a Learning Century*. London: Kogan Page.

McClenaghan, P.A. (2000). 'Social Capital: Exploring the Theoretical Foundations of Community Development Education'. *British Educational Research Journal*, 26, 5.

McClenaghan, P.A. (1996). *ESF/University of Ulster Transfrontier Community Economic Development Project*. Department of Adult and Continuing Education, University of Ulster.

McClenaghan, P.A. and T. Robson (1996a). *Training for Community Development: The North West Initiative: Achievements and Prospects*. University of Ulster. Northern Ireland.

McClenaghan, P.A. and T. Robson (1996b). 'Training for Community Development: The North West Experience', in S. Hill and B. Merrill (eds.), *Access, Equity, Participation and Organisation Change*. ESREA Warwick.

McKevitt, D. and A. Lawton (1995). *Public Services Management: Theory, Critique and Practice*. London: Sage.

McLaren, P. (1995). *Pedagogy and Predatory Culture: Oppositional Politics in a Postmodern Era*. London: Routledge.

Mezirow, J. (1991). *Transformative Dimensions of Adult Learning*. San Francisco: Jossey-Bass.

Ministerial Working Group (1998). 'Communities Learning through Change'. Quoted in *Learning, Planning and Evaluation*. Scottish Community Development Centre, 2000.

Minkler, M. (ed.) (1998). *Community Organizing and Community Building for Health*. Piscataway, NJ: Rutgers University Press.

*New Start* (2001). 'Bringing Together the Partners in Community Regeneration'. 3, 134.

Nisbet, R.A. (1967). *The Sociological Tradition*. London: Heinemann.

Powell, F.W. and D. Guerin (1997). *Civil Society & Social Policy: Voluntarism in Ireland*. Dublin: Farmar.

Powell, M. (1999). *New Labour, New Welfare State? The 'Third Way' in British Social Policy*. Bristol: Policy Press.

Rhodes, R.A.W. (1998). 'Understanding Governance: Comparing Public Sector Reform in Britain and Denmark'. Inaugural lecture.

Ronnby, A. (1995). *Mobilizing Local Communities*. Aldershot: Avebury.

Rose, N. (1996). 'The Death of the Social'. *Economy and Society*, 25, 3.

Salamon, L., L.C. Hems and K. Chinnock (2000). 'The Non-profit Sector: For Whom and For What? *Working Papers of The Johns Hopkins Comparative Non-profit Sector Project*. Baltimore: Johns Hopkins University.

Salling Olesen, H. (1996). *Adult Education and Everday Life, Adult Education Research Group*. Roskilde University Centre, Viborg, Denmark.

Shaw, M. and Crowther, J. (1995). 'Beyond Subversion', in M. Mayo and J. Thompson. *Adult Learning Critical Intelligence and Social Change*. Leicester: NIACE.

Strydom, P. (1999). 'The Challenge of Responsibility for Sociology', *Current Sociology*, Vol. 47, No. 3.

Welton, M.R. (ed) (1995). *In Defense of the Lifeworld: Critical Perspectives on Adult Learning*. New York: SUNY Press.

White, S.K. (1988). *The Recent Work of Jürgen Habermas, Reason, Justice and Modernity*. Cambridge: Cambridge University Press.

# 11
# Welfare, Gender and Political Agency: Comparing Strategies in the UK and Denmark

*David Etherington*

## Introduction: poverty, power and women's agency

This chapter explores the strategies deployed by women and social movements in the pursuit of gender equality. The chapter focuses on welfare and workfare, comparing the UK and Denmark.

I wish to highlight the role of women's agency and interest articulation as a struggle against the politics of workfare or activation. By comparing the UK and Denmark the chapter will consider similarities and differences in the gender politics of exclusion within quite diverse welfare contexts. Choosing cities as case studies enables us to illuminate how struggle and contestation are shaped by and grounded in space and place (see Andersen and Larsen, this volume, chapter 13). The research poses the following questions. In what way is there a common ground of experience between the two countries? How do strategies and agendas differ, and why? By addressing these questions it is hoped that a richer understanding of the role of political agency in the struggle around welfare restructuring will be developed. Before elaborating the comparative framework (in the next section) some general theoretical comments and context are helpful.

There has been a recent revival of work in the UK that draws on Marxist or critical realist theories of class and struggle in relation to social inequality, welfare and society (Byrne, 1997; Bradley et al., 2000; Ferguson, Lavalette and Mooney, 2002; Lavalette and Mooney, 2000) and in particular develop a more detailed analysis of the dynamics of social struggle and mobilisation (Miliband, 1989; 1995; Kelly, 1998; cf. Bourdieu, 1998). This approach views women's poverty as an integral part of processes of class power inequalities and mechanisms of oppression which have been central to Marx's original critique of capitalism (Marx, 1976). Social struggle is derived from perceptions of injustice and the processes of discrimination and exclusion which are inherent under capitalism (see Young, this volume, chapter 2).

Birte Siim has argued that 'women's agency in civil society and in relation to formal politics has in some cases been able to influence the discourse, and politics of citizenship and improve women's civil, social and political rights' (Siim, 2000: 161). In this respect women engage with social and political movements and organisations which are crucial for addressing exclusion and poverty in the work place (for example, trade unions) (see Bradley, 1999) and in the 'community' where self-help and voluntary organisations will act as buffers and shelters against market inequalities and welfare restructuring (Jones and Novack, 2000).

Space and place are intertwined with social processes, and places differ in terms of culture, traditions of labour organisation, levels of poverty, labour reserves (and their components), and so on (Massey, 1996). Localities and local economies can possess their own 'local coherence' in terms of a distinct pattern of industrial structure, class/gender/ethnic and patriarchal relations, local traditions of organisation and mobilisation. Cities are the terrain of oppositional politics against neoliberal welfare reforms and women are key actors in this political process (see Harvey, 1996; Andersen and Siim, this volume, chapter 1). Globalisation processes and economic restructuring have changed the gender division of labour in the workplace between men and women, as redundancies and unemployment have in some areas disproportionately affected men whilst women have benefited from new employment opportunities (McDowell, 2001). This has had a profound impact on gender and class relations and on reproductive politics in terms of gender roles in the home.

Whilst ideology and discourse are not a central focus of this chapter, their role is seen as crucially important. The social relations of gender have a strong ideological and discursive element in that social elites are able to impose their definition of what is a social problem (that is poverty, unemployment) and what constitutes gender roles (men and women). Social groups, including subordinate classes, will also produce their own discourses (for example, minority ethnic groups, women and labour movements) which challenge ruling ideologies. This is a useful model in that it helps us to understand how discourse or discursive practices are constantly shifting and embedded in political struggle (Fairclough, 2000).

## Gender poverty, welfare and activation in Denmark and the UK: a comparative perspective

The notion that welfare systems are configured and shaped by labour and social movement power and mobilisation is one of the compelling features of Esping-Andersen's approach to comparative welfare analysis (Esping-Andersen, 1992; 1996). In the case of Denmark, the welfare system is primarily social democratic in Esping-Andersen's typology because of its strong orientation to redistribution and universal policies, extensive labour and trade union involvement in policy networks. The liberal welfare systems such as the UK's have been constructed around a 'voluntarist' system of industrial relations whereby wage bargaining is primarily decentralised to workplaces or industries and there is no central machinery through which capital and labour negotiate wages and employment conditions. The fact that trade union organisation and recognition cannot be taken for granted in the UK has enormous implications for both gender and class inequality.

This is a useful starting point, but needs further refinements and modifications in terms of building a more sophisticated analysis of agency into welfare state research. The role of women's agency within an understanding of how welfare settlements are formed enriches the perspective because, as argued above, class formation in itself is shaped through gender and ethnicity. As Siim points out, there are issues about the breadwinner model (the relationship between waged work and caring work) where men are assumed to be the principal earners, and women the carers, for it constitutes the social construction of gender within a welfare settlement. This is particularly strong in the case of the UK and weak in relation to Denmark. Whilst this is useful for comparison, the 'model tends to reduce both the development of social policies and women's wage work to a universal single logic; 'there is a need to discuss the structural factors behind the model as well as the role of actors such as employers, trade unions political parties and women's organisations in the formation of the welfare state' (Siim, 2000: 15; see also Ginsburg, 1992; Warren, 2000).

It is important to consider regimes and settlements not only in a dynamic and changing context, but also at different geographical scales, as a way of comparing cities. The recognition that social life is fundamentally spatial also means that there are geographical and spatial dimensions to regulation and struggle which cannot be read off or deduced from national 'characteristics' and typologies. Both place and space are vital to any analysis of exclusion and contestation. Building this into comparative state analysis has its difficulties, but Jessop is useful in that he links the two – or, perhaps more importantly, sees spatial scale and state restructuring as dialectically interlinked.

Jessop argues that a shift has occurred from a Keynesian Welfare National State (KWNS) to a Schumpeterian Workfare Post-National Regime (SWPR), which is related to the crisis in the traditional postwar welfare settlement of redistribution and regulation. A more contradictory and unstable regime is emerging based on the subordination of policies to the needs of economic competitiveness, which involves a more neo-liberal politics based on privatisation and re-commodification (Jessop, 2000).

Under the SWPR the national political territory is no longer the sole 'power container'. Policy-making functions are being shifted (or 'hollowed out') upwards, sideways and downwards. Policy-making devolution to the urban scale means that local politics is important in shaping regulation, and the different trajectories and forms of policy restructuring are contingent on the balance of social/class forces, institutional legacies and changing economic and political conjunctures. What is key about the shift in the post-Keynesian welfare state is that activation and workfare become the dominant policy discourse, but also different modes of political representation arise in the new emphasis on governance. Forms of governance and corporatism (as models of political representation) will depend on institutional and political legacies and a balance of social forces. This explains the different dynamics and forms of political representation in the UK and Denmark as illustrated in Table 11.1.

## The UK – increasing workfare and the politics of gender mobilisation

### The New Deal for the unemployed – mechanisms of exclusion?

New Labour's welfare reforms underlie a *laissez-faire* approach, set by previous Conservative governments, which provides the basis for subordinating the interests of capital over labour and its social partners within the formulation and implementation of employment agendas. Local government functions and responsibilities are increasingly circumscribed within the structure of urban partnerships responsible for 'steering' local employment policies (Jones and Ward, 2002; Etherington and Jones, forthcoming).

Basically, the welfare-to-work strategy, first implemented in 1997, involves a number of New Deal for unemployed programmes targeted at

*Table 11.1*  Interest representation and welfare states in the UK and Denmark

| | Denmark | UK |
|---|---|---|
| **Industrial relations** | Co-regulation collective bargaining recognising trade union rights to collective bargaining. Most sectors covered. Legal right for recognition. | Voluntarist and decentralised with limited coverage. Union recognition limited under law. |
| **Trade union involvement in labour market policy** | Unemployment Trusts managed by unions provide advice services in relation to labour market policy and training. Work-based training integrated into collective agreements. | Ad hoc involvement in relation to work-based negotiation. No formal links with unemployed except through TU sponsored Unemployment Centres and individual union initiatives. |
| **Mode of social reproduction and access to work** | Relatively generous benefits, comprehensive maternity child care provision – access to all pre-school children, integrated and subsidised public transport (public controlled or tightly regulated), housing mobility through regulated private and subsidised social housing | Social benefits low, heavily means-tested and linked to working tax system. Only limited child care provision does not guarantee 100 per cent pre school coverage. Dependent on private provision. Transport system deregulated and privatised does not guarantee mobility. Market private/public rents limits mobility |
| **Labour market policy stakeholders and forms of political representation** | Trade unions, local government and private employers. Tripartism operating within labour market institutions | Private employers, voluntary sector and public sector. Representation modelled on company board within Local Strategic Partnerships – business-dominated |
| **Institutions and delivery** | Regional Labour Market Councils and vocational training institutions run by social partners. | Local Learning Skills with limited budgets for vocational training. New Deal heavily oriented to contract system involving private and voluntary sectors. Limited role for local government. |
| **Urban policy and representative democracy** | Increasing role for local government in activation. Shift to governance in strategic policy making bringing in more 'actors'. User service groups still influential. | Decreasing role for local government due to 'enabling' role of Council. Councils have to bid for contracts in new deal. 'Cabinet' government in town halls centralises power. |

different groups – young people, long-term unemployed, lone parents, disabled people – involving subsidised employment and training. The New Deal is primarily managed by the Employment Service and is implemented through local partnership structures involving public, voluntary and business organisations. In addition to the New Deal, employment and training policies are formulated through the various government policies for regenerating cities via area-based programmes such as the Single Regeneration Budget (SRB) and the New Deal for Communities (NDC) (Diamond, 2001).

The narrative of the New Deal Welfare to Work programme is of work as the vehicle for inclusion. In this respect there are strong similarities with Denmark. It also carries an 'underclass' discourse focusing on lone parents, and the New Deal for Lone Parents makes sure that women are put under pressure to accept work offers. The policy has stigmatised lone parents, as lone motherhood, economic inactivity and benefit dependency are 'behavioural' norms which the policy will address; the lessons to be drawn are the value of paid work in terms of an exit from poverty (Grover and Stewart, 2000: 240).

The underlying structure of the New Deal programme is discriminatory because its core strategy is that of moving claimants from benefits into work. Katherine Rake argues that more men are taking part in the New Deal programme because women who have an employed partner are not entitled to claim the Job Seekers' Allowance (JSA – a form of unemployment benefit). Where both partners are unemployed, the man is more likely to register for the JSA. Although elements of the New Deal programme target women, the vast proportion of spending is on the component which benefits men (Rake, 2000). Furthermore, the programme relies on the role of the private sector and jobs being available, yet in areas of low labour demand its success rate is open to question. If women are registered as unemployed they *may* have opportunities to gain access to training and unemployment programmes, but it is a fact that large numbers of women are hidden from the unemployment tally (see Beatty et al., 2002).

In relation to child care, when compared with other European countries, the UK has the lowest level of provision. Rosemary Crompton argues that the relative lack of child care reinforces a more exploitative women's labour market because part-time jobs or non-standard employment will be taken up by women who have to combine household and child care responsibilities with work (Crompton, 1999).

In terms of interest or stakeholder involvement, New Labour's welfare policy sees the third (or voluntary) sector as a crucial element to new forms of urban governance. As Ruth Levitas comments, 'the role of the community is to mop up the ill-effects of the market and to provide the conditions for its continued operation, while the costs of this are born by individuals rather than the state' (Levitas, 2000: 193). Women play an important role in the development of the third sector, yet, as Lister argues, their contribution is not generally valued or given recognition despite the fact that there is considerable amount of 'unpaid' work. Unlike in Denmark, there is no set framework for representation within urban partnerships which will *guarantee* that the interests of specific groups – particularly those excluded from the labour market – are represented in local forums. The New Deal does not in anyway highlight the need for local government and the trade unions to be involved in local partnerships (Herd et al., 1998). In fact, despite local government often being one of the largest employers in localities, it does not have a prescribed role as a manager of programmes, which emphasises the marginalisation of the public sector as a New Deal provider (Jones and Ward, 2002).

### Gender and the urban political landscape: the struggle for representation and inclusion

Within Jessop's concept of the 'hollowing out' process of the state it is indicative that New Labour has sought to decentralise its economic and social programmes within a tightly centralised monitoring and steering structure. In this respect it is important to note at the outset how much of the nationally-focused social and economic programme of the New Labour administration retained, in its underlying essentials, elements from the previous Conservative regime. This amounted to a modified, neoliberal regime rather than an entirely new template for the national policy programme – an approach variously described as 'pragmatism and populism', 'stakeholder policies', 'social integrationism' or the 'new paternalism' (McGregor, 1999). These social and political dynamics of a Schumpeterian workfare state are shaping the contours of power and conflict in cities.

Against these political changes it is important to note that in the industrial cities of the North and Midlands, generally controlled by the Labour Party, there is an historic legacy of municipal socialism which was a vehicle for oppositional politics during the 1980s against Thatcher's political programme and which gave some weight to inclusion of diversity in the debate and agenda-setting of economic and social policies (Wainwright, 1987).

The focal point of struggle around the New Deal is on representation within partnerships and the way policies themselves exclude women.

Taking representation first, Geddes' study of local partnerships and social exclusion in the UK revealed that many partnerships were dominated by men with a focus on how the partnerships could serve private interests. He also indicates that these processes were regularly challenged by local organisations. He describes the position of women in terms of partnership arrangements as follows:

> As has already been indicated, there was a major disparity on the board and the executive committee between the predominance of (white middle class) males as representatives of public and private sectors partners, and of women as community representatives. In the view of one person interviewed, this reflected the macho 'business' ethos of the development industry to which partnership is primarily orientated . . . traditional gender roles have been replicated by the confinement of women to community roles, and the partnership had not given real priority to women's issues in its strategies and activities.                                              (Geddes, 1997: 65)

In essence, the practice of urban policy in the UK has been to mobilise class interests around agendas of growth and containment. The policy mix tends to focus on private accumulation and the management of the ever-growing surplus population in the cities which involves a mixture of repressive and coercive policies (for example, workfare) as well as paternalism ('empowering communities', the language of 'partnerships'). The result is that local politics are being increasingly shaped by corporate interests and the private sector, and representative democracy as such is becoming sidelined. These political processes and orientations towards the private sector are configuring struggles and mobilisations in British cities. As Mayo observes, (similar to Geddes) communities – in particular women – tend to contest the partnership and power structures assembled to decide, allocate and distribute urban funding (Mayo, 2000). Such struggles embrace diversity in terms of experience, goals and objectives.

Research undertaken by the University of Birmingham (Centre for Urban and Regional Studies, 1997) has revealed that women are actively engaged in partnerships in terms of shaping agendas and project funding. For example, there was a women-led Single Regeneration Budget (SRB) bid undertaken by a group of women who were experienced community activists and some were paid workers in the voluntary sector connected to a local community centre. The SRB partnership assisted in developing a local forum where some of the concerns which the partnership could not address could be tackled by the forum.

The Birmingham example is not unique. In Sheffield a coalition of women's organisations were formed around the Women's Forum which has engaged with local partnerships in negotiating funds for labour market initiatives and is acting as a voice in representing women's interests in the city (Etherington, 2003a). There is a problem with the role of the voluntary sector. New Labour see it as having a key role in the implementation of social policy which raises issues about resources and capacities and dangers of being institutionalised and losing its independent status (see Taylor et al., 2002).

In relation to the policy regimes connected to the New Deal, the New Deal for Lone Parents has been particularly contentious. It was launched with a fanfare declaring a national child care strategy whereby lone parents (mainly women) would be offered work benefits (to maintain minimum income) and child care subsidies. In many respects this has failed to integrate most lone parents into the labour market, because of the inflexible arrangements around working time and a lack of resources to meet individual contributions to child care costs. Furthermore, there are other, more subtle barriers relating to material and area-based poverty (housing, basic education and transport) which act as barriers to women's inclusion in the labour market (Speak, 2000).

Women's organisations have engaged directly with the New Deal. An example is SCOOP Aid, an organisation which represents one-parent families in south Yorkshire which has developed strategies for increasing funds for projects which assist one parent (usually a woman) in the labour market. At the same time the organisation has played an important role in lobbying on the provision of child care, rules on benefits and the minimum hours rule (36 hours' work per week) which acts as a barrier to women obtaining work (SCOOP Aid, 2001). Much of this work is closely linked to national-based organisations campaigning around welfare and child care (for example, the National Council for One Parent Families).

Whilst trade unions are not directly engaged in many of the New Deal partnerships, even where they are excluded, it is important to note that unions still have a presence in localities, in particular through the medium of local Trade Union Councils, and are heavily organised in the public sector which is also the main employer in most urban centres. These dynamics are important in relation to equality politics where the main public sector union, UNISON, has sought to develop a politics of diversity which has given independent voice for women, black and gay and lesbian groups (Colgan and Ledwith, 2000). This type of mobilisation is important because of the 'spillover' effects on local politics. UNISON is the main local government trade union, and women activists have (in some cases) tended to incorporate their union politics within local government policy discourses. An example of this is Sheffield City Council, one of England's largest metropolitan councils, which produced a report that highlighted not only the extent of women's poverty in the city, but also the deficiencies of the current New Deal for unemployed for women (Etherington, 2003a; Sheffield City Council, 2003).

In conclusion, the governance of employment policy through Local Strategic Partnerships has brought more women's organisations into the political arena, but at the same time, as Geddes argues, the construction of the partnerships has given precedence to business and other elite coalitions. The relationship of local government to these partnerships can be ambivalent; this in itself has had implications for how women and other oppressed groups can be incorporated or 'included' into policy agenda-setting (Etherington, 2003b).

The voluntary sector is a key agent of mobilisation, self-organisation and mutual support for women in the UK. It is more geographically embedded because of the focus on area regeneration programmes. Some voluntary organisations are developing innovative social and employment projects and have effective campaigning and networking experiences. However, struggles tend to be fragmented because of the proliferation of many groups (which often lack sufficient funds to develop) compete for limited resources.

## Denmark – activation as a politics of inclusion?

### Denmark's welfare to work reforms: decentralisation and regulating corporatism

For Denmark, most workplaces are covered by collective agreements, there are high trade union densities, a highly developed welfare system in relation to social reproduction, and corporatist modes of decision-making dominate employment and training policy. Furthermore, local government has a major role in decision-making and management of activation, through its responsibilities for administering social assistance to unemployed claimants. The 1990s welfare and labour market reforms represent a modified form of workfare; whilst benefit entitlements are tied to activation offers, many other elements of universal social policies have been retained. Labour market policies have been decentralised to Regional Labour Market Councils, and more recently include an increasing role for local government. The reforms had a profound impact on women in that the introduction of leave schemes relating to education, child care and sabbaticals (which were later abandoned) enabled the establishment of a balance between home and working life. The child care schemes have been extremely popular, allowing paid leave (the equivalent of unemployment benefit) for carers (Etherington, 1998).

The women's movement has played an important role in the construction of Denmark's welfare model (Christensen, this volume, chapter 6) and has tended to support or modify the social solidaristic discourse which has encompassed work sharing and changing the balance between work and family life (Compston and Madsen, 2001; Moller, 1999: 172–80). Individual unions such as Specialarbejderforbundet i Danmark (SID), a large union representing unskilled workers, has consistently opposed the element of compulsion and called for a more public sector role in delivering training (SID, 1995; see also the response by the Nursery Workers Union, PMF, 1999). The public sector unions in particular have been suspicious about these special employment schemes, particularly job training, because of the potential substitute effects of their introduction (Bredgaard, 2001).

However, the reforms had adverse impacts. A disproportionate number of women have participated in this scheme (approximately 85 per cent), which suggests the sexual division of labour in care responsibilities in the home is replicated in the labour market (Loftager and Kongshoj Madsen, 1997: 128–9; see also Siim, 2000). A consequence of this is that more women, as a result of the carrot of the child care schemes for balancing family and work life, are feeling the stick in terms of labour market disadvantage. Furthermore, the distribution of schemes tends to be biased towards the public sector, with the negotiation of child care schemes more difficult in the private sector (Lind, 1999). Paradoxically, the leave schemes have developed job rotation, an instrument of labour market policy pioneered by the labour movement involving unemployed replacements for those on vocational education leave. These replacements are given on the job employment and vocational training (Etherington and Jones, 2003; see below).

It is important to emphasise the (territorial) decentralised nature of the Danish welfare state in that major welfare functions are carried out by the municipalities and county authorities. This is relatively unique in the European context in that all major functions relating to social reproduction, environmental regulation and infrastructure are under elected democratic control. Furthermore, the representative organisations of the county and local authorities have had (in most cases) major political influences in shaping welfare policy.

However, in the 1990s the shift from government to governance was characterised by an increasing role and influence of non-directly elected institutions. The 1994 labour market reforms involved the administration of labour market programmes by the 14 regional Labour Market Councils (whose boundaries are coterminous with the county council system). The LMCs are corporatist-style institutions, with planning and implementation undertaken by the 'social partners' – local government, trade unions and the employers – who have equal representation in the 14 regions. This mirrors the composition of the Central Labour Market Council, where local government is represented by the KL (National Local Government Association). LMC boards have executive status, are supervised by the central government Labour Market Authority, and their policies and plans are subject to approval by central government.

During the late 1990s the government established a social inclusive labour market policy (rummelig arbejdsmarkedpolitik) with the aim of reducing the number of claimants on social assistance. As local government administers social assistance, it was charged with setting up local coordinating committees involving appropriate 'actors' and social partners in the management of activation programmes.

**Women contesting activation?**

As Table 11.1 (p. 190 above) shows, there are significantly different 'spaces' of political representation in the labour market policy at the local level in Denmark. I will briefly explore here the gender dimension. Similar to the UK case study I will address two aspects – interest representation and engagement with policy regimes.

The strengthening of tripartite corporatism in regions and cities has given a greater voice for the unions and to some extent that this can have had some impact on gender interest articulation. However, studies by Hansen and Hansen (2000) and Hansen (2000) have stressed that there have been adverse democratic consequences around the operation in the LMCs in terms of three areas. There tends to be a lack of transparency and openness in the decision-making process, and there are barriers to public accountability and remoteness of Executive Council members from their 'constituencies'. This form of political mobilisation could have implications for how specific interests can be articulated. Etherington (2003a), in his study of Aalborg and North Jutland, found that women's groups and women trade union activists were sensitive about the development of a gender dimension to regional labour market policy given the high levels of occupational segregation and unemployment.

Within the activation policy regime, there is no doubt that, at the local level, high levels of unionisation and women's engagement with the various leave programmes – especially job rotation – has brought about considerable benefits for training and employment (see Etherington and Jones, 2003). Like Sheffield, Aalborg's City Council's Equality Committee (Ligestillingsudvalget) has been in the vanguard in developing a debate and policy for gender equality in relation to employment and pay. A recent report, appropriately titled 'Hvor meget er kvinders arbejde vaerd?' (How much is women's work worth?), has developed a critique of common notions of women's work and pay (Aalborg Kommune, 2001a). Furthermore, the Equality Committee has been the driving force behind tackling other issues such as occupation and vertical segregation within the local authority (Aalborg Kommune, 2001b). The Equality Committee has forged links with trade unions within the city council in order to promote equal pay policies in the unions in terms of developing national pay guidelines (interview with Chair of Equality Committee, 2002).

It is important to understand the local government system in terms of interest articulation and political struggle. There are several aspects to this. First, there is a highly developed system of service user groups which act as 'watchdogs' in relation to how services are delivered. Second, the public sector trade unions politically lean to the left and are organised to resist reforms that undermine the collective and social solidarity principles of welfare provision. It is important to note that women play an important role in this mobilisation (Siim, 2000). Third, the local government organisations (such as the Kommunernes Landsforeningen (KL) – National Association of Local Government) are represented in the corporatist networks and act as important pressure groups around local government issues (Etherington, 1997).

The social inclusion labour market policy (SILM) has been constructed around a discourse of marginalisation relating to welfare claimants, including ethnic groups. The new forms of partnerships and local networks evolving from the local coordinating committees have been represented as a new form of 'network steering', creating possibilities for a more pluralistic governance (Andersen and Torfing, 2002).

There are tensions and paradoxes in this development. On the one hand, *more* actors and groups are engaging in the local policy arena about how to integrate marginal groups into the labour market. On the other, this engagement has a specific and narrow focus about getting claimants of social assistance and sickness benefits. It is this focus which actually generates a (potentially) more tightly controlled and disciplinary regime of activation (Larsen et al., 2001). There are two issues which have implications for gender mobilisation and interest articulation. Networks to a large extent are driven by top-down, state-initiated actions and in fact are 'embedded in hierarchical state structures' (as in the hollowing-out process, as described by Jessop), and networks themselves exhibit tendencies towards inequality, imitation and exclusion (see Leitner and Shepperd, 2002). To a large extent, the degree to which the SILM incorporates a gender perspective and challenges to inbuilt labour market discriminations will largely depend on how the dominant discourse will be shaped by mainstream politics of equality in local government.

## Conclusion: reformulating gender mobilisation and exclusion

In this section I discuss some of the salient issues of convergence and divergence in the UK and Denmark. In terms of *convergence* – or common threads of struggles and agendas lies with the following:

The importance of equality policies and politics for agenda-setting and as a focus for mobilisation cannot be overstated. Their limitations are also being realised as the 'dynamics of class is adversely affecting the lives of many employees, both men and women' (Bradley, 1999: 109). The focus on gender inequality is, therefore, inevitable and raises issues about other forms of social disadvantage – young men, minority ethnic women, older women, older men – and how these issues can be linked. Although referring to Britain, Irene Bruegal's observations on the gender dimensions of local development also have application to Denmark:

At the same time without effective local authority women's committees, local economic development and urban regeneration policy have become disengendered to a remarkable degree. . . . The charge is not so much rank sexism; rather a failure to understand what the gendering of local economic policy might entail. This might appear a side issue in Britain, now that women have become more visible in political parties, in the media and as commentators on economic trends, and when the future for boys in areas of high deprivation can seem bleaker than for girls. Widening disparities between women, and between men, make gender inequality less prominent as a policy issue.                                                                (Bruegel, 2000: 2–3)

One women trade unionist in Denmark considered that activation and training programmes were not designed to benefit women or combat discrimination in the labour market and that the shift to the Right by the current Liberal-Conservative government has meant that access to training will be even more restricted. The question is how the Danish labour movement reacts, or whether there will be a reaction at all (interview with TU officer, PMF Union, Aalborg, December 2002).

If we focus on *divergence* the following main issues can be highlighted. In the UK, the almost total lack of (formal) union engagement with the New Deal welfare to work programme has led to a more oppressive workfare regime. The spotlight has been put on issues of capacities and capabilities and how women can *access* participation to training and the New Deal. The high costs of child care and lack of adequate provision is a key area of struggle by both trade unions and community/voluntary sector. Community organisations in British cities involved with the various Urban Regeneration Partnerships are increasingly taking on responsibilities for welfare and social policy-making (cf. Michel, 1998).

The lack of a direct link between the voluntary sector and trade unions and the lack of representation of unions in local partnerships have implications for women's mobilisation. Unions in the cities still have an important presence and the strongest unions – the public sector unions – have high women memberships, and their struggles around welfare reforms (and against privatisation) do have direct impacts on women's social well-being. In Danish cities the trade unions are heavily involved with labour market policies in both the political arena and in the management of activation programmes. However, unions do not generally have a strong tradition around gender and equality so their role in promoting women's interests in the labour market can be problematic. The politics of activation generates different types of struggles and mobilisations. In urban contexts, the UK New Deal for the Unemployed is paradoxically focusing the spotlight on the inadequacies of basic welfare services and social reproduction which will combat poverty and exclusion but are essential for women's and men's access to the labour market. Thus many voluntary organisations are concerned with child care provision, training programmes sensitive to women's needs, transport and mobility, and so on. In Danish cities, this may become a pressing issue given the new dominance of liberal politics, but the dominant discourse around welfare and activation focuses on marginalisation around ethnicity. This has parallels with the 'lone parent' discourse in the UK – activation programmes are being designed around integrating immigrants into the labour market. Social assistance claimants are also included as being vulnerable to marginalisation. As Siim (2000: 147) points out, this is challenging social movements to develop their own counter-discourses of social solidarity, which will unite oppressed groups in the labour market.

There are different historic legacies in terms of politics of diversity. Compared with Denmark, there is a *relatively* more developed coalition of women's and community organisations with a clear political and social agenda as well as equality politics which embrace different forms of social oppressions in UK (perhaps with the exception of Copenhagen; see Andersen and Larsen, this volume, chapter 13). This can be explained by the remnants of municipal socialism, but also the national struggles over institutionalised racism and campaigns against violence against women. The role of the union movement in both countries is crucial, but the relatively advanced developments of women's self-organisation (or the integration of diversity) within the larger British unions must be seen as crucial in shaping equality agendas. This tradition has not been embedded in the Danish TU movement to the same degree (Hansen, 2002), which may also explain why greater union involvement in corporatist networks does not guarantee that equality policies will be put on the policy agenda or prioritised.

To sum up, the framework introduced in this chapter opens up the space for considering the variation in the changing role played by political struggle and mobilisation in the welfare state across different national (space) contexts. So, the implication for our understanding of gender exclusion is contextualised within the constitution and reconstitution of the social proletariat, organisation of the welfare state and social regulation, the labour and trade union, women's movement, other social movements, and so on I suggest that such an approach opens up a line of enquiry which integrates notions of exclusion to concepts of social and class mobilisation which focus on women as actors and resisters rather than passive victims.

## References

Aalborg Kommune (2001a). *Ligestillingsredegørelse* [Equal Opportunities Statement]. Aalborg: Aalborg Kommune Ligestillingsudvalget.

Aalborg Kommune (2001b). *Hvor meget er kvinders arbejde værd?* [How Much is Women's Work Worth?]. Aalborg: Aalborg Kommune Ligestillingsudvalget.

Andersen, J. and J. Torfing (2002). *Netværkstyring i velfærdssamfundet: de lokale koordinationsudvalg*. Aalborg: CARMA, Aalborg University Centre.

Beatty, C., S. Fothergill, T. Gore and A. Green (2002). *The Real Level of Unemployment 2002*. Sheffield: Centre for Regional Economic and Social Research, Sheffield Hallam University.

Bourdieu, P. (1998). *Acts of Resistance*. Cambridge: Polity Press.

Bradley, H. (1999). *Gender and Power in the Workplace*. London: Macmillan Press.

Bradley, H., M. Erickson, C. Stephenson and S. Williams (2000). *Myths at Work*. London: Blackwell.

Bredgaard, T. (2001). *A Danish Jobtraining Miracle? Temporary subsidised employment in the public and non-profit sector (National Report for the MESANOM Project)*. Aalborg: CARMA, Aalborg University Centre.

Bruegal, I. (2000). 'Getting Explicit Gender and Local Economic Development'. *Local Economy*, 15, 1.

Byrne, D. (1997). 'Social Exclusion and Capitalism: The Reserve Army across Time and Space'. *Critical Social Policy*, 50.

Centre for Urban and Regional Studies (1997). *Gender Report: Women and Regional Regeneration in the West Midlands*. Birmingham: University of Birmingham.

Colgan, F. and S. Ledwith (2000). 'Diversity, Identities and Strategies of Women Trade Union Activists'. *Gender Work and Organisation*, 7, 4.

Compston, H. and P.K. Madsen (2001). 'Conceptual Innovation and Public Policy: Unemployment and Paid Leave Schemes in Denmark'. *Journal of European Social Policy*, 11.

Crompton, R. (1999). 'Non-standard Employment, Social Exclusion, and the Household: Evidence from Britain', in J. Lind and I.H. Moller (eds.), *Inclusion and Exclusion: Unemployment and Non Standard Employment in Europe*. Aldershot: Ashgate.

Diamond, J. (2001). 'Managing Change or Coping with Conflict? Mapping the Experience of a Local Regeneration Partnership', *Local Economy*, 16, 272–85.

Esping-Andersen, G. (1992). 'The Emerging Realignment Between Labour Movements and Welfare States', in M. Regini (ed.). *The Future of Labour Movements*. London: Sage.

Esping-Andersen, G. (ed.) (1996). *Welfare States in Transition: National Adaptions in a Global Economy*. London: Sage.

Etherington, D. (1997). 'Trade Unions and Local Economic Development – Lessons from Denmark'. *Local Economy*, 12.

Etherington, D. (1998). 'From Welfare to Work in Denmark: an Alternative to Free Market Policies'. *Policy and Politics*, 26, 2.

Etherington, D. (2000). 'A Question of Space and Place? Gender, Class Mobilisation and Exclusion'. Paper to Gender Empowerment and Politics Conference, 18–20 August, Vilvorde Kursus Centre, Denmark.

Etherington, D. (2003a). 'Women Experiencing Poverty and Exclusion: Comparing Strategies in Aalborg (DK) and Sheffield (UK)'. Paper to the International Research Conference on Marginalization and Social Exclusion, Aalesund, Norway, 21–23 May.

Etherington, D. (2003b). 'Welfare Reforms Local Government and the Politics of Social Inclusion: Lessons from Denmark's Labour Market and Area Regeneration Programmes'. Roskilde, Denmark: Roskilde University Centre, *Reseach Paper no. 4/03*.

Etherington, D. and M. Jones (1999). 'Practising Class and Social Mobilisation: Welfare *through* Work – An Alternative to Workfare?' Paper presented to the Annual Conference of the Royal Geographical Society/Institute of British Geographers, University of Leicester, January.

Etherington, D. and M. Jones (2003). 'Beyond Contradictions of the Workfare State: Denmark, Welfare-*through*-Work, and the Promises of Job-Rotation'. *Environment and Planning C: Government and Policy.*

Etherington, D. and M. Jones (forthcoming). 'Whatever Happened to Local Government? Local Labour Market Policy in the UK and Denmark'. *Policy and Politics.*

Fairclough, N. (2000). *New Labour New Language?* London: Sage.

Ferguson, I., M. Lavalette and G. Mooney (2002). *Rethinking Welfare: A Critical Perspective.* London: Sage.

Geddes, M. (1997). *Partnership against Poverty and Exclusion – Local Representation Strategies and Excluded Communities in the UK.* Bristol: Policy Press.

Ginsburg, N. (1992). *Divisions of Welfare A Critical Introduction to Comparative Social Policy.* London: Sage.

Grover, C. and J. Stewart (2000). 'Modernizing Social Security? Labour and its Welfare to Work Strategy'. *Social Policy and Administration*, 34, 3.

Hansen, C. (2000). 'Democratic Challenges to Policy Networks'. Paper to GEP International Conference, Vilvorde Kursus Centre, Denmark.

Hansen, C. and A. Hansen (2000). *Democracy and Modern Governance Exemplified by the Danish Labour Market Steering System.* Aalborg: Aalborg University Centre, Department of Economics, Politics and Public Administration.

Hansen, L.L. (2002). *Does the Future of Unions Depend upon the Integration of Diversity?* Mimeo, Roskilde: Roskilde University Centre.

Harvey, D. (1996). *Justice, Nature and the Geography of Difference.* London: Blackwell.

Herd, D., J. Peck and N. Theodore (1998). 'Union Representation in New Deal Partnerships'. A briefing paper prepared for the TUC, Manchester: University of Manchester, School of Geography New Deal Monitoring Project.

Jessop, B. (2000). 'From the KWNS to the SWPR', in G. Lewis, S. Gewirtz and J. Clarke (eds.), *Rethinking Social Policy.* London: Sage/Open University.

Jones, C. and T. Novak (2000). 'Class Struggle, Self Help and Popular Welfare', in M. Lavalette and G. Mooney (eds.), *Class Struggle and Social Welfare.* London: Routledge.

Jones, M. and K. Ward (2002). 'Excavating the Logic of British Urban Policy: Neo-Liberalism as the Crisis of Crisis Management', in N. Brenner and N. Theodore (eds.), *Spaces of Neoliberalism Urban Restructuring in North America and Western Europe.* Oxford: Blackwell.

Kelly, J. (1998). *Rethinking Industrial Relations Mobilization, Collectivism and Long Waves.* London: Routledge.

Larsen, F., N. Abildgaard, T. Bredgaard and L. Dalsgaard (2001). *Kommunal Aktivering – Mellem disciplinering og integration.* Aalborg: CARMA, Aalborg University Centre.

Lavalette, M. and G. Mooney (2000). 'Introduction: Class Struggle and Social Policy', in M. Lavalette and G. Mooney (eds.), *Class Struggle and Social Welfare.* London: Routledge.

Leitner, H. and E. Sheppard (2002). ' "The City is Dead, Long Live the Net":

Harnessing European Interurban Networks for a Neoliberal Agenda', in N. Brenner and N. Theodore (eds.), *Spaces of Neoliberalism Urban Restructuring in North America and Western Europe*. Oxford: Blackwell.

Levitas, R. (2000). 'Community, Utopia and New Labour'. *Local Economy*, 15, 3.

Lind, J. (1999). 'Labour Market Flexibility and Regulation', in J. Lind and I. Moller (eds.), *Inclusion and Exclusion: Unemployment and Non-Standard Employment in Europe*. Aldershot: Ashgate.

Loftager, J. and P. Kongshoj Madsen (1997). 'Denmark', in H. Compston (ed.), *The New Politics of Unemployment: Radical Policy Initiatives in Western Europe*. London: Routledge.

MacGregor, S. (1999). 'Welfare, Neo-liberalism and New Paternalism: Three Ways for Social Policy in Late Capitalist Societies'. *Capital and Class*, 67.

Marx, K. (1973). *Capital*. Vol. 1. Harmondsworth: Penguin.

Massey, D. (1996). 'Space/Power, Identity/Difference', in A. Merrifield and E. Swyngedouw (eds.), *The Urbanisation of Injustice*. London: Lawrence and Wishart.

Mayo, M. (2000). 'Exclusion, Inclusion and Empowerment: Community Empowerment? Reflecting upon the lessons of strategies to promote empowerment'. Paper to GEP International Conference, Vilvorde Conference Centre, Denmark.

McDowell, L. (2001). 'Father and Ford Revisited: Gender, Class and Employment Change in the New Millenium'. *Transactions of the Institute of British Geographers*, NS 26.

Michel, S. (1998). 'Childcare and Welfare (In)Justice'. *Feminist Studies*, 21, 1.

Miliband, R. (1989). *Divided Societies: Class Struggle in Contemporary Capitalism*. Oxford: Oxford University Press.

Miliband, R. (1995). *Socialism for a Sceptical Age*. London: Polity.

Moller, I.H. (1999). 'Trends in the Danish Social Mode of Economic Regulation', in J. Lind and I.H. Moller (eds.), *Inclusion and Exclusion: Unemployment and Non Standard Employment in Europe*. Aldershot: Ashgate.

PMF (Paedagogisk Medhjaelper Forbund) (1999). *Hvad ligger der bag den arbejdsmarked reform?* [What Lies behind the Labour Market Reforms?]. Aalborg: PMF.

Rake, K. (2000). 'Men First'. *Guardian*, 20 June.

SCOOP Aid (2001). *Lone Parents in South Yorkshire*. Sheffield: SCOOP Aid.

Sheffield City Council (2003). *Women Living in Poverty*. Briefing paper for the Sheffield First For Inclusion Partnership Board. Sheffield: Sheffield City Council.

SID (1995). *Voksenuddanelseereformen – vision eller vanetaekning* [Adult Education Reforms – Vision or Illusion]. Copenhagen: SID.

Siim, B. (2000). *Gender and Citizenship Politics and Agency in France, Britain and Denmark*. Cambridge: Cambridge University Press.

Speak, S. (2000). 'Barriers to Lone Parents' Employment Looking Beyond the Obvious'. *Local Economy*, 15, 1.

Taylor, M., G. Craig and M. Wilkinson (2002). 'Co-option or Empowerment? The Changing Relationship Between the State and the Voluntary and Community Sector'. *Local Governance*, 28.

Wainwright, H. (1987). *Labour: A Tale of Two Parties*. London: The Hogarth Press.

Warren, T. (2000). 'Diverse Breadwinner Models: A Couple-Based Analysis of Gendered Working Time in Britain and Denmark'. *Journal of European Social Policy*, 10, 4.

# 12
# The Politics of Marginal Space

*Jørgen Elm Larsen*

## Introduction

Denmark is internationally known for its mature welfare state covering almost all people in need of cash benefits or social services. Relatively speaking, Denmark has a high degree of socio-economic equality among its citizens, although recent developments in Danish politics towards immigrants and refugees challenge this rosy picture. In the late 1990s and at the beginning of the new millennium, Denmark and a few other countries like Ireland and the Netherlands were known as the 'European miracles', with low unemployment rates and low inflation. Paradoxically, however, despite the low unemployment rate in Denmark, there seems to be a rather large group of marginal people who are almost impossible to employ in the regular labour market. At the same time, the active role of Danish citizens is stressed more than ever and most forcefully demonstrated through the activation policy that demands of everybody that they have to participate on the labour market (Larsen, 2002a). The discrepancy between the totalising activation line and a large group of hard-to-employ has marked a second front-line in social policy. There is a growing recognition of the difficulties that social and labour market policies face in relation to bringing the hard-to-employ into the regular labour market. Instead of a hardcore activation policy, different types of 'social activation' have been implemented aiming at some kind social and spatial integration of marginal people.

This chapter presents a study of this second front-line of social policy as it is carried out in the city district of Kongens Enghave in Copenhagen. It is a study of drop-in centres and places-to-be for marginal people, for example mentally ill people, drug addicts, problem beer drinkers and long-term unemployed social assistance claimants.

Although this study is local in scope, the aim of this chapter is to frame the empirical results within a broader theoretical and conceptual context related to the social policy discourses on social integration and empowerment.

The concept of the *politics of marginal space* is employed to emphasise an increasingly important form of social integration of the most marginal and vulnerable people. The politics of marginal space is, however, an ambiguous phenomenon. On the one hand, the politics of marginal space could be interpreted as a politics of displacement or of neglect. On the other hand, it could been seen as a response to a need of differentiated social integration – that is a particularistic policy approach towards those who do not, cannot or are unwilling to fit within a universal or normalising social policy approach. The politics of marginal space can be seen as recognition of marginal people's special needs and lifestyles. However, it can easily turn out to be a politics of displacement or of neglect if this recognition is not complemented by a willingness to provide the necessary space and resources to accommodate and provide for these people (Larsen, 2002b).

## Normalisation and social integration

Social integration through normalisation has been the prime objective in social work with marginal people over at least the last 25 years in the Danish and many other welfare states. The normalisation principle holds that all citizens, irrespective of their physical, social or psychological limitations, are to be as far as possible supported and assisted to function in the normal, everyday life of the local community and of society in general. Normalisation has been perceived as a prerequisite for integration into the family and social networks, into the workforce and into political participation. The normalisation principle has been based on the belief that it is desirable to break down the barriers between ordinary citizens and those that are different or marginal. Those that are different or marginal should not be isolated from 'normal' people and be institutionalised into special enclaves.

Paradoxically, the normalisation principle has for many marginal people resulted in them becoming 'homeless'. The closure of total institutions (Goffman, 1961) and the placing of marginal people in local communities has created new types of social integration problems. To inhabit a physical place, a 'home' is not the same as feeling at home and having the home function socially and practically. The de-institutionalisation of marginal people was not met with adequate offers of housing, treatment and social opportunities as these people moved into the local communities. Consequently, marginal people not only experienced a lack of care arrangements but also lacked 'fields of care' (Tuan, 1996). By 'fields of care' I mean places in which marginal people can feel emotionally or otherwise particularly connected – that is places they dream of and wish to belong to. A drop-in centre can be perceived as a chink in that type of normalisation and integration practice marginal people most often meet, and drop-in centres may create a space for other practices of being and living.

## Drop-in centres as communities

It was particularly during the 1990s that drop-in centres were established in many local communities as an opportunity for marginal people to have their own places-to-be. Drop-in centres are a way of accommodating people who, in one way or another, cannot or will not adjust to the framework of normality. The renewed importance of drop-in centres is, however, due not least to the increasing concentration and visibility of vulnerable and marginal people in certain local areas such as Kongens Enghave. Drop-in centres can generally be seen as frameworks supporting marginal people's communities in marginal places. These are places for people who are socially isolated in their everyday life, and who have a need for support in order to handle their lives.

The former Minister of Social Affairs, Karen Jespersen (2000), pointed out that the lack of communities, especially for vulnerable and marginal people, is the major challenge for a new welfare project. When emphasis is placed politically on the generation of strong communities, it is not coincidental that simultaneously much greater emphasis and faith are placed on the idea that voluntary social work can solve a number of social policy challenges that are seen to lie outside the scope and capacity of public social work. When it is pointed out that marginal people become strong and resourceful only through being part of strong communities where they can take joint responsibility, then there is also an increased emphasis on local and localised issues for social work. In the main, marginal people are confined to the local area in which they live. They are not connected to a workplace, and many have a weak or non-existent family and/or social networks both within and outside their local area. In addition, they often do not have the economic or personal resources to participate in social or cultural activities, and in other communities outside their local area. Those communities that could socially integrate marginal people and contribute to having them become responsible for their own and others lives must thus first be developed locally. Simultaneously, the community that is to create meaning and identity for those within it must also be connected to spaces and places where the communities can engage in fellowship and activities.

## Different modes of social integration

Disciplining, controlling and punishing poor people are often seen as an intrinsic part of social policy. Modern prisons and workhouses certainly had such functions and some scholars and politicians also regard some of the contemporary workfare or activation programmes in the same way.[1] However, self-discipline and self-control work much more indirectly, smoothly and often cost less than external discipline and control. The kind of social technologies that are employed in contemporary social policy to produce 'conduct of conduct' are in most cases based on the ability to promote self-discipline and self-control among marginal people. Social technologies and/or technologies of the self that promote self-discipline and self-control often appear to marginal people as more indirectly and less compelling than external discipline and control.[2] Identity or self-identity is a central condition for self-control and self-discipline. When work disappears or if it never became an option, the wage-earner identity either fades away or is never established as part of a person's identity. Some unemployed and 'unemployable' people find other ways of coping and creating an identity. But many marginal people without family, kinship or other close social relations often feel rootless. In this context, various types of drop-in centres can function as identity-creating entities and can thus contribute to the creation of self-discipline and self-control. The centres promote and regulate interaction between people at the margins of society, as well as relationships between marginal people and others in local communities. The various types of drop-in centres create the potential for social contact and a certain amount of regularity in daily life.

At the same time, the various types of drop-in centres and places-to-be have their own raison d'être and their own ways in which they operate, which promote or discourage different types of social integration. In this context, we can differentiate between three types of integration: *normalising integration, segmented integration* and *communicative integration*.

*Normalising integration*, as it can, for example, be expressed in the activation enterprise, intentionally builds on trying to integrate marginal people into a normal working life. A secondary goal, connected with the former, is to educate or re-educate marginal people to turn up and remain in a specified place during certain hours of the day. The activation system's focus on normalisation, however, makes it difficult for this system to observe, understand and act in relation to the lifestyles that proliferate in a local area's tribal communities. Tribal communities are here defined as groups that occupy certain territories, where there is a clear distinction between those who belong to the tribe and those who are 'outsiders'. Tribal communities are characterised by the specific and exclusive subculture that the members share, for example, a certain type of 'abuse culture', related to certain places where this subculture is practised. The beer drinkers in Kongens Enghave, for example, comprise such a tribal community.

The beer drinkers' tribal communities are based on user developed and unorganised places-to-be (for example, worksheets, open spaces and the harbour foreshores) and they build on a type of *segmental integration*. The places-to-be coexist with the other physical and social spaces in the locality, but there is a marked division between the tribe that inhabits the area and the rest of the local population. The normalising and the segmented integration types display very poor communication. The tribal communities represent a social problem culture, which the activation system aims to address and hopefully eliminate, because participation in the problem culture is often seen as preventing participation in the labour market. In both Kongens Enghave and many other suburbs and municipalities in Denmark, there is an attempt for example to persuade or force alcoholics to take the drug antabus (which, if taken in combination with alcohol causes vomiting) whilst they are being activated. Communities based on addiction are assumed to prevent both participation in activation and integration in normal and healthy communities. One important reason for why tribal communities are still tolerated is that at least in these communities the beer drinkers are under some kind of control and at the same time located in marginal places where they create the least amount of inconvenience for the other local inhabitants and shopkeepers.

Drop-in centres for the mentally ill were primarily founded with the purpose of establishing a differentiated type of integration or *communicative integration*, which is a mode of integration based on recognition of differences between people and their different needs. It aims at establishing a framework for the community that can accommodate these differences. Drop-in centres for the mentally ill who frequent Kongens Enghave function first and foremost as places where it is possible to receive care in contrast to the activation projects that primarily function as places-to-be where marginal people are forced to stay, and where there are various types of disciplinarian and normalising rituals in place.[3] The communicative integration at the drop-in centres for the mentally ill builds on an attempt to avoid segregation by attempting to build a bridge between different lifestyles, without necessarily striving towards a normalising integration. This modus operandi signifies what has also been termed 'the politics of a differentiated universalism' (Williams, 1999).

## Marginal spaces as homely spaces

A drop-in centre for mentally ill people can first and foremost be seen as an intimate space. That is, a space where people share everyday experiences and where in particular mentally ill people with a weak or non-existent network experience their only daily social interaction. It is a space that, through the community, offers an opportunity for social integration, which occurs and is created there. This is a space that in this way takes on the characteristics of a 'home'.

Their dwelling place or their home is often not the place where interaction with others can occur, and the home is thus often experienced as a place of loneliness or boredom (Larsen and Schultz, 2001). For many of the mentally ill, their home is actually a harbouring place for fear and obsessive-compulsive thoughts, whilst the drop-in centre is associated with homeliness in the shape of food, care and social contact. For some their accommodation ('the home') is therefore just a place to be, whilst the drop-in centre is the place where one can feel at home. The drop-in centre is the place where there is social contact, where one can eat a hot meal with others, and the place where the social aspects of life can develop. Even though there may be chaos around the users and in their lives, the drop-in centres represent a kind of 'normality' in terms of a welcoming environment, cooked meals, a well-laid table and the serving of the meals. This creates a kind of 'symbolic order of everyday life' and provides a way of creating some type of order in an otherwise chaotic and problematic life. It can be understood as a type of symbolic glue that influences the user in a positive manner by installing a kind of normality and dignity in their daily lives. If the drop-in centre provides a person with a self-identity and a place-identity, then the drop-in centre is a part of the home; that is, the place where one feels at home.

## Place, identity and community

A sense of place is created by the socialisation of space. Therefore, spaces are never just a physical condition, but are to a large degree made up of the ways that people place themselves socially. This social placement in a space brings with it borders and distinctions around that which is associated or not associated with the space. Borders and distinctions that at first appear as 'natural' and 'self-explanatory' are the result of complicated negotiations around the rights to the space. Those people that move in for the short or long term inhabit the public space. Public spaces convert to private spaces, and are thus never neutral zones but spaces that always change in importance, interpretation and relevance in relation to those people that occupy them (Goffman, 1971). The social construction of meaning in relation to places is created, for example, through different institutions, social relations and discourses. In this sense, places are not stable entities but are created and re-created by historically processes. Places represent values, perceptions and practices, which together constitute socially constructed communities.

Thus, the place defines a space that has taken on significance through those cultural processes that individuals and groups experience in relation to this space. Attachment to places, and the people who are found there, are a significant part of individuals and groups' life and identity. The attachment means that people have a sense of belonging, that they feel included, establish roots there, and also have a sense of community in relation to these places (Low and Altman, 1992). A central part of belonging is thus the feelings and emotions that the place elicits, and is associated with. Belonging is thus not primarily about the physical characteristics of the place (for example, beautiful landscapes), but about relationships and interactions with other people, who are part of creating those impressions, experiences and feelings that are associated with specific places. Places are thus contexts that elicit the crystallisation of people, community and cultural relationships. It is to these social relationships and not 'place' as a 'space' that people feel attached to. The place attachment can underpin the experience of security and can connect social communities in an open and obvious manner. Place attachment contributes to the fact that people and groups share experiences, impressions and opinions that define a sense of a unique community (Low and Altman, 1992).

The above highlights that spaces and communities are defined in part through their positioning in the hierarchy of power and the way they represent themselves, and in part through the feelings and importance that are associated with them (Gupta and Ferguson, 1992). Abstract spaces are redefined through social practice and those classifications and representations that highlight both similarities and differences between places and people. However, places are also the starting point for the creation of differentiating interaction spaces (Certeau, 1984).

Local communities are thus not only places with shared practices and frames of reference for the development of feelings, meaning and identity. Moreover, the local community stands not only in relationship to other communities, but is in itself a composition of internal differentiating social practices and communities that again are internally differentiating, and so on. Thus, there are both internal and external classification processes within the local communities in relation to these differentiation processes. Structures in social space become an expression in a number of ways in the form of spatial contradictions, where the occupied or acquired space functions as a form of apparent symbolisation of the social space (Bourdieu et al., 1999). When society is hierarchical (for example, among those that work and do not work, among those that are beer drinkers and those that are not beer drinkers, between the mentally ill and drug addicts, and so on) then the physical space also becomes hierarchical.

## Marginal spaces

Marginal people are rarely associated with positive place attachments. Being marginal is an indication that people are outside or on the fringes of the arenas, institutions or places that are normally associated with being of positive value in society – especially having a job or being part of a family. However, meaning, identity and community exist not only within the framework of normality.

Places-to-be and drop-in centres for marginal people are not only 'badlands', even though most people would avoid such places, either because they appear threatening and repulsive or remind them of how bad things can turn out if they lose their job and are socially derailed. However, for those people that frequent these places, it can often be a case of a positive attachment. Attachment to a place can often contribute to individuals and groups being able to share symbolic meaning that promotes a sense of a special and unique community.

Places where marginal people live and develop their identity can be seen as both problem areas and as pockets of resistance. However, they are also sites of ordering (Hetherington, 1997). The social order is not least maintained by place politics that creates meaning and identity in the local space. The relationship between marginal places and their inhabitants and other places and their inhabitants is not only or even mainly one of conflictual relations but also one of ordering relations. The mere existence of marginal places might actually produce a kind of ordering of social relationships in a community with heterogeneous groups and people. Such places can be symbolised by another set of values and impressions than those that are the norm in society, and these places can present a fulcrum for their identity and the way in which they want to be identified. Such places can take on a central role for reproduction of marginal or outsider identities (Shields, 1991; Hetherington, 1998). These places can create possibilities for individuals and groups being able to exist and interact in a different way and that they eventually can constitute new identities and narratives among the individuals that congregate in the places. Foucault (1986) has termed these indeterminable places, and the practices that constitute these special places-to-be by various types of alternative activities, 'heterotopia'.

Heterotopia does not exist 'in the order of things', but rather is constituted through the ordering of things of which they are co-producers. Heterotopia occurs in places where those who are forced out, marginal, excluded or where ambivalent things are represented, and where this representation becomes the basis for a changing of the order of things. This has the effect of presenting a contrast to the dominant representations of the social order. There are no 'innate' characteristics of particular places that in themselves should determine that they are referred to as heterotopia. Heterotopian relationships are created, rather, through the relationship between places that contain different types of social order and representations.

Attribution to and/or the emergence of a certain place as being 'different' occurs when such a place starts to be compared with other places with different arrangements and representations. The arrangements and representations that are associated with heterotopia are perhaps not stable or locked in, but are part of the process that can create meaning in the way people see themselves in the sense of who they are and how they relate to others – in relationship to both the group they belong to and other external groups.

However, who the outsiders are and who the insiders are is dependent on the position of the observer. Becker (1973), for example, points out that for people who are branded as outsiders, the orientation can be completely reversed. Perhaps the outsider does not accept those rules and norms from which the construction of 'outsider' is defined.

Furthermore, he/she will not accept that those people that define him/her as an outsider has the competence or a legitimate right to carry out this labelling. For the one who breaks the rules, these 'others', those that judge and carry out the labelling, can be perceived as outsiders themselves. He/she perceives himself as an insider in the group, which has the same identity and way of functioning as him/herself.

Although the insider and the outsider view of such heterotopic or marginal places may be in total opposition to each other, they none the less create an ordering of spatial and social relations. Social relations may without such a spatial ordering be much more conflictual and destructive for the community. However, the paradox around these marginal places is that they serve as identity creating and, at the same time, the community at large sees them as marginal places. Marginal places are those that function as a symbolic centre for outsider groups or groups that are, or consider themselves to be, on the periphery of society. These individuals and groups can become or be experienced as the 'others' or the 'strangers' and 'foreigners' by the surrounding community create identities in such places, and eventually some resistance to the conduct of conduct imposed on them by the rest of the community or the society at large.

## The small ghetto

The ghetto is often used as a derogatory term – something that should not be found in our city or as a symbol of the dangerous and evil in city life. However, in certain instances, the ghetto does fulfil very positive functions for its inhabitants. There is a need for differential spaces so that the right to be different is recognised (Lefebvre, 1991). The small ghetto is not to be conflated with the concentration and segregation of, for example, immigrants, refugees or marginal people in certain areas and housing estates in the city. However, in particular, these groups are often not rooted in powerful networks with easy access to economic, social, cultural and political capital. 'Integration' policies that aim to disperse these people throughout the city and in housing estates to avoid segregation are basically a way of denying them a place of their own: a place where they can share common narratives, community feelings and identities. Even with the best of intentions, strong anti-segregation policies can create processes whereby the socially excluded are further marginalised and end up being isolated in their own restricted physical and social space.

The city dwellers of today – and especially those who belong to the most mobile part of the working population – live a rather individualised life. Many studies have shown that they do not necessarily wish or need intimate social relations with their neighbours or the community. Many want to live an anonymous life among strangers (Pløger, 1999). They are based in networks of which only a few are local (see also Castells, 1997; Bauman, 1998). However, those strangers that they want to live among should be like them and not potentially dangerous and deviant strangers.

Those who have a real need for community-building and identity are first and foremost the non-mobile: elderly people, handicapped people and others who are much more territorially rooted. But the kind of community they are most strongly oriented to is the 'small ghetto'. In this sense, it is perhaps difficult to maintain the idea of a joint local community that secures a strong social integration for all its members. On the other hand, there is an obvious danger in placing too much emphasis on difference, because it may lead to a counterproductive social fragmentation and to tribalism. Acknowledging differences and differential space should not lead to mechanisms and processes of closure, where certain tribes are denied access to common goods – common resources, decision-making and narratives. In today's society there may no longer be an overriding model of social integration, but to put too much emphasis on tribalism may create hostility and a lack of social cohesion. Instead of having mutual recognised differential spaces in a local community, the lines between differential spaces could become confrontational spaces.

## The politics of marginal space

The politics of marginal space is a new specific mode by which urban and social policy seeks to create integrative spaces for marginal people. The politics of marginal space is an expression of subpolitics that is in contrast to the general normalising policies that are practised through, for example, activation arrangements where the people implementing them are not primarily interested in eliminating the marginal or deviant. In contrast, these policies are aimed at creating the space and possibilities for people to live marginal lives. This is about an attempt to create an alternative order based on the potential for creating different types of social integration of marginal people. Rather than attacking or removing what is deviant from the local social and physical space, there is an attempt to position and integrate these people in marginal places in the local area. The basis for the social integration of marginal people in a local area is, on the one hand, a willingness by the local community to create space for them (Andersen and Larsen, 2001), and, on the other, that these spaces provide a sense of meaning and identity, and as such become places where they can live.

Thus, the politics of marginal space demonstrates a new type of 'conduct of conduct', where marginal people need to be dealt with within a local context, and where the emphasis is on promoting quality of life rather than 'normality'. Improvements in the quality of life are simultaneously about activating and passivaisting behavioural influences. The modus operandi of drop-in centres is, however, also about surveillance and control. But it is not an institutionalised kind of discipline as it works as a part of everyday practices (Deleuze, 1995). Those practices and symbolic orders that are associated with the drop-in centres facilitate a conduct of conduct and are mediators between marginal people and the local community. Individuals' readiness for interaction is activated by improving the quality of life via participation in a community. By building up the interaction by positive energy and feelings within the community, negative interactions with the remainder of the (local) community can perhaps be minimised and, in the best-case scenario, even be turned into positive interactions and relationships. At the same time, by political activation of ethical (local) communities, the everyday world of normality is made responsible for dealings with marginal people. Where employers are expected to create a more accommodating labour market, then volunteer organisations and local actors are expected to create a more accommodating civil society, which actively attempts to include rather than exclude that which is 'different'.

The politics of marginal space can be viewed as a way of building bridges to marginal people and those places they frequent, either by seeking them at street level or by establishing special drop-in centres and places-to-be. The rationale of this governmentality is to establish contact, help and provide care, promote treatment, and influence behaviour by attempting to prevent 'wildly' deviant activities.

The politics of marginal space is different from earlier attempts at organising marginal spaces, in that earlier marginal spaces were established with the purpose of separating the deviant from the normal. Mental institutions, hospitals and different types of treatment, holding, improvement and penal institutions were all used for the containment and handling of the deviant and criminals. One can explain the difference by saying that 'border control' and bridge-building between the normal and deviant has changed from being centralised and institutionalised separating to being decentralised in local open spaces.

Marginal spaces play a central and unique role in dealing with marginal people in local communities by different methods of including their marginality rather than making marginality the subject of treatment. Rather than trying to prevent marginal people's participation in marginal cultures and networks, this type of spatialised and culturalised social policy supports these subcultures and networks. But the collection of marginal people in certain places and in certain subcultures also makes possible a certain degree of supervision and control in the local community. However, this form of supervision and control is more socially integrative and cheaper than the type that would occur in closed institutions. At the same time, these spaces open up the potential for various types of interventions, but these interventions are chosen selectively and are not by definition intended to normalise. Thus it is important to differentiate between different types of intervention and the way in which they attempt to influence behaviour: from care in drop-in centres for the mentally ill, to street-level work attempting to establish contact with the homeless and others that live in public spaces, the right to activation arrangement implementation plans and demands for activation.

Putting emphasis on quality of life rather than normalisation is, however, based on the assumption that there can perhaps be small improvements made, which in the longer term can open up the possibility for a more normal existence. By working with and through individuals, rather than working with people putting up 'resistance', there is an attempt to create empowerment which gives marginal people the power to handle themselves in a more rational and less destructive manner. The best way to achieve this is in different types of communities where some have social therapeutic and/or care personnel and others do not. The strength of these 'free places' is typically formulated as places where the participants can 'function on their own terms'. Furthermore, the drop-in centres create and maintain social networks. However, the different types of marginal spaces are also controlled by various inclusion and exclusion mechanisms. Partly, there are more or less clear guidelines and criteria for what it means to be a member, and partly, there are also various types of behavioural expectations and demands. Something-for-something principles are also in operation, for example, whose obligations one has to meet to obtain methadone, or in association with parole from prison. Activity agreements for social assistance claimants are a particularly active form of mutual obligation, but there are also more moderate examples of mutual obligation with respect to particularly difficult or vulnerable people.

## Marginal spaces as fields of empowerment?

Empowerment was originally defined as a remedy and a process whereby powerless and disadvantaged groups could attain power and self-determination. However, the concept of empowerment has in recent times enjoyed a ripple effect and, in the various forms in which it exists today, it is being applied in the management of both public and private firms, as well as in social work with marginal people. Cruikshank (1999) has demonstrated how empowerment – understood as an instrument used to combat social exclusion and powerlessness – can be compared with other instruments and social technologies, in that the intention is to influence people's behaviour and thus improve their ability to deal with their situation so that they take more responsibility for their own and others' lives. As a social technology, empowerment is a way of acting in relation to others' actions. Empowerment is something that professional facilitators need to help marginal people deal with, so that they manage to gain control over themselves and their lives. Empowerment is no longer something that only marginal and underprivileged people are fighting to attain, but something that others are trying to apply to marginal people (Baistow, 1995). Empowerment is, therefore, not only a question of whether marginal people gain the power to challenge or change the existing order of things, but also to create order. This is a form of governmentality that works through and with, rather than against, marginal people's subjectivities.

To create a connection between the personal self and a 'disturbed' identity requires an active interpretation, which is conditional on the environment in which the interpretation is carried out (Gubrium and Holstein, 2001). Loseke (2001) calls this 'identity work' and Gubrium and Holstein (1995) call it 'biographical work'. Empowerment is a key word in connection with such 'identity work'. The aim of social and social pedagogical work is to activate and (re)establish individuals' capacities, feelings, practices and ethical ability to take responsibility for their own rational self-determination. These empowerment initiatives and those activities that need to be generated to create empowerment are not localised to specific disciplinary spaces, but occur in various guises in more or less controlled cultural communities, where professional aid functions as a facilitator for the rebirthing of active and moral individuals.

Via these empowerment initiatives, individuals are given the capacity to avoid, on the one hand, the risk of exclusion from communities, which they are exposed to if they are incapable of rational self-control. And, on the other hand, they avoid the dangers the individual may pose for the community. Autonomy is now promoted as a question of having personal power, and the capacity to accept responsibility. For those that cannot or will not be included – and for those that are too risky to deal with in open circuits – the control will be in the form of more or less permanent confinement (Rose, 1999). Confinement will thus always be a part of the type of 'border control' utilised. But to what extent, how and what groups are confined, varies historically (Foucault, 1979). However, there is an ambiguity in the governmentality rationale of social policy towards marginal people. The social work approach to marginal spaces includes approaches that tend both to be aimed at individuals and the collective group. Whilst psycho-and social therapeutic work tends to place the single individual at the centre of 'identity work', in other instances place politics acts collectively on the 'identity work'.

In the politics of marginal space, those who have gained better control over themselves, or have completely overcome their destructive habits, or have totally been able to break free of a marginal existence, play a special role. Some of these people become integral keys in the bridge-building and border control between marginality and normality. The 'competent user' has become a new role model in social work, in that it is a person who has been able to break free of their destructive habits, and who can speak about their experiences in a way that appeals to the practical sense of active alcoholics or drug addicts. The 'competent user' fits eminently well into the empowerment model within social work, in that the competent user appears as a previous abuser who has reached a level of self-control and empowerment needed to act out rational self-control. At the same time, the competent user is able to position themselves within an abuser's universe and can thus achieve the necessary contact and trust required for getting active abusers motivated to change their lifestyle. Competent users are particularly included in voluntary social work, and they are indicative of a type of intervention that is based on equal worth and common experience parameters. The philosophy is to meet marginal people as they are and where they are.

## Conclusion

In the analysis of the drop-in centres and their users, it has been illustrated that spatial and cultural social policies contribute to the creation of communities for marginal people. These 'small ghettos' or communities for marginal people are most likely to be the only spaces available where these people are able to have social contact and fellowship. Rather paradoxically, the politics of marginal space may facilitate rather than counteract 'marginal cultures' and 'risk communities'. Social integration into marginal communities may lead to disintegration in relation to 'normal cultures'. Therefore, there seems to be a tension or ambivalence built into this new urban and social policy. On the one hand, the overall governmental policy aims at the reintegration of marginal people into the normal labour market and other normalising social institutions. It is perceived as the best or only way of combating poverty and social exclusion. Everybody is to be self-supportive and self-conductive. On the other hand, there is a growing awareness among certain social policy actors and agencies of the impossibility of normalising all people. Mentally ill people, drug addicts, alcoholics and socially disabled people are not easily inserted into the normal chaos of the labour market, the family and social networks. The different types of drop-in centres and places-to-be for marginal people can be seen as ways of accommodating marginal people in local communities. Drop-in centres for mentally ill people, for example, are committed to an equal moral value and the inclusion of each user on the basis of their diversity. Such a differentiated universalism and claims of recognition, however, renders the risk of producing and legitimising structural differences and inequalities if such an recognition is not combined with claims for redistribution. The politics of marginal space may become a relatively cost-effective way of containing, entertaining and conducting marginal people in the local public space instead of developing more comprehensive and coherent programmes to combat social exclusion and create social integration. The politics of marginal space can thus contribute to ensuring the continuing existence of different coexisting spaces, with very large differences in living conditions, within the local 'community' as well as between poor and more affluent local communities.

A critical perception of the politics of marginal space is that it represents a new confinement of marginal and deviant people. It is not a physical but a symbolically violent confinement as marginal spaces may produce a common-sense perception about the limitations one is subordinated to in the social and physical space. Poor communities with poor people are self-evidently experienced as being condemned to have poor services. The social and spatial differences and hierarchies can thus be perceived as normal and unchangeable. The world exists as it is, and how it should be. Thus ideas about alternatives become unworkable and disappear. Marginal people and marginal places will, however, generally present a challenge for 'normal' people and their idea of how society should function. By representing that which is different and deviant, marginality, demonstrates that which is right and normal. On the other hand, marginality can also present a challenge for the existing orientations and arrangements of people and spaces.

## Notes

1. Workfare and activation programmes should, however, not be conflated since they are often based on different means and goals and on different political ideologies (Barbier, 2001; Larsen, 2002a).
2. For the concept of 'conduct of conduct' and the distinction between the different types of technologies of government, see Foucault (1983; 1988).
3. Although disciplinarian and normalising rituals are central to the activation approach, the activation policy in Denmark has many faces and it varies greatly both among and within the municipalities. In some local activation projects, there is a strong commitment to individual empowerment instead of strictly to labour market participation (Larsen, 2002a; 2002c; 2002d).

## References

Andersen, J. and J.E. Larsen (2001). 'Social bæredygtighed i byudviklingen'. *Medlemsblad for Foreningen Dansk Byøkologi*, 5, 3.

Baistow, K. (1995). 'Liberation and Regulation? Some Paradoxes of Empowerment'. *Critical Social Policy*, 14, 3.

Barbier, J.-C. (2001). *Welfare to Work Policies in Europe. The Current Challenges of Activation Policies*. Paris: Centre d'études de l'emploi.

Bauman, Z. (1998). *Globalization: The Human Consequences*. Cambridge: Polity Press.

Becker, H.S. (1973). *Outsiders: Studies in the Sociology of Deviance*. New York: Free Press.

Bourdieu, P. et al. (1999). *The Weight of the World. Social Suffering in Contemporary Society*. Oxford: Polity Press.

Castells, M. (1997). *The Information Age: Economy, Society and Culture*. Volume II: *The Power of Identity*. Oxford: Blackwell.

Certeau, M. de (1984). *The Practice of Everyday Life*. Berkeley: University of California Press.

Cruikshank, B. (1999). *The Will to Empower. Democratic Citizens and Other Subjects*. Ithaca, NY: Cornell University Press.

Deleuze, G. (1995). *Negotiations*. New York: Columbia University Press.

Foucault, M. (1979). *Discipline and Punishment*. New York: Vintage Books.

Foucault, M. (1983). 'The Subject and Power', in H. Dreyfus and P. Rabinow (eds.), *Michel Foucault: Beyond Structuralism and Hermeneutics*. Brighton: Harvester.

Foucault, M. (1986). 'Of Other Spaces'. *Diacritics*, 16, 1.

Foucault, M. (1988). 'Technologies of the Self', in L.H. Martin, H. Gutman and P.H. Hutton (eds.), *Technologies of the Self. A Seminar with Michel Foucault*. Amherst: The University of Massachusetts Press.

Goffman, E. (1961). *Asylums: Essays on the Social Situation of Mental Patients and Other Inmates*. Harmondsworth: Penguin.

Goffman, E. (1971). *Relations in Public: Micro-Studies of the Public Order*. London: Penguin.

Gubrium, J.F. and J.A. Holstein (1995). 'Life Course Malleability: Biographical Work and Deprivatization'. *Sociological Inquiry*, 65.

Gubrium, J.F. and J.A. Holstein (eds.) (2001). *Institutional Selves. Troubled Identities in a Postmodern World*. Oxford: Oxford University Press.

Gupta, A. and J. Ferguson (1992). 'Beyond Culture. Space, Identity and the Politics of Difference'. *Cultural Anthropology*, 7, 1.

Hetherington, K. (1997). *The Badlands of Modernity. Heterotopia and social ordering*. London: Routledge.

Hetherington, K. (1998). *Expressions of Identity. Space, Performance, Politics*. London: Sage.

Jespersen, K. (2000). 'Her er det nye velfærdsprojekt'. *Dagbladet Politiken*, 22 January.

Larsen, J.E. and I. Schultz (2001). 'Marginale steder', in J. Goul Andersen and P.H. Jensen (red.). *Marginalisering, integration, velfærd*. Aalborg: Aalborg University Press.

Larsen, J.E. (2002a). 'The Active Society and Activation Policy', in J. Andersen and J.E. Larsen, *Coping with Social Polarization in the Urban Landscape – Reflections upon the Politics of Empowerment*. GEP Report No. 1–2002. Aalborg: Aalborg University.

Larsen, J.E. (2002b). 'Who Cares about and for Marginal People?', in J. Andersen and J.E. Larsen, *Coping with Social Polarization in the Urban Landscape – Reflections upon the Politics of Empowerment*. GEP Report No. 1–2002. Aalborg: Aalborg University.

Larsen, J.E. (2002c). 'Marginale mennesker i marginale rum', in M. Järvinen, J.E. Larsen and N. Mortensen (red.), *Det magtfulde møde mellem system og klient*. Århus Aarhus University Press.

Larsen, J.E. (2002d). 'Aktiveringspolitikkens mange ansigter', in J. Andersen, A.-M. Tyroll Beck, C.J. Kristensen and J.E. Larsen (2003). *Empowerment i storbyens rum – et socialvidenskabeligt perspektiv*. Copenhagen: Hans Reitzels Forlag.

Lefebvre, H. (1991). *The Production of Space*. Oxford: Blackwell.

Loseke, D.R. (2001). 'Lived Realities and Formula Stories of "Battered Women"', in J.F. Gubrium and J.A. Holstein (eds.), *Institutional Selves. Troubled Identities in a Postmodern World*. Oxford: Oxford University Press.

Low, S.M. and I. Altman (1992). 'Place Attachment. A Conceptual Inquiry', in I. Altman and S.M. Low (eds.), *Place Attachment*. New York: Plenum Press.

Pløger, J. (1999). ' "Det lokale" som grundlag for bypolitikken – en illusion?'. *Samfundsøkonomen*, 99/7.

Rose, N. (1999). *Powers of Freedom. Reforming Political Thought*. Cambridge: Cambridge University Press.

Shields, R. (1991). *Places on the Margin: Alternative Geographies of Modernity*. London: Routledge.

Tuan, T.F. (1996). 'Space and Place: Humanistic Perspective', in J. Agnao, D.N. Livingstone and A. Rogers (eds.), *Human Geography. An Essential Anthology*. Oxford: Blackwell.

Williams, F. (1999). 'Good-enough Principles for Wlefare', *Journal* 331 of *Social Policy* 28(4): 667–87.

# 13
## Social Polarisation and Urban Democratic Governance

*John Andersen and Jørgen Elm Larsen*

### Introduction

This chapter looks at social struggles over citizenship and democratic participation in relation to urban policy and governance in Denmark and in Copenhagen in particular. If one agrees, as we do, with the general message propounded by Young, Phillips and others in this volume that the analysis of democratic participation and political citizenship cannot be separated from issues of (re)distribution and social citizenship, then urban policy is very useful to highlight this issue in empirical studies. The complexity of urban policy is clearly illustrated by the relationship between inclusive democratic governance and its linkages to different scales of politics and space ranging from neighbourhood to city, regional, national and transnational levels. The message of this chapter is that contemporary urban democracy can be characterised by a striking duality between:

1. New urban entrepreneurial governance in the form of neo-elitist/ corporative market-driven strategic growth strategies, which target investors and operate on a transnational scale. This type of 'growth governance' is based on notions of the entrepreneurial city.
2. The new urban social ('neighbourhood welfare') governance consisting of empowering inclusion-oriented community strategies, which target deprived districts and neighbourhoods and create a new democratic terrain open to social mobilisation. This 'empowerment governance' (Fotel and Andersen, 2003) trend is based on notions of the inclusive city. In many cases, it involves elements of deliberative democracy and politics of empowerment and inclusion.

The tension – and a possible mediation – between the elitist market orientation and the bottom-up welfare orientation presents a theoretical and empirical challenge to research dealing with the politics of empowerment and inclusion not only at the level of local government, but also at the regional, national and transnational levels.

The chapter first outlines a broader framework for the understanding of present forms of social polarisation in the city. The American and European discourse on social polarisation in the city is related to the Danish context in order to highlight the specific features of the urban policy regime in Denmark – including the relation between welfare regimes and urban poverty.

The second section illustrates the duality of urban democracy and contextualises the regime changes emphasising how the transition towards a new post-industrial economy and urban form was mediated via political and institutional struggles over the form and content of urban policy in Copenhagen from the late 1970s to the present.

The concluding section discusses potentials for overcoming the dualism of present urban governance between neo-corporate growth regimes and participatory and community welfare-oriented policies.

## Social exclusion in the urban context

Since the 1980s, social exclusion in cities has become a central issue. Globalisation, industrial decline, migration, social exclusion and segregation are the key words employed to explain processes of polarisation of the social geography (Madanipour et al., 1998).

In the United States, there has been a long-standing discourse and research interest in urban poverty. In the 1980s, the much debated concept of an urban 'ghetto underclass' was developed to describe the inhabitants of urban inner city areas with high concentration of, among other phenomena, poverty, unemployment, crime, teenage pregnancy and lone motherhood (Wilson, 1987). The underclass debate also crossed the Atlantic in the late 1980s (Macnicol, 1987). While the underclass debate was heated in UK, it never gained the same hegemony in Continental Europe. Here, instead, the concept of social exclusion was at the centre of the mainstream discourse at least in the EU institutions (Silver, 1994; Andersen and Larsen, 1995a).

Wacquant (1996) dismisses the idea that there are ghettos in the large European cities on the same scale and segregated way as they exist in larger American cities. But he argues very convincingly that it is possible to point out a number of characteristics that have led to the development of what he terms as 'advanced marginality' in the larger cities of Western nations.

'Advanced marginality' is characterised as follows. First, there is a breakdown of employee contracts – in particular for male unskilled workers. Second, a functional separation from the macro-economic trends occurs in that better employment opportunities generally do not affect the job opportunities of the ghetto inhabitants. Third, a territorial fixation and stigmatisation occurs through a concentration of socially excluded people that develops within distinctive geographical areas. Fourth, alienation in relation to space occurs in that a consequence of the stigmatisation of an area can be that people lose connection, and no longer feel safe, in the geographical area and the social and physical environment that this represents. Fifth, there is a loss of network resources and social capital, in that the majority of people in the ghetto are unemployed and outside mainstream society. This makes it difficult for people to support each other and establish a social economy. Increasingly, the situation is 'everyone for him/herself'. Sixth, a symbolic fragmentation occurs in that the absence of a common method of expression, which symbolically can create spatial connectedness, accentuates the fragmentation of the new urban poor. Furthermore, there are no organisations that are powerful enough to represent the excluded. Hence, the physical space demonstrates and implements the exclusion and suppression mechanisms that constitute the social space. Underprivileged housing areas collect the excluded and the suppressed, and thus intensify their exclusion and suppression.

## Welfare regimes and social exclusion

The possible negative impact of post-industrial urban development in terms of increased inequality and social exclusion depends, in part, on the efficiency of inclusion and redistribution policies. Entrepreneurial city strategies (see later) can have different impacts on social polarisation and living conditions depending on the type of welfare regime and the broader regulatory framework in which such strategies are implemented (Moulart, Swyngedouw and Rodriques, 2003).

In universalistic and redistributive welfare state regimes like the Danish one, the relation between social class or market position and living conditions is to some extent decommodified (Esping-Andersen, 1990). Hence, for example, the impacts of socio-economic change and urban policy concerning labour and housing markets are, therefore, modified or 'filtered' by the operation of the welfare state regime. In residual welfare state regimes like the British, where the 'welfare state filter' or buffer between market position and living conditions is weak, the impact of urban policies on living conditions will be more direct. In much of the debate about the welfare state, the Social Democratic and social liberal forces argue that a strong universal welfare state is not only just but also functional with reference to the stimulation of economic growth; this is precisely because it 'socialises' the costs of socio-economic (including spatial) change. In other words, the universalistic type of welfare state creates a regulatory framework, which modifies the possible socio-economic polarisation effects of market forces.

As in most EU member states, the battle for full employment in Denmark was lost in the late 1970s. In the 1980s, the welfare state project became much more defensive. The advantages of the developed postwar welfare state, which to some degree emancipated the individual from the forces of the market, were translated into 'disincentives' and 'market imbalances' by the offensive neo-liberal and neo-conservative forces.

In 1982, a Conservative–Liberal coalition government came to power after decades of Social Democratic rule, but the changes implemented were moderate and the overall welfare regime was still closest to the universalistic type. In a comparative perspective, the Danish case is an example of a relative stable regime. Unlike many other countries industrial relations are still heavily influenced by strong trade unions. The problem of the 'working poor' is relative marginal and minimum wages have been kept at a relatively high level.

In the 1990s, the most important reorientations within the Danish welfare regime were: (1) A strong emphasis on activation and education schemes for the unemployed; (2) the introduction (since the mid-1990s) of experimental, bottom-up social action schemes targeted at deprived urban districts; and (3) a strong emphasis on regional strategic growth policy which embodied a new type of state-led entrepreneurialism – this was particularly so in the Copenhagen region (see later).

Even though there are, today, common trends in European countries concerning the concentration of socially excluded people in certain urban districts and the emphasis of community renewal in the overall policy approach, there are still major differences between the European welfare states. The specific way in which social and housing policy confronts social exclusion in cities depends on earlier policy traditions in each country, a path dependency in policy developments (Pierson, 1998). The rhetoric about revitalising communities may be very similar in, for example, Denmark and the UK, but existing socio-economic structures, institutions and actors shape the way in which urban restructuring is taking place. Different welfare regimes often approach the same phenomena with different means, or they apply the same governmental technology, for example, 'workfare', in rather diverse ways (see Etherington, this volume, chapter 11).

During the past decade, most European welfare states have adopted some kind of workfare or activation policies in their overall employment policy. The new active line in labour market and social policy has been introduced under different names in the different European welfare states. These active measures have become of prime importance in reforming the welfare systems and in stimulating or forcing the labour market participation of the unemployed and other social benefit claimants (Berkel and Møller, 2002). The apparent parallel international trend in workfare/activation policies does not, however, follow a common path, and activation policies do not lead in the same direction. It is often misleading to treat activation and workfare as one and the same thing, because workfare and activation *in principle* refer to rather different approaches and strategies (Larsen, forthcoming). Most studies of workfare/activation broadly distinguish between two types of approaches, for example, 'work first' or 'social investment'. In general, 'work first' approaches are connected to liberal welfare states and the 'social investment' approaches are especially linked to the Scandinavian welfare states. According to Barbier (2001), the two polar examples in Europe are the United Kingdom representing the purest form of workfare and Denmark representing the purest form of activation social investment type. The Danish activation approach aims, in principle, at improving the employability of those out of work by offering opportunities for training, better skills, work experience, and so on, while the workfare approach tends to restrict access to benefits, reduce levels of compensation and restrict the duration of payments (European Foundation, 1999).

## Socio-spatial polarisation and gender differences

Although Denmark is, comparatively speaking, a relatively egalitarian society, a closer look at the social landscape shows increased spatial concentration of the less affluent, labour market excluded and otherwise marginalised groups. In particular, the City and Region of Copenhagen has crystallised this new social division (Munk, 1998).

From 1995 to 1999 there was an increase of 25 per cent in the number of unemployed people participating in activation measures and in the same period the number of unemployed dropped considerably (from about 12 to 6 per cent). This development shows how strong the political commitment is to activate unemployed people. However, the activation policy has in recent years had little success in bringing the persistent long-term unemployed into the labour market. Many of those who remained unemployed during the employment boom are characterised by having other problems than being unemployed. At the same time, the economic recovery has to a large extent bypassed the deprived districts and their residents. That is to say, socio-spatial polarisation has grown in a period of increased economic growth. The gender and age composition of the long-term unemployed has also shifted and is now much more clearly concentrated among middle-aged and elderly unskilled women and men. In particular, elderly unskilled men seem to represent a distinctive new type of social exclusion (Andersen and Larsen, 1998) that policy-makers and welfare institutions have not been able to respond to. Whereas women's risk of economic impoverishment (in terms of lack of economic resources/income poverty) is still slightly higher than men's risk, the exposure to 'hard-core social exclusion' in terms of alcoholism, the breaking down of everyday life routines, and so forth is much greater among men.

One of several reasons for the change in the gender profile of social exclusion has to do with the (overlooked) fact that the most innovative policies of social empowerment were developed for and largely carried out by women. Whereas a range of experimental social action programmes targeted marginalised women, for example, the successful daytime high schools, innovations with regard to excluded men have been more or less absent (Andersen and Larsen, 1998). In fact, there is strong empirical evidence in Denmark that women – including low-income marginalised women – are more active in day care and school boards, local associations and community work and local politics than men (Andersen et al., 2003; Larsen, 2003). In other words, a trend towards the 'feminisation' of local politics can be observed.

## Policy responses at the national level

Since the mid-1990s the political response to the new social division in urban areas has been a long-term social action programme targeted at 'deprived' urban areas. According to the official 'Social Atlas' 5 per cent of the Danish population lives in deprived areas, approximately half of which is located in Copenhagen.

Until 1993, urban policy was not defined as a distinct policy field. The design of the first multidimensional Urban Social Action Programme in 1993/94 was a manifestation of attempts to stimulate bottom-up empowerment orientation in deprived urban areas.

The programme was inspired by EU Poverty 3 (1989–94), which emphasised experimental local action against social exclusion. It was the first time, in Denmark, that a large-scale urban programme was launched, based on principles of multidimensional area-based action, participation (including participation of the Social Housing Associations) and partnership. The programme quickly became an innovative and experimental part of public planning and welfare policy. It had elements of a 'politics of positive selectivism' and 'social mobilisation' approach. In the implementation, the National Urban Committee ('Byudvalget') has, in the negotiations about project contracts with the Municipalities and Housing Associations, insisted that citizen participation and empowerment orientation in the projects should be taken seriously.

All the major parties supported the programme in parliament. One important background for this consensus in the Danish parliament was a long-lasting and contradictory public discourse about social segregation and, in particular, about the emergence of 'ethnic ghettoes' in social housing estates. Social Democratic mayors in municipalities with a large share of social housing estates argued in public that the proportion of ethnic minorities had reached a level that posed a major problem for the local welfare state. These mayors also accused the Liberal-Conservative municipalities of being 'free riders' with regard to the inclusion of immigrants and other socially excluded people. In this climate, a vague consensus that 'something needs to be done' was gradually established in the Danish parliament, but the design of the content and institutional form of policy interventions was left to actors like the social housing associations, the Social Workers' Union and civil servants in the ministries. Despite the 'negative' point of departure in the public discourse – the negative labelling of social housing estates with ethnic minorities as a 'burden' and sometimes with clear connotations of a 'Muslim underclass' – what happened in the practical policy design process was a transformation to a broader social inclusion problematique that recognised the need for government resources to handle the growing spatial inequalities in a more holistic (physical, social and cultural) manner. As can be observed in many policy areas from the 1990s up until the present, the policy design players very often use 'communitarian rhetoric' as a tool to construct a temporary 'beyond left and right slippery consensus'. This is done at the right time and place in order to give a policy field the image of being beyond ideological conflict. In the *practical* policy-making processes, where the crucial point first and foremost is to get money from the state budget, this can sometimes be an efficient strategy.

Compared with most other European countries, the formation of ethnic minority communities is a new phenomenon and the public discourse about the ethnic or 'ghetto problem' in the 1990s was the first of its kind in Denmark. The major reason for the willingness of the liberal and conservative forces to allocate additional resources to a range of regeneration and social action programmes in deprived areas was that they saw the new urban policy as a way handling ethnic tensions.

For the Social Democrats and leftist forces, the dominant rationality for supporting the creation of a new urban policy was the recognition of spatial inequality as a national political issue to which the state should allocate resources.

This part of urban policy has introduced the rhetoric of experimentation, participation and partnership with strong parallels to the Corporate Social Responsibility campaign for making firms more socially responsible for creating a more encompassing labour market. In policy documents like 'The City of the Future' (Ministry for Housing and Urban Affairs, 1999) concepts like the 'Inclusive City' (Young, 1990), the 'Creative City' and the 'Green City' (which relate to the Agenda 21 movement) were introduced.

The 'City of the Future' document underlines that the social, cultural and economic problems of deprived districts should be addressed in a multidimensional and coherent manner. It is explicitly acknowledged that long-lasting multidimensional programmes are necessary due to a lack of coherent planning in the past and the long-term impact of socio-spatial concentration of unemployment and social exclusion. Partnerships with local companies are suggested as tools to improve labour market integration of excluded groups. In practice, the latter has played only a marginal role in the implementation of the programmes.

McClenaghan (see this volume) argues that 'community participation' and 'empowerment' are increasingly expressed as the twin pillars of social policy interventions aimed at social inclusion and based on synergetic partnerships between community groups, governmental bodies, statutory authorities and other organisational agents.

Despite some common elements in the political rhetoric – namely, the communitarian language of rights and duties, the active society, and so on – it is extremely important to distinguish between the political content and outcome of the inclusion orientation in different regime contexts: (1) The neoliberal/conservative welfare regime *retrenchment* context; and (2) the inclusion orientation in the Social Democratic context with welfare regime stability.

In the first case, more 'government through community' (Rose, 1996) to some extent *replaces former citizenship rights and politics of redistribution*. In the later case, the basic architecture of the welfare regime is not transformed and hence politics of inclusion and empowerment – for example, local empowerment projects – is 'added value' to existing welfare policy. As we will argue in the following, the new Danish urban policy was until 2002 (to a large extent) an example of what could be termed politics of positive selectivism with regard to spatial inequality.

However, as the new urban governance in Copenhagen illuminates, the economic growth policy and the area-based social and housing policies are not well orchestrated and integrated. Instead of representing one inclusive face, they manifest themselves as two separate faces of the new urban governance, especially in Copenhagen. In the following, the social struggles in the last decades that led to the present two-faced urban governance regime in Copenhagen will be outlined.

## From urban movements to city entrepreneurialism and community empowerment

The political, social and economic context in which the Copenhagen urban regime was transformed can briefly be summarised as follows (Andersen, 2003). In the 1970s, the Social Democratic hegemonic urban regime, which had dominated local government since the beginning of the twentieth century, was robustly challenged by the growing strength of the new urban movements and the New Left (Socialist Left Party and the Socialist People's Party) who held 30–40 per cent of the seats in the city council. The 'rainbow coalition' between militant working-class segments, the new urban movements and new and old left political radicals created a unique 'post-68' political climate in the city throughout the 1970s. The New Left forces heavily criticised the Social Democrats for a 'top-down' authoritarian urban renewal and planning policy which was based on the interest of the (imagined) 'standard working- and middle-class family', and, according to the New Left, did not take 'particularism', the social and cultural diversity of the urban space into account. The urban movements successfully criticised the top-down planning in its rigid bureaucratic forms. In short, their nodal point was a welfare city in which a diverse civil society and notions of direct democracy held a much stronger position vis-à-vis the monolithic local government administration.

The tensions between local government and the new urban movements became manifest around 1980. The pinnacle of this dislocation was a week-long fight between locals and the police that took place in the streets of Nørrebro in 1980. The event was provoked by the decision to remove a popular playground ('Byggeren') in the area. In reality, the conflict was also about the authoritarian non-participatory style used in the implementation of urban renewal schemes. After this episode, the political climate deteriorated even more, and on the national political scene, the municipality of Copenhagen was labelled as partly 'ungovernable'. The popular Villo Sigurdson from the Left-Socialist Party had controlled the department for urban planning, but from the mid-1980s, the authority of this important department was moved to the direct control of the Lord Mayor. The Left claimed that this removal was illegal and a year-long battle took place in the courts in the mid-1980s about the administrative responsibility for urban planning. This unstable situation paralysed the Copenhagen urban planning system for years.

The political polarisation and institutional dislocation fused with growing budget deficits due to a shrinking tax base caused by demographic change and industrial decline. Copenhagen was hit much harder than the rest of Denmark because the general employment crisis fused with a long-term trend that had existed since the 1960s which saw a massive loss of industrial manual work. The level of public investment in Copenhagen was also shrinking compared to the rest of Denmark. This was in part due to a national decentralisation policy, which was the dominant paradigm until the late 1980s. Furthermore, the municipalities outside Copenhagen have benefited most by the growth in high-paid service sector jobs, which indeed occurred in recent decades due to a growing number of commuters.

Due to the strength of the left-wing parties and the strong Social Democratic position the financial problems were not managed by dramatic cuts in welfare services but largely by accumulation of dept and low levels of public investments. The policy responses during the 1980s consisted of three components: (1) Political pressure for additional state grants until the mid-1980s; (2) a gradual changed housing policy favouring middle and high income households; and (3) attempts to develop a coherent regional strategy for employment and infrastructure development within the framework of the regional authority the Greater Copenhagen Council (founded in 1974).

The Social Democratic national government in office until 1982 had recognised the need for serious negotiations. When the Conservative-Liberal government came to office in 1982, after a decade of Social Democratic rule, an expert commission appointed by the Liberal Home Secretary was created. The commission pointed towards two negative self-perpetuating mechanisms of the socio-economic crisis: (1) industrial decline, lack of new growth and employment sectors; and (2) an expensive demographic composition of the population (many elderly and young) including increasing concentration of socially excluded and other low income groups. Despite the political pressure, the system of municipal reimbursement and state grants remained almost unchanged. The result was a foreseeable increasing in municipal debt.

Since the town hall had been run by the Social Democratic Party from the beginning of the twentieth century, social housing and municipal-owned housing had from this time been an important part of Social Democratic housing policy. Social housing in Denmark dates back to the beginning of the twentieth century when the first Social Democratic-controlled municipalities supported housing cooperatives, which became closely linked to the labour movement (Kolstrup, 1996). The democratic tradition of self-governance in the housing co-operatives is regarded as a unique 'social capital', which constitutes one of the overlooked strengths of the Danish welfare regime (Munk, 1998). In the 1980s, the number of new social housing estates being built decreased, and since the late 1990s has stopped altogether. Furthermore, municipal-owned houses were sold in the mid-1990s. As a way of improving the tax base, the Social Democratic leadership, in a path-breaking alliance with the strengthened Liberal and Conservative members of the city council, gradually accepted this strategic change in housing policy. Hence, the social housing associations were now placed on the periphery. The political changes fused with market changes as the combination of inflation and regulation of tax reduction for private ownership from the 1960s onwards made the purchase of property very advantageous for upper-working-class and middle-class households. The combined result of these changes was that the social geography in the metropolitan region became more polarised because middle-income residents left the social housing sector in which the share of low-income residents rapidly increased. Accordingly, some Copenhagen districts have gradually been gentrified, and the share of private ownership and private co-operative housing in these districts has increased rapidly. Other districts with a greater share of social housing estates moved from the middle to the bottom of the urban hierarchy.

## The role of the regional level

From the beginning, the Greater Copenhagen Council (GCC) was in a functional and financial crisis due to its diffuse legal status. It was also paralysed by struggles between the poor Social Democratic and leftist-governed Copenhagen, and the richer Conservative-Liberal municipalities outside Copenhagen. It was finally closed down by the Conservative-Liberal government in 1987 (parallel to the abolition of the Greater London Council in the United Kingdom by the Thatcher government), and the metropolitan region was left without a political authority. The closure of the GCC only extended the problems of governing Copenhagen and the region.

It was in a context of persistent municipal budget deficits and the political administrative dislocation at the regional level that the national Conservative-Liberal government of the late 1980s held a strong bargaining position vis-à-vis the municipality of Copenhagen. As will be shown, it was in this economic, institutional and political context that the shift towards a more aggressive entrepreneurial city strategy took place.

## The entrepreneurial turn

After years of socio-economic decline and 'ungovernability', a new urban regime of 'state-led city entrepreneurialism' (Harvey, 1989) emerged in the late 1980s. The new Social Democratic leadership gave up its former policy of confrontation vis-à-vis the state, and was less committed to taking the interests of low-income groups in housing policy into account. In the field of urban renewal a more participatory orientation based on ideas of communicative and incremental planning (Sehested, 2002) occurred in the 1990s.

The most pathbreaking change from the late 1980s and onwards was, however, the linkage of the urban regeneration strategy to a metropolitan regional growth strategy. The state–municipal growth alliance has been relatively stable since the beginning of the 1990s when the national Social Democratic leadership was replaced by a more centre-oriented one, and when the Social Democratic Party returned to power in 1992 at the national level (after a decade of Liberal-Conservative rule). The Oerestad project (the creation of a new high-tech-profiled city district) became the flagship project in the implementation of the new strategy (Andersen, 2003). The major change was the emphasis on urban (re)development as a strategic means to compete against other European city regions for investments in the transitions towards the globalised post-industrial economy and urban form.

In 1990, a Metropolitan Committee on traffic investments suggested the establishment of a Copenhagen Metro system and a costly, large-scale Urban Development Plan (UDP) for development of a huge new Copenhagen high-income and international business district – the Orestad district. The key to the plan was to suggest incremental planning, whereby the proceeds from selling land would be used to finance the Metro, and, when it was finished (around 2003), the proceeds would be channelled back to cover outstanding liabilities from the development.

From theoretical perspectives such as growth machine theory (Harding, 1994), neo-Marxist regulation theoretical approaches (Jessop, 1998) or regime theory (Stones, 1993) this initial policy process can be seen as step in the formation of a *neo-corporatist growth regime*. Following Stones, a regime can be defined as a relative stable group with access to institutional resources that enable it to have a sustained role in making governing decisions. For the Liberal-Conservative government the Orestad package was in line with the government's new public management orientation and attempts to introduce more 'business-like modus operandi' in urban planning. The success of the metropolitan growth regime in the initial phase was strongly related to introduction of quasi-market governance instruments.

In the UDP design phase, in the beginning of the 1990s, the Conservative Party was in government together with the Liberal Party, while the Social Democratic Party was the largest party in the parliament and the dominant party in the Copenhagen City Council. At the political level, the key actors in the new ground-breaking state–capital growth coalition were the leaderships of the Social Democratic and the Conservative Parties. Influential professionals in urban planning and opponents of the plan criticised it in the public discourse using terms such as 'elitist corporate planning' and the 'politics of the casino'.

Despite intense criticism, the coalition was powerful enough to speed up the process of implementation. In 1992, a law on the institutional set-up and general terms for the project passed through parliament, where only the United Left and the Socialist People's Party voted against the law. Hence, the Danish UDP represents a clear case of 'exceptionality' (Moulart, Swyngedouw and Rodriguez, 2003) in relation to existing planning instruments and regulations. The new solution was criticised for being a hybrid. It consisted, on the one hand, of an autonomous private shareholder company, and, on the other, of a state–municipal partnership with a financial base in the form of a state guaranteed credit line of some 850 million Euro (which was later to be increased many times). The adherents argued that the Orestad Development Company combined 'the best of two worlds': public control without the 'ensnaring bonds' of politics and capable of operating on market terms. The critical voices argued that the project was not embedded in a coherent vision of a sustainable city of the future, the needs of the neighbourhoods, and that the whole idea of a 'compact hyper-growth district' was not sufficiently substantiated.

## Governance dynamics in the phase of implementation

The major problem of the UDP, evident around 1996/97, was the disappointingly low level of private investments. Therefore, the mobilisation of (semi-)public partners to invest in the project became crucial. The irony is that in the design phase, the project was presented as more or less cost-neutral for public budgets, because urban rent and private investments would finance the development project. The growth coalition had to mobilise investments again, and in the implementation phase there was a massive increase in the use of public credits and costly (re)directions of public investments to the UDP.

One major problem in the implementation of large-scale UDPs is that the 'point of no return' makes it difficult to redirect UDPs once they are set in motion. UDPs have a very strong element of the 'politics of the casino', which tends to follow a logic of *irreversibility*.

In the Danish case, the growth coalition became successful in constructing the agenda as a choice between the defensive stagnation scenario and the offensive globalisation scenario. The critics, however, claimed that the presentation and calculation about benefits and risks were too optimistic and seductive.

## New social urban governance: community empowerment in deprived areas

The other face of the new urban governance, as we have noted, has been the initiatives and urban renewal programmes undertaken by the National Urban Committee established in 1993 with the purpose of addressing problems related to social housing estates.

The Urban Committee's work has been an indicator of an administrative strategy where the government's main goals are to be proactive against 'ghettoisation' and improve the quality of life in the city and housing areas. This strategy was combined with identifying the problems and solutions of the local participants and institutions. In line with these new trends in urban administration, the National Urban Committee launched a programme that utilised two strategies. First, a local networking strategy aimed at improving living conditions for tenants and reducing social problems by mobilising locally-based resources and initiatives. Second, a strategy of an improved competitive position aimed at improving the locality's competitive position in the housing market so as to attract more resource-strong groups into the localities.

In general, the evaluation reports conclude that segregation processes have been contained or prevented from escalating due the initiatives of the Urban Committee, even though the social problems have not yet been solved.

A common initiative in the housing estates has been the employment of housing estate counsellors. These counsellors became part of preventative social work attempting to strengthen the social life and networks on the estates. The co-operation, on a permanent basis, in the municipalities between the local welfare state and tenants' associations as well as other local participants and organisations has been one of the most important outcomes of the local network strategy launched by the Urban Committee (H.S. Andersen, 1999). Today, there are many more social activities in the estates and this has improved community life generally, making the estates better places to live. The programme has also resulted in a redirection of social work in some municipalities towards a more neighbourhood-oriented approach. But holistic-oriented approaches targeted towards a neighbourhood as a whole rarely reach those with the greatest need for help. They require specially targeted efforts to benefit from these efforts (on this issue, see Larsen, in this volume, chapter 12).

The strategy of improved competitive position has led to important and very visible physical improvements on the housing estates. It has also been possible to reduce rents on some of the housing estates. In combination with a reduction in visible social problems, the twofold strategy has improved the image of many housing estates. In effect, the characteristics of those that move onto the estates have changed, and the rate of turnover has decreased.

The evaluations show that the most successful parts of the programme are centred on community-led socio-cultural projects, whereas the efforts to create efficient partnerships with the business community focusing on job creation programmes are much less successful. Therefore, a very important counterproductive factor for the deprived areas is that they have not experienced a decrease in unemployment to the same degree that less deprived areas have. Some of the initiatives from the National Urban Committee can therefore be interpreted as initiatives to create housing areas where it is possible to live a decent life outside the labour market.

## The inclusive and the entrepreneurial city – can they coexist?

Present urban governance is characterised by ambivalence and conflicting agendas: The two faces of the present urban policy and governance are:

1. the strategic growth orientation, which sets the dominating agenda at state, regional and local government level; and
2. The mobilising and welfare-oriented orientation expressed in 'politics of positive selectivism and empowerment' and reinvented participatory planning instruments, which echoes the notions of deliberative democracy (see Ulrich, this volume, chapter 4), supported by national-funded social action programmes.

The missing links between the dominating strategy for economic growth and the programmes for social renewal and community empowerment in the deprived urban areas concerned with social sustainability and the avoidance of polarisation of the social geography constitute the most striking paradox in Danish – and EU – urban policy.

Seen from today's perspective, it is obvious that the urban movements in Copenhagen were much less powerful in influencing the orientation and management of growth policy and the larger revitalisation strategy. This part of the political landscape was excluded from the new powerful growth policy networks. On the other hand, the voice of community activists has re-entered the urban scene since the mid-1990s, not least due to the state-initiated implementation of area-based social action programmes in deprived districts inspired by former social renewal projects and by the EU Poverty 3 programme (Andersen and Larsen, 1995b).

However, the limits of these action programmes are their localist and socio-cultural orientation. Structural socio-economic issues and the linkage to the broader revitalisation strategy are almost non-existent, despite the fact that the national programme has a strong rhetoric about the necessity of such linkages. Hence, the social action and social renewal programmes for the deprived districts live a life of their own with marginal links to the city and regional entrepreneurial growth strategy. Thus, an ambiguous duality can be identified between the strategy for economic revitalisation dominated by neo-corporative, elitist governance and the area based programmes for the deprived districts influenced by ideas of urban planning such as social mobilisation (Friedman, 1987) and community empowerment (Craig and Mayo, 1995).

The different types of urban renewal programmes seem to have established two entirely different political and administrative forums of new urban governance. The separation of the economic and the social face of new urban governance are indeed not democratically inclusive since this way of governance does not secure the 'inclusion of and attention to socially differentiated positions in democratic discussion' and it does not 'tend to correct biases and situate the partial perspective of participants in the debate' (Young, this volume, chapter 2).

Furthermore, this type of governance expresses a type of recognition that is combined with negative redistribution effects, since the growth policy largely favours the work and income-rich, and bypasses the work and income poor people and districts. Full citizenship rights are not completed with the recognition of people's needs and rights to political inclusion, since economic equality is a pivotal condition for political equality. Severe inequality restricts poorer people's capabilities of making the most of their political citizenship rights (for an extension of these issues see Phillips, this volume, chapter 3).

Since the late 1990s, however, this duality has been challenged by the Ministry of Housing and Urban Affairs (1999), which promoted a new, holistic-oriented urban policy. This political agenda to some extent echoes the participatory and welfare-oriented planning paradigms of the 1970s in order to avoid a market-driven city entrepreneurialism and to (re)link economic, social, spatial and physical objectives and rationalities of urban development. At the state administrative level, this policy orientation also follows an institutional logic because the Ministry of Urban Affairs and Housing wanted to challenge the monolithic role of the Ministry of Financial Affairs, which had the dominant role in the design of the Entrepreneurial City strategy including the flagship project of the Orestad.

## New government – new ideology – new policy

The change in the national government at the end of 2001, when the Liberal and the Conservative Parties came to power, has completely changed the political climate and institutional framework for the Danish urban policy. In general, the new government has favoured/ upgraded the entrepreneurial side of urban policy and downsized the holististic and social dimensions. At the institutional level, the change has been dramatic. The new government, for the first time in Danish history, abolished the Ministry of Urban Affairs. This was a clear signal that there would be less emphasis on the social dimension of urban policy: physical planning was transferred to the Ministry of Business ('Erhversministeriet'), and the 'Kvarterløft' programme was transferred (with some budget cuts) to the new Ministry of Integration.

Compared to the initial holistic social action programmes in deprived neighbourhoods, this was a clear signal about redefining and *reducing* the issues about social cohesion and integration in deprived neighbourhoods to a question about *ethnic-related tensions* in these neighbourhoods. The signals from the government with regard to urban policy are, therefore, that urban policy is no longer a comprehensive, holistic district policy field, but should be split into separate entrepreneurial issues and ethnic issues. This will most likely lead to a further widening of the gap between the two faces of urban policy.

## Conclusion

Adequate inclusive and empowering policy responses should be directed at combating the polarising mechanisms in central arenas, such as the labour market, the housing market, social services and education. Macro-level policies must, however, due to the complex and multi-dimensional forms of present exclusion mechanisms with regard to class, gender, ethnicity and social geography, be combined with policy responses at the meso and micro level.

From the empowerment and social inclusion angle, we identify the challenge as, on the one hand, developing holistic policy objectives (taking social, ecological, aesthetic and economic considerations into account) in order to secure that Urban Programmes are part of a coherent inclusive (regional) socio-economic strategy; and, on the other, to (re)develop participatory policy instruments, which stimulates local participation/community empowerment and transparency of good practice and learning across the local, regional, national and transnational levels. In terms of governance, this includes efforts to include partners usually excluded from growth policy network – for example, the third sector, social housing associations and agencies representing deprived neighbourhoods and socially excluded people.

From a social polarisation angle, the lack of collective action from the bottom is the major problem. The ability to organise collective action (empowerment) and political representation from the bottom – and therefore the presence of organised conflictive relationship and communicative 'agora' between the affluent and the less affluent – is a condition for reaching sustainable development: social inclusion and integration is impossible without both social conflict and truly democratic dialogue based on a willingness to listen seriously and take others' interests and perspectives into consideration in order to achieve a more just and cohesive society. *Socially productive and transformative conflicts* can be defined as conflicts which encourage the social learning of collective and individual actors and hence reduce transactions costs and enhance social capital; and the norms and networks facilitating collective action for mutual benefit (J. Andersen, 1999).

Empowerment is not entirely a matter of political will and disposal of social capital (see this volume Mayo, chapter 9; and McClenaghan, chapter 10). Economic and material resources do matter – and so do politics of redistribution to empower the least privileged to enhance their political inclusion and participation. Generally speaking, this could be supported by a *combination* of universalistic social citizenship rights and politics of 'positive selectivism' – including empowerment-oriented urban social action programmes in deprived neighbourhoods. When they work well, they empower local actors and transform the public agencies in a more supportive direction and give rise to empowering or 'inclusive' localism. But without more far-reaching changes in the socio-economic regime, which can break the trend towards polarisation of the social geography local empowerment strategies are likely to fail.

The remaining challenge is the development of a holistic and participatory form of government and governance with emphasis both on sustainable growth and on the (re)distribution of the total set of living conditions. In Denmark, there were attempts to develop this type of planning in the late 1970s and since the 1990s these ideas have re-entered the discourse in the language of inclusion, but so far without linkages to the neo-corporative entrepreneurial discourse.

# References

Andersen, H.S. (1999). *Byudvalgets indsats 1993–98. Sammenfattende evaluering.* SBI-Rapport 320. Hørsholm: Statens Byggeforskningsinstitut.
Andersen, J. (1999). 'Post-industrial Meritocracy or Solidarity'. *Acta Sociologica,* 42, 4.

Andersen, J. and J.E. Larsen (1995a). 'The Underclass Debate – A Spreading Disease?', in N. Mortensen (ed.), *Social Integration and Marginalisation*. Copenhagen: Samfundslitteratur.

Andersen, J. and J.E. Larsen (1995b). 'Post-Industrial Solidarity – Future Challenges and Poverty III Lessons', in N. Mortensen (ed.), *Social Integration and Marginalisation*. Copenhagen: Samfundslitteratur.

Andersen, J. and J.E. Larsen (1998). 'Gender, Poverty and Empowerment'. *Critical Social Policy*, 18, 2, Issue 55 May.

Andersen, J. (2003). 'Gambling Politics or Successful Entrepreneurialism? – The Orestad in Copenhagen', in F. Moulart, E. Swyngedouw and A. Rodriquez (eds.), *The Globalised City*. Oxford: Oxford University Press.

Andersen, J., A.M. Tyroll Beck, C.J. Kristensen and J.E. Larsen (2003). *Empowerment i storbyens rum – et socialvidenskabeligt perspektiv*. Copenhagen: Hans Reitzels Press.

Barbier, J.-C. (2001). *Welfare to Work Policies in Europe. The Current Challenges of Activation Policies*. Document de travail, No. 11, November 2001, Centre d'études de l'emploi.

Berkel, R. v. and I.H. Møller (2002). 'The Concept of Activation', in R. van Berkel and I.H. Møller (eds.), *Active Social Policies in the EU. Inclusion through Participation?* Bristol: Policy Press.

Craig, G. and M. Mayo (eds.) (1995). *Community Empowerment*. London: Zed Books.

Esping-Andersen, G. (1990). *The Three Worlds of Welfare Capitalism*. Cambridge: Polity Press.

European Foundation for the Improvement of Living and Working Conditions (1999). *Linking Welfare and Work*. Dublin: European Foundation.

Fotel, T. and J. Andersen (2003). 'Social mobilisering og forhandlingsplanlægning kvarterløfterfaringer fra Kgs. Enghave', in K. Sehested (ed.), *Bypolitik og Urban Governance*. Copenhagen: Akademisk Forlag.

Friedman, J. (1987). *Planning in the Public Domain: From Knowledge to Action*. Princeton: Princeton University Press.

Harding, A. (1994). 'Urban Regimes and Growth Machines Towards a Cross-National Research Agenda'. *Urban Affairs Quarterly*, 29, 3.

Harvey, D. (1989). *From Managerialism to Entrepreneurialism: the Transformation of Urban Govenance in Late Capitalism*. Geografiska Annaler, series B: Human Geography, 17 B, 1.

Jessop, B. (1998). 'Globalisation, Entrepreneurial Cities and the Social Economy', in P. Hamel, Lustiger-Thaler and M. Mayer (eds.), *Urban Movements in a Global Environment*. Urban Studies Yearbook. London: Sage.

Kolstrup, S. (1996). *Velfærdsstatens rødder*. Viborg: SFAH.

Larsen, J.E. (2003). 'Danskernes faglige og politiske deltagelse', in B.H. Andersen (red.), *Udviklingen i befolkningens levekår over et kvart århundrede*. Copenhagen: Socialforskningsinstituttet.

Larsen, J.E. (forthcoming). 'The Active Society and Activation Policy – Ideologies, Contexts and Effects', in A.M. Guillemard et al. (eds.), *Social Policy, Marginalisation and Citizenship*. Bristol: Policy Press.

Macnicol, J. (1987). 'In Pursuit of the Underclass'. *Journal of Social Policy*, 16, 3.

Madanipour, A., G. Cars and J. Allen (1998). *Social Exclusion in European Cities. Processes, Experiences and Responses*. London: Jessica Kingsley Publishers.

Ministry of Housing and Urban Affairs (1999). *The Future of the City* [Fremtidens By]. Copenhagen: Ministry of Housing and Urban Affairs.

Moulart, F., E. Swyngedouw and A. Rodriquez (eds.) (2003). *The Globalised City*. Oxford: Oxford University Press.

Munk, A. (1998). *Succession and Gentrification Processes in Older Neighbourhoods*. SBI-Report 305. Hørsholm: Statens Byggeforskningsinstitut.

Pierson, P. (1998). 'Irrestible Forces, Immovable Objects: Post-Industrial Welfare States Confront Permanent Austerity'. *Journal of European Public Policy*, 5, 4.

Rose, N. (1996). 'The Death of the Social? Re-Figuring the Territory of Government'. *Economy and Society*, 25, 3.

Silver, H. (1994). 'Social Exclusion and Social Solidarity: Three Paradigms'. *International Labour Review*, 133, 5–6.

Stones, C. (1993). 'Urban Regimes and the Capacity to Govern: a Political Economy Approach'. *Journal of Urban Affairs*, 15. 1.

Wacquant, L.J.D. (1996). 'The Rise of Advanced Marginality: Notes on its Nature and Implications'. *Acta Sociologica*, 39.

Wilson, J.W. (1987). *The Truly Disadvantaged. The Inner City, the Underclass, and Public Policy*. Chicago: The University of Chicago Press.

Young, I.M. (1990). *Justice and the Politics of Difference*. Princeton: Princeton University Press.

# Name Index

# Subject Index